MODERN PIRACY
& MARITIME
TERRORISM

THE CHALLENGE OF PIRACY
FOR THE 21ST CENTURY

M. R. HABERFELD

JOHN JAY COLLEGE

AGOSTINO VON HASSELL

THE REPTON GROUP

Kendall Hunt
publishing company

Front cover images:
Top: courtesy of the U.S. Navy.
Middle: skull and crossbones © Luca Bertolli, 2009. Used under license from
Shutterstock, Inc.
Bottom: pirates on ship U.S. Department of Defense photo by Mass Communication
Specialist 2nd Class Kitt Amaritnant.

Back cover image:

Pirates surrendering: U.S. Navy photo by Mass Communication Specialist 2nd Class
Jason R. Zalasky.

Kendall Hunt
publishing company

www.kendallhunt.com
Send all inquiries to:
4050 Westmark Drive
Dubuque, IA 52004-1840

Printed in the United States of America
10 9 8 7 6 5 4 3 2 1

To my daughters, Nellie and Mia, whose love of the seas should never be disturbed by criminal acts.

—M. R. Haberfeld

To the brave men and women of our United States Marine Corps and the United States Navy who have been fighting pirates since 1800.

—Agostino von Hassell

CONTENTS

PREFACE

While the editors of this book could not have hoped for a better timing for its release from the perspective of the current events evolving around the world, it is the wisdom of the many contributors of this volume that truly needs to be recognized. The previously published contributions, together with chapters written for this anthology, represent a wide range of timelines and situations that brought about the actions of the actors involved in the maritime attacks and the possible responses to their criminal activities.

The idea of looking at the modern piracy and the maritime terrorist events through the prism of different themes is rooted in the background of the editors and the profound belief that only through a very eclectic approach this evolving phenomenon of modern terrorism can be curbed and minimized. We aimed at bringing together a balanced approach to a long-ignored problem that seemed to capture the imagination and the attention of many in the recent days but appeared to be disregarded by most of the policy makers and even the academics. The ones who wrote about the problem and alerted the others to its complexities were either this field's practitioners or a handful of scholars for whom the area of maritime piracy was, in most cases, peripheral to their interest in the larger problem of terrorism and its various incarnations. Our goal was to bridge that attitudinal gap by bringing together the writings of practitioners and academics whose knowledge in the area of understanding and combating terrorism brings an insightful approach to the counter-maritime terrorism response.

James N. Rosenau, a renowned scholar in the field of social sciences, in his attempt to explain the phenomenon of bifurcated politics, compared it to a water cascade whose scope, impact, and duration go far beyond a given cascading event. In this venue the understanding and response to maritime terrorism or modern piracy is treated by the editors as a cascade that needs to be contained before its scope, impact, and duration will get out of control.

We wish you, the reader, an insightful and thought-provoking journey that will expose you to many different perspectives and allow for a proper understanding of the romanticized notion that in reality is far from romantic and represents one of the challenges that democratic countries around the world will need to deal with in the very near future, before the waterfall will cascade into too many, serious impact bearing directions.

—Maria (Maki) Haberfeld
—Agostino von Hassell

Acknowledgments

It is the most gratifying time in the editors' and authors' hectic and stressful lives when they can finally acknowledge the people who helped them make the project come to life.

It is our distinct pleasure to thank Sue Saad, whose insightful understanding of the somewhat dispersed ideas we presented her with created this volume and enabled us to get more clarity regarding what we wanted to accomplish. Stephanie Moffett, the project coordinator, exemplifies the professional idea of book publishing and her help and patience certainly relieved much of the pressures we were exposed to. The production staff of Kendall Hunt Publishing Company assisted us during the many facets of the production hurdles and we would like to acknowledge their endeavors and the valuable contributions.

We owe our gratitude to the original contributors of this volume, who generously allowed us to reprint their work, and to the new contributors who found the time and the passion to add their expertise and thoughtful analysis.

Finally, we would like to acknowledge all the women and men who devote their life to the fight against criminal activities, wherever they take place, in the belief that a world built upon democratic rules and laws is the only way to sail forward.

CHAPTER 1

INTRODUCTION

1.1
Operational, Legal, and Policy Challenges

M.R. HABERFELD
AGOSTINO VON HASSELL

Extraordinary commands would have to be created if Rome was to recover control of the sea from pirates. It was Pompey who benefitted most from the restoration of tribunician initiative. After his consulship, he waited in Rome while rival nobles undermined the position of Lucius Licinius Lucullus, who was campaigning against Mithradates in Anatolia, and made halfhearted attempts to deal with the pirates. Finally, in 67, the tribune Aulus Gabinius forced a bill through the popular assembly empowering Pompey to settle the pirate problem.[1]

In the autumn of 68 BC, the world's infamous military power was subjected to a devastating attack by maritime terrorists. Ostia, a Roman port, was attacked, a consular war fleet was destroyed, and two prominent senators were kidnapped. The perpetrators of this daring attack were loosely organized pirates, the only ones who would dare to attack the Roman Empire at its time of glory.[2]

Is the threat posed by modern piracy real? This would be a good, yet very simplistic, research question to ask at the onset of this volume. Prior to the attacks of September 11, 2001 (9/11), one author of this volume was looked at with a serious dose of skepticism and sheer disbelief as a result of research into modern piracy.

However, as the opening quote of this chapter hints, the problem of piracy was a very real issue to tackle for the powerful Roman Empire. Pompey, one of its notorious generals, was charged with

---

1. Encyclopedia Brittanica: Pompey the Great. Retrieved May 1, 2009, from *http://www.britannica.com/EBchecked/topic/469463/Pompey-the-Great*
2. Harris, 2006.

3

finding an adequate solution as early as 67 BC As the United States (U.S.) is frequently compared to the Roman Empire—as a result of its military, political, social, and economic influence on the world—recent events, including Somali pirates hijacking a U.S. vessel, might have just have been the proverbial straw that broke the camel's back. The time has come to empower the U.S. military, the contemporaries of the Roman popular assembly, to respond to this growing threat. Yet, the question remains: Is piracy a serious and growing threat, or an iconization of a number of incidents that, in the grand scheme of other threats, are just a peripheral menace to world security? As some of the authors in this volume posit, the latter might be the case and, as such, the reaction of the injured parties should not be exaggerated or taken out of proportion.

Piracy, in popular imagination, had been relegated to the world of fables and history, the cinema, and children's stories. Yet piracy is alive and well and now, in some regions, has connections to Islamic fundamentalism and its related terrorism. Today, pirates have recaptured the headlines, emerging from dusty pages of history into the crystallizing sharpness of CNN's "Breaking News" and the ledgers of maritime insurance companies. The English word *pirate* is an ancient term, whose origin can be found in the dawn of human history and navigation of the seas. The term is as common as the old saying, much quoted by German Grand-Admiral Alfred von Tirpitz: *"Navigare necessere est; vivere non est"* (Navigation is essential, life not so).

The original term is derived from the Latin term *pirata,* which developed from the Greek τειρατής *(peirates)* "brigand," and ultimately from τεῖρα *(peira)* "attempt, experience," implicitly "to find luck on the sea." The word is also cognate to *peril.* In the seventeenth and eighteenth centuries, sources often rendered the word as "pyrate." However, the term does not exclusively relate to robbery committed at sea, as other similar origins have a broader definition.[3]

Pirates have captured popular imagination and are seen as cult figures, such as Bonnie and Clyde—infamous robbers from the Great Depression period of the United States. The popular glorification of groups of criminals, such as pirates, has led to children's games involving pirates and numerous movies, such as Disney's *Pirates of the Caribbean,* which has spawned two sequels to date. There is glorification of these bands of criminals long thought to be extinct even within major U.S. sports franchises. For example, Pittsburgh, PA, has a professional baseball team named the Pirates; Tampa

---

3. *http://www.etymonline.com/index.php?term=pirate*

Bay, FL, has a professional football team named the Buccaneers; and many high school and college sports teams use similar names that glorify this type of activity.[4]

Piracy, as a criminal enterprise, has occurred through the ages ever since the first ships were launched upon the waves. From the earliest days of maritime trade, criminals preyed on merchant shipping. Any commodity of value, either to the pirates or to those who would pay for their criminal ventures, was stolen or destroyed. Homer wrote about pirates; luminaries such as Julius Caesar were kidnapped by pirates. There is nothing truly new. Piracy is a fancy word for robbery—whether it be software "piracy" as practiced all over the world or capturing a ship and people for gain and ransom.

> *The man who had seduced her asked her who she was and where she came from, and on this she told him her father's name. 'I come from Sidon,' said she, 'and am daughter to Arybas, a man rolling in wealth. One day as I was coming into the town from the country some Taphian pirates seized me and took me here over the sea, where they sold me to the man who owns this house, and he gave them their price for me.'*[5]

Piracy is a tool of terrorism and, often, government-sponsored terrorism is equally common throughout the ages. Drake—on behalf of the Virgin Queen Elizabeth—was instructed to use piracy to defeat the Spanish Empire. In its early years, the United States engaged in piracy against the superior naval forces of the United Kingdom. Despite the desire of the injured parties to pursue, throughout history, pirates escaped their hunters by seeking sanctuary in havens where they could ply their booty and relax without fear of prosecution. Nowadays, very much like the days past, such feral cities offer a similar lifeline to the contemporary pirates.

Interestingly enough, some of the best-known pirate havens in existence during the Golden Age of Piracy (1690–1730), such as the Caribbean, have become "hot spots" for today's maritime terrorists. What made these havens so appealing to pirates back then and equally appealing over 300 years later? Possibly the location, possibly the proximity of unstable governmental structure on land, or possibly the local population that was or may still be sympathetic to some of the causes espoused by these "freedom fighters."

---

4. The official site of the Pittsburgh Pirates: *http://pittsburgh.pirates.mlb.com/index.jsp?c_id=pit*. The official website of the Tampa Bay Buccaneers: *http://www.buccaneers.com/splashFL.aspx*
5. *http://homer.classicauthors.net/odyssey/odyssey15.html*

Pirate activities virtually ceased in the nineteenth and twentieth centuries for a number of reasons:

- the increase in size of merchant vessels; thus they became harder to attack
- naval patrolling of most major waterways: major European naval powers, eager to protect colonies rich with natural resources, patrolled the seas
- regular, mostly colonial, administration of most islands and land areas in the world
- general international recognition of piracy as an international offense[6]

However, recent years have brought about a resurgence in maritime terrorism, although some experts still express a dose of skepticism regarding the existence of a real threat. Prior to reaching any conclusion with regard to the scope, intensity, or possible duration of this new/old phenomenon one needs to understand the magnitude of the operational, legal, and policy challenges involved in responding to the semi-romanticized notion of piracy.

Operational Hurdles

In order to respond with any degree of effectiveness to a threat posed on the high seas, the responding actor needs to be prepared for such a response. What seems to be evolving from the accounts of the incidents covered by various media outlets is a picture of a semi-coordinated, multinational effort that is accompanied by the individual response of a given country or a private owner of a specific vessel. Here are just a few examples from 2009:

- On April 18, 2009, the Associated Press reported that pirates, who attacked a tanker in the Gulf of Aden, were detained by the NATO forces that were called to the rescue. A Dutch frigate (from a nation that itself engaged in massive piracy in the days of Spanish domination of the "Spanish Netherlands"), part of the NATO force, spotted the pirates fleeing on a small boat, intercepted the pirates, and then boarded the Yemeni vessel that was under duress, freeing twenty Yemen fishermen.[7]

---

6. Vallar: *Pirates and Privateers: The History of Maritime Piracy.*
http://www.cindyvallar.com/pirates.html
7. Houreld & Pitman, 2009.

- On April 27, 2009, Yemeni special forces freed a Yemeni oil tanker that was seized by Somali pirates in the gulf of Aden, killing three pirates and capturing at least nine. The ship, *Qana*, was seized by the Somali pirates off Yemen's cost.[8]
- On Saturday, April 26, 2009, an Italian cruise ship, *Melody*, with 1500 passengers on board, was attacked by Somali pirates who fired wildly towards the passengers and the crew on board. What they did not expect was the operational response from the cruise line. The private Israeli security forces aboard MSC Cruises ocean liner fired on the pirates with pistols and water hoses, preventing them from boarding. According to the Associated Press "They (pirates) didn't expect such a quick response. They were surprised."[9]

The three incidents depicted exemplify the operational hurdles that nations, governments, and private owners faced and will face in the future with regard to adequate response to the maritime threats that, despite some academic dispute, pose a real problem to both private and public interests. Some of the operational questions that this volume attempts to deal with are:

1. What is the "right" response to a modern piracy phenomenon?
2. Is there a "right" response to a phenomenon of modern piracy?
3. Is there a difference between an effective response to an individual, stand-alone incident of piracy versus an incident of maritime terrorism that has ties to structured terrorist groups on land?
4. Who should be charged with the decision-making process once the incident is in progress?

From the operational hurdles to legal impediments, we might know what to do, but are we allowed from the legal standpoint to engage in such responses?

The Legal Impediments

Although our legal systems go back as far as our maritime security problems, it is not clear that we were ever in a position to enact all

---

8. Hammond, 2009.
9. Callimachi & Winfield, 2009; BBC (2009, April 26): Italian cruise ship foils pirates.

the laws necessary to counter the maritime terrorism. Similar to the case of 9/11, once an attack of a certain magnitude takes place, governments of many countries mobilize their legal systems to provide for an adequate response. In this speedy attempt to tackle a problem long in existence, governments and nations tend to overreact and, as Kraska (2009) refers to the problem, they tend to "miss the boat."

According to Kraska (2009) since 1994 the United States has considered joining the convention that outlines the legal rights and duties of the coastal states and nations. Fifteen years later, we are still "considering." How many more incidents like the recent crisis with the *Maersk Alabama* at the Somali coastline in 2009 do we need to encounter before we stop considering and just join?

Right now from a legal standpoint, we are experiencing a mixed reaction to international treaties as well as our own inability to decide which laws would apply and which are relevant for the operational response to and prosecution of maritime attacks. Another issue is the public perception of governmental responses to the romanticized notion of piracy. Abdi Wali Abdulqadir Muse, the pirate captured subsequent to the hijacking of the *Maersk Alabama,* has been described as a misguided juvenile whose only crime, according to by civil rights lawyer Ron Kuby, was to enter the vessel "under a flag of truce to negotiate."[10]

Do we need an event equivalent to 9/11 and the following enactment of the Uniting and Strengthening America by Providing Appropriate Tools Required to Intercept and Obstruct Terrorism (USA PATRIOT) Act to determine what is the proper legal response and one that will, at minimum, deter and minimize the current increase in this particular form of criminality?[11] Finally, in addition to the operational and legal hurdles there are, first and foremost, the policy issues.

The Policy Challenges

As one of the authors of this chapter experienced firsthand over years of dealing with maritime security challenges, operationally sound practices that are legally justified do not always make for the acceptable policy recommendations. Historically, certain nations, like Japan for example, refuse to arm their crew members on board

---

10. Guardian, 2009.
11. US DOJ: U.S. PATRIOT Act. *http://www.usdoj.gov/archive/ll/what_is_the_patriot_act.pdf; http://www.usdoj.gov/archive/ll/docs/text-of-paa.pdf*

their vessels. In this respect, despite the convincing and effective operational response by the Israeli security forces on the Italian cruise liner to the recent Somali attack, neither the Japanese government, nor the major Japanese shipping lines, would endorse contracting with the Israeli private security forces to provide for an adequate response to the threat.

Policies, especially those of governments, can be tricky and serve as the major impediment to operational effectiveness. Hacker (1977) provided a typology of terrorists and divided them into three categories: crusaders, criminals, and crazies.[12] The operational response to the different typologies should be very different. However, this operational wisdom has not translated to either legal or policy recommendations, as politics is often a major obstacle to effective operational response.

In the similar venue, private industries are measuring their investments in maritime security in dollar signs that have to do with the purely mathematical equation of juxtaposing risk versus liability. As Greenberg, Chalk, Willis, Khilko, and Ortiz (2006) clearly identify, it is all about risk and liability when policy issues are concerned. This anthology is presented to the reader based on a discussion of some themes that emerged and evolved from our understanding of modern piracy and maritime terrorist threats in the twenty-first century.

The themes help organize the analysis of what is happening and what could possibly be done to properly respond to a threat that appears—on the surface—a bit romantic and for some downright archaic but can pose a real existential problem to the world's economy and peace. The modern threat of piracy and maritime terrorism is very much akin to the threat that almost brought ancient Rome to its knees in 67 B.C. The threat of piracy to Rome's survival has since been compared to the threat for the United States resulting from 9/11.

This introductory section outlines and discusses the operational, legal, and policy challenges as presented by different authors throughout the chapters of this volume. Their overview is tied to the initial outline of the problems inherent in combating maritime terrorism or modern piracy, from the definitional problems through the politically proper response (that is not always operationally sound) to the legal and jurisdictional impediments.

In Chapter 2-1, Murphy discusses the concept of "unwanted challenge" when the powerful nations are challenged by the seemingly

---

12. Hacker, 1977.

marginal groups or individuals who, despite their diminutive stand in the world of global politics, manage to create havoc and embarrassing inaction on the part of the most potent and influential countries. Murphy does not see maritime terrorism as a serious threat, although he does see the potential of more serious ties between the various disjointed insurgent groups and more structured and well-established terrorist groups around the world and warns that the maritime forces need to be prepared for this emerging challenge.

In Chapter 2–2, Brookes discusses in more detail the challenges of modern piracy and warns about the complacency that can lead to much greater problems in the future. Although possible remedies are already identified and some of them put in place, such as the multinational Combined Task Force (CTF) 150, the response is still somewhat fractured and brings us back to the Barbary pirate problem that the United States faced close to 200 hundred years ago and managed to solve in a rather successful manner.

In Chapter 2–3, Lunsford identifies the five factors that made piracy and maritime terrorism alive and well through the more distant and recent history. From the golden age of piracy in the sixteenth century to the Somali insurgents, the reader can trace the strengths and the weaknesses of this criminal modality. The models presented by the author provide some badly needed templates for an up-to-date analysis of the maritime terrorist activities taking place as this volume goes to print, and offer some possible solutions to address this unwanted and rather embarrassing challenge.

From definitional, operational, and conceptual hurdles the next theme of the volume concentrates on the magnitude of the real threat. Shan and Ho, in Chapter 3–1 address the problems of armed robbery and piracy in Southeast Asia. While attacks in other areas of the world appear to surge, the number of incidents in Southeast Asia tend to be on the decline. The authors analyze these trends vis-à-vis the number of the attempted attacks in the area that provide for a different picture than the sheer number of reported attacks.

Tomberlin, in Chapter 3–2, warns us about the dangers of maritime piracy for the energy markets and the stability of our oil and gas supply. This real threat to our most critical commodities necessitates better intelligence gathering and response to the maritime shipping industry. The most interesting slant of his article touches upon the differences between the old-time piracy problems and modern maritime terrorists. While the pirates of the past had a quick financial gain as their primary goal, the contemporary maritime terrorists have a much broader ideological basis that raises more concerns than their predominantly economically motivated counterparts of the past.

In Chapter 3–3 Commander Patch raises the concept of the "overstated threat." His argument, in contrast to Tomberlin, centers on the difference between pirates and maritime terrorists and the implication of implying that they are one and the same. The author refers to the piracy problem as yet another type of criminality with relatively little impact on the world's welfare, nor any real link or evidence between the pirates and well-organized terrorist groups. The author posits that piracy, in its current scope, poses no real danger to the vital national security interests of the United States.

From a more academic perspective, Gunaratna, in Chapter 3–4, ponders the real level of terrorist threat to the maritime domain. The analysis of the real threat is presented from the perspective of a lack of understanding of the interface between the organized terrorist groups and the maritime threat. Gunaratna explores the development of maritime terrorism and how various terrorist and guerilla groups have penetrated and exploited these new territories to support their goals and ideologies.

From a more speculative angle of trying to address the real and/or perceived magnitude of the danger we move to the theme of countering the threat through interoperability and targeting of the support systems on land.

In Chapter 4–1 Allen and Stockton discuss interoperability problems inherent in international cooperation measures to secure the maritime commons. The planning for multinational cooperation in the maritime domain needs to be addressed from a number of angles and needs to take into consideration a multitude of factors. The role of NATO and the UN Security Council are discussed and analyzed from the perspective of the theater security cooperation plans. The need for greater intelligence sharing appears to be the common thread rooted in any successful interoperability based counterterrorist response.

In Chapter 4–2, Vice Admiral Feldt emphasizes the importance of the ultimate goal that needs to be established in anticipation of international cooperation to counter the maritime threat. The factors that create an effective framework for international cooperation need to be clearly spelled out in order to maximize the relevant and efficient response. The author emphasizes economic prosperity as the major driving factor in mobilization of an international cooperation.

In Chapter 4–3, Lieutenant Commander Frick discusses the importance of the support systems on land for the effectiveness of piracy
related operations. The primary focus is on the impact of a "feral
city," one in which the state government's ability to maintain the
rule of law has deteriorated. The main premise of this chapter is the
necessity to concentrate on the piracy lifelines, as found in these
feral cities, and the need to eradicate their ability to support the
maritime terrorism.

From the pragmatic solutions to the more problematic legal and
policy challenges, in Chapter 5–1 Commander Kraska addresses
the issues of countering piracy from the legal standpoint. On the
high seas, outside the jurisdictions of a state, any nation may seize
a pirate ship, arrest the pirates, seize the property, and proceed by
referring the matter to its civil or criminal courts. However, this right
is limited only to the warships and military aircrafts or vessels in
governmental service, therefore rendering any other response is
technically illegal. This chapter raises the concerns about any other
than the governmentally endorsed response to instances of maritime terrorism.

In Chapter 5–2, Lieutenant Martin focuses on the fluid boundaries
and the impediments to enforcement of the international laws at
sea, within the framework of political realities. Subsequent to 9/11,
there was an amplification of ambiguity of the definitions and determination of who will respond and how they will respond. The importance of the smaller states' willingness to cooperate must be
stressed by identifying core common denominators in the fight
against the mutual enemy.

Gutoff, in Chapter 5–3, discusses the interface between the laws of
piracy and the popular culture. Much of what lay people know about
piracy is influenced by television and the movies, but not much of
what we know from these sources focuses on the legal issues inherent in dealing with maritime terrorism. Our "understanding" is
shaped as much by the fiction as it is by the real-life events.

In Chapter 5–4, Commander Kraska and Captain Wilson stress the
importance of U.S. partner nations to make the sea safer in light of
the surge in the Somali maritime terrorism. The main problem identified by the authors centers around the uncertainty of actionable
options once the pirates are actually caught by the authorized parties. What to do with the "PUCs" or "persons under control" appears
to be the key legal question.

Next, we move from the legal hurdles and definitions to the ways the
response is actually handled in the hot spots around the world's

oceans. In Chapter 6–1, Lieutenant Colonel Mitchell addresses the counter-maritime terrorism response in the Caribbean Sea. The chapter, drawn from Mitchell's master thesis, concentrates on the more practical and pragmatic options to minimize the threat in the Caribbean Sea area.

In Chapter 6–2, Cheloukhine and Lieberman trace the origins of Russian maritime attacks and terrorism, discussing both its historical role addressing piracy and contemporary responses to the issues surrounding the security of the waterways of the world. Although they do not advocate for the adoption of the tactics and strategies successfully employed by Russian forces, the authors outline the unequivocal response that is so characteristic of this area of the world.

Finally, Walker, in Chapter 6–3, tackles the most recent events, including the Yemen and Somali attacks, from the larger perspective of the failed states and the international coalition to battle piracy. His most recent accounts of the maritime piracy cases address the issues of the use of technology and the tactics used by the pirates.

The final theme of the volume addresses future considerations and concerns. Chapter 7–1, by Greenberg, Chalk, Willis, Khilko, and Ortiz, touches upon the "sacred cow" issues of risk versus liability equations. The long history of maritime security, very much like the history of any type of security problems and the relevant response, is always replete with the concepts of risk versus liability drives.

In Chapter 7–2, Shane and Lieberman tackle the contribution of criminological theories as one possible solution in the attempt to combat maritime terrorism. The chapter provides a theoretical overview of a number of theories that fit the circumstances that brought about the most recent proliferation of modern piracy. This contribution to the volume adds an additional layer of concepts to ponder with regard to a more proactive and long-term solution.

These considerations provide for an adequate framework for Chapter 7–3, the last chapter, where von Hassell and Haberfeld draw some conclusive remarks about lessons learned from the past, the current events, and the possibilities in the future. As much as can and should be learned from historical contexts, the military response, and the legal hurdles, it is always advisable to include as many angles as possible to arrive at a solution that might be not the most appealing one but appears to be the most efficient and effective for the future of secure and tranquil high seas.

REFERENCES

Greenberg, M., D., Chalk, H. H. Willis, I. Khilko, and D. S. Ortiz. 2006. Maritime Terrorism: Risk and Liability. Rand Center for Terrorism Risk Management Policy. RAND Corporation, Santa Monica, CA. Retrieved May 1, 2009, from *http://www.rand.org/pubs/monographs/2006/RAND_MG520.pdf*

Guardian Staff. 2009. Teenage Somali pirate arrives in US facing trial over Maersk Alabama attack. April 21, 2009. Retrieved May 1, 2009, from *http://www.guardian.co.uk/world/2009/apr/22/somali-pirate-trial-maersk-alabama*

Hacker, F. J. 1977. *Crusaders, Criminals, Crazies: Terror and Terrorism in our Time.* New York: W. W. Norton & Co.

Hammond, A. 2009. Yemen frees ship, captures pirates. *Reuters,* April 27, 2009. Retrieved May 1, 2009, from *http://news.yahoo.com/s/nm/20090427/wl_nm/us_yemen_ship_release*

Harris, R. 2006. Pirates of the Mediterranean. *New York Times,* September 30, 2009. Retrieved May 1, 2009, from *http://www.nytimes.com/2006/09/30/opinion/30harris.html*

Kraska, J. and B. Wilson. 2009. Fighting piracy: International coordination is key to countering modern-day freebooters. *Armed Forces Journal,* 24. Retrieved May 1, 2009, from *www.armedforcesjournal.com*

Pitman, T. and K. Houreld. 2009. NATO frees 20 hostages; pirates seize Belgian ship. *Associated Press,* April 18, 2009. Retrieved May 1, 2009, from *http://news.yahoo.com/s/ap/20090418/ap_on_re_af/af_piracy*

Winfield, N. 2009. Cruise ship fends off pirate attack. *Associated Press,* April 26, 2009. Retrieved May 1, 2009, from *http://abclocal.go.com/wpvi/story?section=news/national_world&id=6780941*

Chapter 2

Definitional, Perceptional and Conceptual Hurdles

2.1
The Unwanted Challenge

MARTIN N. MURPHY

Maritime Insurgency Presents a Far Greater Challenge to World Naval Forces than Random Acts of Terrorism at Sea

Maritime terrorism is not a serious threat. Acts of terrorism at or from the sea, that is to say acts of violence committed by politically motivated groups to inspire their supporters or induce feelings of fear among their enemies, have been rare and are likely to remain so. Insurgent groups do, however, use the sea. The maritime domain might offer few opportunities for terrorist acts but some insurgent groups have used it extensively.

The reason for the low incidence of maritime terrorism is that the risk-reward ratio rarely computes. The resources groups need to undertake acts of violence at sea tend to be specialized and therefore cost more than the resources needed to mount equivalent attacks on land. More important, the rewards terrorists look for, publicity in particular, are hard to achieve at sea because of distance, which limits press access, and because the effect on the audience is limited by the fact that few people think that what happens at sea affects them directly.

"The Unwanted Challenge," by Martin N. Murphy. Reprinted from *Proceedings,* December 2008, Vol. 134, No. 12, with permission; Copyright © 2008 U. S. Naval Institute/*www.usni.org.*

Limited Success

With the exception of the October 2000 attack on the USS *Cole* (DDG-67), which had resonance for all advanced navies, no act of maritime terrorism has come close to achieving anything like the effect of attacks perpetrated on land. The incident that is cited most often, that of the *Achille Lauro,* an Italian cruise liner hijacked in the Mediterranean in 1985 by the Abu Abbas wing of the PLO, was probably a mistake. It appears that the terrorists intended to attack the Israeli port of Ashdod, but once a steward caught them in their cabin cleaning their weapons they were forced to hastily concoct another plan. They took over the ship but their attempt to force Syria to give them sanctuary was rebuffed. Although they did conclude a deal with Egypt that allowed them to fly to Tunis where the PLO's headquarters was then located, their plane was intercepted by U.S. carrier jets and forced to divert to Italy where they were imprisoned (minus Abu Abbas who the Italian authorities allowed to slip away).

The attack on the French supertanker *Limburg* off Yemen in 2002 is frequently cited as an example of how terrorists could disrupt the world's oil market. The reason it is mentioned so often is because it is the sole example of an attack on an oil tanker. It undoubtedly had limited success but the ship did not sink—in fact it was renamed the *Maritime Jewel* and continues to trade under that name—and most of the economic consequences of the attack were confined to Yemen.

However, it is worth acknowledging the failed attack on the Iraqi oil terminals in 2004 in which three U.S. servicemen died. All of Iraqi's oil export flowed through these terminals and it is likely that the loss of these supplies would have had a considerable effect on oil prices, although evidence from other disruptions suggests that this would have been temporary as other suppliers compensated for the shortfall. The longer-term consequence might have been that the attack would have sparked unrealistic demands for increased security for oil installations worldwide.

The attack on the Philippines inter-island vessel *Superferry 14* in 2004, the most recent noteworthy attack, also caught the world's attention as the result of a probable error. The perpetrators, the Abu Sayyaf Group (ASG), are undoubtedly a vicious, murderous band, but it is uncertain whether they intended to inflict the carnage they did. Inter-island ferries in the Philippines are attacked regularly by politically-motivated groups intent on extorting money from the companies that operate them. The company that operated the *Superferry 14* had received an extortion demand that it refused to pay. It is likely that the bombing, made worse by a poor fire suppressant system, was intended to send a message to the company to pay up in the future, not to kill as many as 114 people and send a message to the Philippine government. The consequences for the ASG since then have been disastrous: with U.S. assistance, the Philippines armed forces have hounded them almost to the point of extinction.

Despite this history of questionable success, certain types of vessels are attractive targets for terrorists. Naval vessels, U.S. Navy ships especially, have iconic status as symbols of state power. USNS support ships, although of less iconic value, might also be vulnerable as they are not as well defended and often sail alone. Passenger ships offer mass-casualty potential. Cruise ships are reasonably secure from internal seizure but vulnerable to suicide boat attack, and the U.S. Coast Guard's concerns about the use of small craft for this purpose in U.S. waters remains very real.[1] Ferries, because they depend on open access, are much harder to defend and in the case of Roll on-Roll off (Ro-Ro) vessels, with open decks, present terrorists with the opportunity to drive large car or truck bombs on board.

The Right Incentives

Most insurgent groups have had no reason to use the sea, and those that have elected to do so out of *choice* rather than out of *necessity* have generally backed away pretty quickly. Only those who have used the sea as the result of a geographically determined imperative have been successful because they possessed the incentive necessary to overcome the manifest difficulties of operating in the unforgiving maritime environment.

A number of factors appear to influence success: a permissive legal regime, inadequate security, access to secure base areas and maritime expertise, state support, and leaders who are persuaded of the seas' importance to their cause. These factors interact with each other and while circumstances determine which predominate, it is usual to find the majority are present in varying degrees.

For example, maritime operations demand more complete base facilities closer to the location of an attack than land operations. The al Qaeda cell that attacked the USS *Cole* and the *Limburg* was well led tactically and operationally, probably had access to local

1. Eleanor Stables. "Mines, small boats may pose threat to US ports." *CQ Homeland Security,* 14 May 2007.

maritime expertise, and was able to take advantage of the weak legal and security environment prevailing in Yemen. Although it planned a number of other maritime assaults, including major operations in the Straits of Hormuz and Gibraltar, only the operations launched from Yemen were carried through. Al Qaeda's failure to continue its maritime campaign is clearly inseparable from the disruption to its operations globally, but its lack of secure bases in the areas where it hoped to mount its maritime attacks appears to have limited its options significantly. More important, success at sea was not fundamental to its overall success, meaning there was no imperative to overcome the obstacles associated with such operations.

In contrast, all the key success factors were in place to benefit the Sea Tigers wing of the Liberation Tigers of Tamil Eelam (LTTE): weakness and indecision have characterized the Sri Lankan government and navy for much of the campaign, and this precluded them from mounting an effective counter to Sea Tiger activities; the insurgents benefitted from substantial Indian support during their formative years and although this was withdrawn following their 1991 assassination of the former Indian Prime Minister Rajiv Gandhi, it was not replaced by forthright opposition; their base areas in southern India continued to operate, albeit more discreetly, and were supplemented by secure territory on Sri Lanka and new locations around the Indian Ocean littoral; they were able to draw on the centuries-old Tamil seafaring tradition; and had leaders who were utterly convinced of the need for a maritime capability.

The Sea Tigers fought the Sri Lankan Navy to a virtual stalemate and came to be rated as the most capable non-state naval force in the world, reflected in the fact that when the LTTE proposed during the 2003 peace talks that the Sea Tigers should be given semi-official status, the proposal was rejected by both Sri Lanka and India out of concerns that the recognition of a third force could have a destabilizing effect on the region. Without the Sea Tigers the Tamil insurgency as a whole would have been impossible. Success at sea was imperative to the LTTE's success and drove the group to develop the broadly based maritime competency that al Qaeda lacked.[2]

---

2. The U.S. State Department lists the LTTE as a foreign terrorist organization, not an insurgency. That gives the U.S. government greater latitude in the measures it can invoke against it. However, the organization considers itself to be an insurgency and has always acted as such.

Worth Their While?

Given these factors and experience of what makes some groups successful, how might maritime insurgency develop in the years to come.[3] There is no reason to believe that insurgents will take to the water any more willingly in the future than they have in the past. They will only do so if driven by political necessity, and the political changes required would need to be of sufficient magnitude to make the investment of money, time, and skills worthwhile.

Observation of the Sea Tigers, the Acehese-seperatist movement GAM, Palestinian and Philippine insurgent groups, and al Qaeda suggests strongly that the sea is primarily of benefit to insurgents as a transport medium. Greater use of the sea is therefore likely to focus on developing the capacity to move more cadres, equipment, and funds. New instability or political change in vulnerable regions might allow insurgents to operate with greater freedom than they can at present. If such changes took place where the sea offered significant strategic opportunities, such as maritime Southeast Asia, the West African littoral, or the Gulf of Aden bounded by the Horn of Africa and Yemen, insurgent groups might be inclined to invest in the development of a maritime capability to supplement and support their strengthened presence on land, perhaps looking to the Sea Tigers as a model.

Though the possibility of insurgents developing anything more substantial than an enhanced logistical capability at sea might seem remote, time and again non-state groups have been able to depend on the skepticism of military and political analysts about their capabilities to spring successful surprises. According to the head of the Indian Navy, Chief Admiral Sureesh Mehta, the security situation across the entire Indian Ocean has become "complex, fluid and significantly challenging" with a "dramatic increase in asymmetric threats," a view with which the United States concurs.[4]

The most significant insurgent challenge in the near term might well come from jihadist groups. One of the distinguishing features of jihadist insurgency is its global outlook. Organizations such as al Qaeda are skilled at opening new fronts in their war where they

---

3. Part of what follows is based on the discussion in Martin N. Murphy, *Small Boats, Weak States, Dirty Money: Piracy and Maritime Terrorism in the Modern World* (New York & London: Columbia University Press/Hurst, 2008), pp. 402–8.
4. "Maritime terrorism gains roots in Indian Ocean." *The Times of India,* 9 August 2008; "India's fears of terrorists using sea routes well-grounded: US." *The Times of India,* 24 August 2007.

detect opportunity, observe weakness, or are able to find local allies. The al Qaeda strategist Al-Suri has written about mounting attacks in the Strait of Hormuz and the Bar el-Mandeb, about targeting ships and of blocking passages using "mines and sinking ships in them, or by threatening the movement there by piracy, martyrdom operations, and by the power of weapons."[5]

Chatter on jihadist Web sites, which has been echoed by more covert sources, has indicated that they have looked closely at what the Somali pirates have achieved. Despite the presence of more than ten warships from a number of countries, and the declaration of a maritime safety zone through the Gulf of Aden, pirates using boats no larger than Boston Whalers, in some cases deployed from mother ships, managed to capture a significant number of targets including ships up to 50,000 dwt, large trawlers, luxury yachts and, in the case of the MV *Faina,* a 10,000 dwt Ro-Ro seized in September with 33 T-72 Soviet-era battle tanks on board, before sailing them into Somali territorial waters and holding them there, with their crews, while they waited for ransom to be paid.[6] Coalition commanders admitted that naval action alone could not solve the problem.[7] At the beginning of November 2008 it was believed there were 11 vessels being held at various points off the Somali coast.[8]

A contributor to one jihadist Web site makes the point that Yemen and the Horn of Africa "represents a strategic point to expel the enemy from the most important pillars of its battle." The success of the Somali pirates in hijacking vessels is noted and the implication drawn that "the area is beyond the control of the arsenal of the Crusader Zionist campaign."[9] With this experience in mind it is not inconceivable that insurgents in maritime theaters might build on existing maritime expertise and assemble the capability to harass commercial shipping and possibly even military supply ships to a degree that hinders their free movement without the deployment of scarce and expensive escorts, thus rendering some coastal regions high-risk areas for vessels of all kinds.

---

5. Brynjar Liar, *Architect of Global Jihad: The Life of Al-Qaida Strategist Abu Mus'ab al-Suri* (London: Hurst & Co, 2007), p. 401.
6. See, for example, Jerry Frank. "Somali pirates strike deeper on the high seas." *Lloyd's List,* 28 August 2008; David Osler. "Ro-ro with 30 tanks onboard is seized off Somalia." *Lloyd's List,* 29 September 2008.
7. David Osier. "'We are not the solution' to piracy, says Somalia coalition navy chief." *Lloyd's List,* 25 September 2008.
8. "Pirates seize Danish ship, 13 crew near Somalia." Associated Press, 8 November 2008.
9. "Jihadist website commentary argues 'maritime terrorism' strategic necessity." *Biyokulule Online,* 29 April 2008.

'Black Holes'

Maritime Southeast Asia is another potentially vulnerable region. While currently passing through a period of relatively low pirate activity, and where groups such as the Indonesian-based Islamist organization Jemaah Islamiyah (JI) have for the moment at least turned away from acts of ostentatious violence, the arc of islands that runs from the southern Philippines to southern Thailand is an area of porous borders where operatives and contraband can be moved with relative ease. It is a region that has spawned groups such as the ASG and where it has been demonstrated that "black holes"—areas in which political or criminal groups are able to challenge or even replace the authority of a state—can be created, such as the Moro Islamic Liberation Front (MILF) camps on Mindanao in the Philippines.

Black holes also appear to be emerging in some of the states edging the Gulf of Guinea. Although these countries might not be comfortable nesting grounds for jihadists, the region has seen governments that degenerate into politico-criminal enterprises as the recent histories of Liberia and Sierra Leone have demonstrated. The possibility that Nigeria could fail, weighted down by corruption and the inequitable distribution of the country's oil wealth, is a matter of deep concern, as is the fear that the effects could spread to Cameroon and Fernando Po (an island in the Gulf of Guinea) as oil extraction increases in those countries.

The Movement for the Emancipation of the Niger Delta, the principal politico-criminal group in that area, is probably the most effective maritime insurgent organization operating currently. It has proved capable of striking at night up to 75 nautical miles from the coast, coordinating swarms of 30 boats or more, and of achieving strategic effect by cutting Nigerian oil production regularly by around 15–20 percent, and up to 30 percent on occasion. It is known to have supported at least one separatist raid on Cameroonian territory and is believed to have planned an assault on Fernando Po.

This instability could be exploited by state proxies. These proxies could also work to deny navies access to littoral areas of interest to their sponsors. Hezbollah is the prime example, although because its relationship with Iran is not straightforward it might be better described as a "partial proxy."[10] Regardless of the details,

---

10. Daniel Byman. "Rogue Operators." *The National Interest,* No. 96, July/August 2008, p. 56.

Israel's view is that, in terms of capability, "Hezbollah has everything Iran has."[11] Iran's own irregular maritime capability is considerable. It is vested in the Iranian Revolutionary Guards Corps Navy (IRGCN) with which Hezbollah is known to have trained. The assumption is that if the IRGCN is ever deployed it could cause major navies, including the U.S. Navy, substantial problems in the narrow waters of the Persian Gulf. It is best known for operating small, missile-firing boats in swarms but also operates submarines and has a commando raiding force.[12]

Iranian claims that Hezbollah, too, has a submarine capability might be discounted but it does have a submersible and swimmer capability and a commando force. It was, moreover, the firing of a C-802 antiship cruise missile from Hezbollah-controlled territory in southern Lebanon in 2006 (probably by a detachment sent from Iran for the purpose) that severely damaged an Israeli corvette, the INS *Hanit,* which demonstrated close relationships between states and their proxies were possible. This move suggests that the transfer of sophisticated weapons might take place, including possibly mines, coastal-launched torpedoes, intelligence, surveillance, and reconnaissance systems, UAVs, and USVs, which could make operations in the littoral zone extremely dangerous. Since the end of the conflict the stock of C-802s held in Lebanon is believed to have tripled.[13]

Naval forces have supported counterinsurgency campaigns around the world for the past 50 years but with the exception of the Sri Lankan Navy, to a degree the Israeli Navy, and now the Nigerian Navy, none has had to confront an insurgent presence on water or projected from the coast.[14] In an era of strategic confusion and limited resources, major navies are torn between the demands of possible major conflict against a near-peer competitor and the messy, ambiguous small wars for which their ships and operational meth-

---

11. Harry de Quetteville. "Terrorists' missiles are from Teheran armoury." *Daily Telegraph,* 17 July 2006.
12. Fariborz Haghshenass. "Iran's Asymmetric Naval Warfare." The Washington Institute for Near-East Policy, *Policy Focus* No. 87, September 2008.
13. Barak Ravid. "Israel to UN: Hezbollah has tripled its land-to-sea missile arsenal." *Haaretz,* 31 October 2007.
14. For a review of naval support for counter-insurgency operations see Martin N. Murphy. 'COIN on the Water' in Thomas Rid and Thomas Kearney (eds.), *Understanding Counterinsurgency Warfare* (New York: Routledge (forthcoming 2009)).

ods are ill-suited. In 2006, however, Admiral Mike Mullen, then Chief of Naval Operations, warned that naval forces could not stand off in the deep blue but had to move close to shore if they were to engage the enemy.[15] It is a challenge for which the Navy must be prepared.

---

15. Remarks as delivered by Admiral Mike Mullen, Naval War College, Newport, RI, 31 August 2005 at *http://www.navy.mil/navydata/cno/speeches/mullen050831.txt.*

2.2
The Challenges of Modern Piracy

The thought of pirates usually evokes Hollywood blockbusters involving swashbuckling buccaneers, tropical isles and buried treasure marked on a tattered map with an "X."

To those mindful of history, piracy might conjure up notions of the Barbary pirates, who sailed the Mediterranean Sea and Atlantic Ocean, raiding coastal towns, capturing merchant ships (some American), and ransoming or enslaving their crews in North African ports.

Strikingly, some two centuries later, piracy at sea is back—with a vengeance.

Like their forebears, today's brigands are criminals, holding ship, crew and cargo hostage for payment; or forgoing that tedious arrangement, they'll simply commandeer a vessel, selling the goods—maybe even the ship—on the black market.

The recent incident off Somalia is case in point.

Somali Seizure

Indeed, the September seizure of the Ukrainian merchantman MV Faina off the coast of Somalia highlighted the existence of the modern-day Blackbeard. The ship, reportedly containing 30 T-72 tanks and other heavy weapons, was bound for Kenya when it was pinched by about 60 Somali pirates on the high seas. The boarders, clearly aware of the value of the booty in the ship's hold, initially

"The Challenges of Modern Piracy," by Peter Brookes, *Armed Forces Journal*, December 2008(146):5, pp. 10–12. Reprinted by permission of Army Times Publishing Company.

demanded more than $20 million in ransom to free the ship and crew. (It was later reduced to $10 million.)

The predators promised to kill the crew if a rescue attempt was made and threatened to set the ship ablaze if the ransom wasn't paid.

Unfortunately for the raiders, the cargo's final destination was unknown, drawing the attention of the U.S., which feared the weapons were headed for radicals and extremists in Somalia, some with possible al-Qaida ties. The U.S. Navy and a handful of other ships quarantined the vessel at sea, ostensibly preventing it from delivering its lethal cargo into the wrong hands somewhere ashore.

Just like when the Barbary pirates made the most of the North African coast, an area then rife with lawlessness and criminally complicit rulers, Somalia provides a similarly supportive climate today.

Somalia is a failed, mostly ungoverned state slightly smaller than Texas with 2,000 miles of coastline, bordering the 200-mile-wide Gulf of Aden. Like the Barbary Coast of days past, it turns out to be an ideal place for piracy.

The Gulf of Aden, the shortest year-round sea route between Europe and Asia, connects the Mediterranean and Red seas with the Arabian Sea and Indian Ocean via the Suez Canal and the 13-mile-wide Bab al Mandab Strait.

As one of the world's busiest waterways, as many as 20,000 ships transit it annually—ahead of the Panama Canal at 15,000 ships per year, but behind the Strait of Malacca at 50,000 ships.

Not surprisingly, the Gulf of Aden is also now the world's most dangerous waterway for civilian shipping, according to the International Maritime Bureau, an International Chamber of Commerce group. Just this year, 80 ships have already been attacked by sea-borne bandits in the Gulf of Aden—an increase of 75 percent over 2007—accounting for nearly one-third of the more than 200 reported pirate assaults in 2008 worldwide.

In just one week in mid-October, NATO reported that seven ships were attacked in the pirate-infested waters off the Somali coast. In late October, five attempts were made in just one day. More than 30 ships have been hijacked this year. In fact, the actual number of pirate strikes is probably unknown. While perhaps an over-statement, it's been suggested that as many as 90 percent of pirate attacks go unreported. (Many shipping companies don't report hijackings out of concern for increased insurance premiums or lengthy investigations, which could hold their ships pier-side, despite an estimated $10 billion to $20 billion in annual industry losses to piracy.)

In general, the Somali pirate is in it for the money. No surprise considering half of the Somali people are in need of food after nearly two decades of seemingly interminable conflict, instability and lack of governance. Pirates in these waters can easily net $1 million to $2 million in ransom for a seized ship, a figure that goes a long way in such an impoverished country. Piracy is socially accepted; those who fly under the skull and crossbones live like rock stars in comparison to kith and kin.

Within Somalia, the semi-autonomous region of Puntland, strategically located on the Horn of Africa, is Jolly Roger headquarters, especially the port of Eyl. Piracy has become a pillar—if not the pillar—of the local economy, replacing fishing.

While dead men tell no tales, deceased hostages are worth less to shipping companies than live ones. As a result, special canteens have opened in Puntland to prepare chow for the crews held aboard pirated ships, according to the BBC. But it's not just this area that's afflicted by 21st century privateers. The Strait of Malacca had been considered the most pirate-afflicted waters in the World until it was recently outdone by the Gulf of Aden. Others have pirate problems, too: Tanzania, Bangladesh, Philippines, Brazil and Peru.

Of course, piracy isn't just for treasure. In the areas around Nigeria, Sri Lanka and southern India, local insurgents use acts of piracy to harass governments or gain fame for their movements.

But today's cutthroats don't just sail the Bounding Main, hoping to wander upon potential plunder. Among present-day predators, they're at the peak of the profession.

Pirate Ploys

In fact, today's Long John Silvers often get tip-offs from their network of spies ashore. Harbormasters and ship chandlers chat up skippers about their cargos and destinations before passing it on to the pirates. Some of these same people also help the pirates on the back end of their dirty dealings, negotiating for ransom, laundering money, selling pilfered personal property and cargo as part of an integrated criminal syndicate.

Attacks most often come while a ship is at anchor, but raids can also involve several small speedboats—in some cases launched from larger "mother ships"—that target underway vessels.

While many attacks seem to take place within 20 to 30 miles of shore because of the small size of the pirates' launches, the mother ship scheme allows the marauders a base from which they can operate hundreds of miles at sea.

The raiders, numbering seven to 10 per boat, are often armed with assault rifles and rocket-propelled grenade launchers, aided by satellite phones, GPS equipment, radar and powerful outboard motors.

Medium-sized ships with low freeboard are often targeted because they are the easiest to board and likely to be laden with cargo, since they're sitting low in the water.

While the pirates may try to get a skipper to slow or go dead in the water, threatening the ship in broad daylight with small boat swarming tactics and automatic weapons fire, some approaches aren't so direct. Clever Captain Kidds may even attempt to impersonate officials to get aboard. In fact, some of the sea wolves come from the ranks of corrupt "coastguardsmen," who freelance as criminals, robbing and hijacking ships.

At night, raiders may also try to board a ship at anchor or even while it's underway, using long, hooking ladders made of construction rebar or grappling hooks to hoist themselves over the rail.

Once on board, the pirates, sometimes numbering as many as 100, overwhelm the crew, which are relatively small on today's modern merchant ships. The crew could be held hostage, killed or even set adrift. (No reported incidents of walking the plank, so far . . .)

Depending on their ultimate intent, some of the sea robbers head back to shore or the mother ship after the ship is sized, ready to provide land-based support to the operation or respond with force, if necessary.

Ship captains are warned by international agencies to post 24-hour watches and to use the ship's speed and maneuverability, such as "fishtailing," to swamp the smaller assault boats. Many ships don't carry weapons for fear of escalating violence, preferring to outrun their pursuers, blind them with searchlights or hit them with high-pressure hoses. Some may begin embarking private security teams.

Some shipping companies with deep pockets have actually installed electrical fences along the deck to discourage boarders, but some ships such as fuel carriers can't due to safety concerns.

But perhaps the biggest concern with today's pirate is terrorism ties.

While there have been no direct, publicly reported links between the pirates and terrorism or terrorist groups, the possibility gives security analysts and national security officials pause—and rightfully so.

Indeed, one of the reasons U.S. warships surrounded the Faina was to ensure the weapons on board or any ill-gotten gains didn't fall into the wrong grips, especially Islamist extremists or terrorists with al-Qaida ties based in Somalia.

Moreover, some experts assert that because of international efforts to hinder terror financing, piracy, like narcotics or blood diamonds, could provide a potentially lucrative, alternative revenue stream.

Of course, we've already seen terrorism at sea: The seizure of the Achille Lauro in the Mediterranean in 1985 by the Palestinian Liberation Front; the 2000 al-Qaida attack on the USS Cole in Yemen; and the Abu Sayyaf Group's 2004 strike on a ferry in the Philippines that led to more than 100 deaths.

While maritime terrorism and piracy aren't the same, they could overlap, especially when it comes to targets and techniques, providing opportunities for collaboration.

For instance, al-Qaida identifies the West's economy as a key target. It would come as no real surprise if it were to try to scuttle a ship in a narrow chokepoint, such as the Persian Gulf's Strait of Hormuz, causing a disruption in global energy supply.

While this wouldn't be in the interests of most pirates, al-Qaida could certainly partner with them, using their means and methods to capture a ship in exchange for an appropriate sum.

While perhaps apocryphal, there is at least one report of "pirates" taking control of an underway ship in Southeast Asia, conning it through crowded shipping lanes in what some believe to be similar to the 9/11 hijackers' efforts to learn to fly a plane, but not take-off or land.

Analysts are also concerned al-Qaida now has a number of hijacked, re-registered and renamed "phantom" ships it its possession, including tug boats, which could be used for attacks on ports.

Back to Barbary Wars?

Since governments infrequently negotiate or intervene on behalf of shippers, the UN Security Council recently passed resolutions requesting member states protect shipping off the Horn of Africa, reminiscent of the early 19th century Barbary Wars.

In addition to U.S. naval forces already present as part of multinational Combined Task Force (CTF) 150, conducting regional security operations, NATO deployed three ships to the area in late October.

The NATO operation, Allied Provider, consisting of Greek, British and Italian ships, will be primarily escorting ships supporting U.N. humanitarian and peacekeeping operations in Somalia.

Together, these maritime forces have already thwarted at least two dozen attacks since late August, according to CTF 150.

The European Union is also expected to launch its own escort operation in December, consisting of ships from eight countries. Russia and India have also dispatched vessels to the area to look after their interests.

Moreover, in November, the head of the U.N.'s International Maritime Organization called for the establishment of a United Nations force to combat piracy in the Gulf of Aden, according to the Financial Times.

Adding to the vast operational challenges are legal issues regarding the rights of military forces to conduct counter-piracy operations on the high seas or even in a state's territorial waters (within 12 nautical miles of the coast).

Indeed, the pirates often play upon the limits of sovereignty delineated in the U.N.'s Law of the Sea Treaty involving international and territorial waters, moving in and out of each, or across state jurisdictions, to elude capture.

Another matter is the apparent lack of clarity in international law about the handling of pirates should they be captured, including who has the right to bring them to justice.

The United States helped settle the Barbary pirate problem with military might nearly two centuries ago, in one of the young republic's first demonstrations of power projection abroad. But that sort of major effort isn't likely in the short term.

Due to other more pressing operational commitments such as Iraq and Afghanistan and potential contingences such as a strike on Iran's nuclear program, piracy isn't likely to get the attention it probably warrants.

Unfortunately, the political, economic and security conditions ashore—which allow or drive piracy—aren't likely to improve in the short term in many of these pirate hideaways, especially Somalia.

The problem in the end is that complacency over this emerging challenge, especially its potential to aid and abet terrorism, could prove damning to our national security if not confronted quickly and decisively.

2.3
What Makes Piracy Work?

VIRGINIA LUNSFORD

The Golden Age of Piracy—from approximately 1570 to around 1730—was an era when robbery on the high seas was widespread, lucrative, and threatening. Although nowadays it has been romanticized in such films as Disney's *Pirates of the Caribbean* trilogy, piracy back then was actually violent, frightening, destabilizing, and thoroughly illegitimate, at least from the point of view of governing authorities. Its history provides a variety of case studies and models that illustrate how these groups operated and to what degree their activities continued, despite opposition and military confrontation.

In turn, these models offer ways to analyze the pirates of the contemporary world—including those now operating off the coasts of Africa—so we can ascertain their viability and learn how to combat them. Ultimately, case studies reveal that long-term, intractable, flourishing piracy is a complex activity that relies on five integral factors: an available population of potential recruits, a secure base of operations, a sophisticated organization, some degree of outside support, and cultural bonds that engender vibrant group solidarity. Activities that interfere with the smooth workings of any of these factors weaken piracy's sustainability.

The North Africa Coast

From about 1500 to 1832, the Barbary corsairs of North Africa made the Mediterranean a highly dangerous place, regularly attacking and plundering Western trading vessels. Their ineradicable presence,

"What Makes Piracy Work?" by Virginia Lunsford. Reprinted from *Proceedings,* December 2008, Vol. 134, No. 12, with permission; Copyright © 2008 U. S. Naval Institute/*www.usni.org*.

33

frightening success, and savage violence over three long centuries stemmed directly from their exploitation of the aforementioned five fundamental qualities. Europeans were terrified of these marauders, for the North Africans zealously pursued and looted any and all Western ships, no matter their nationality.

Religious ideology characterized and permeated this conflict, with each side—the North Africans and the Europeans (and later Americans), respectively—citing their Muslim and Christian identities as the primary reason they were locked in a state of opposition. While the loss of trade goods was bad enough, what most terrified the Europeans was that the corsairs routinely seized sailors and passengers from Western ships, using them as slave labor on board corsair ships or in their sponsoring cities, collecting ransoms from their faraway kinsmen and countrymen, or selling them in the slave markets of North Africa and Turkey. People were the corsairs' primary targets. Ships and property were beneficial, but they were secondary objectives.

The corsairs were based in several large North African port cities, including Algiers, Tunis, Tripoli, and Sal and Mamora (later Morocco). While nominally controlled by the Ottoman Empire, the denizens of these settlements were actually granted wide latitude from the Sultan to behave as they wished. The corsairs' origins lay in the Spanish Catholic evictions of Muslims from the Iberian Peninsula (circa 1300–1500), which had created a population of embittered refugees in the North African cities and instigated the early 16th-century Spanish invasions of North Africa.

Lacking a naval response to repel the Spanish aggressors, each of the port cities adopted Ottoman naval technology, combat techniques, shipboard operations, and raiding strategies, and accepted Ottoman financial support, all in exchange for a loose allegiance to the empire.

The resulting arrangement was a win-win situation for both the Turks and the North Africans. The port cities now had the means to combat the aggressive Spanish, and the Ottomans were happy to have a naval bulwark along the southern Mediterranean coast, thereby impeding European endeavors to control the sea.

Muslims versus Christians

Since these events followed closely on the heels of and indeed were inextricably entwined with the tensions stemming from the Crusades and European Reconquest of the Iberian Peninsula, the confrontations that ensued were articulated in the ideological idiom of religious conflict: Muslims versus Christians. At the same time, however, a less obvious but no less important reason for the clash stemmed from the shift in trade patterns from the Mediterranean to the Atlantic and Indian oceans, a change that deprived North African port economies of commercial activity.

Each port city sponsored and sheltered its own fleet of corsairs, pledging financial support and rewards, political protection, and physical refuge. Accordingly, corsairs brought their captured goods, ships, and prisoners to their respective sponsoring city. It was a symbiotic relationship that worked well for the duration of the phenomenon, ensuring the corsairs protection and their city's economic survival.

Over the course of the 16th century, following the Ottoman naval model they had adopted, the corsairs used galleys commanded by local North Africans and rowed by slaves. As the 17th century unfolded, however, they also acquired European sailing ships and began to include an increasing number of dispossessed European sailors in their crews. Many of these so-called renegade Westerners ended up occupying the highest positions in the chain of command and had extremely successful careers as North African raiders.

In keeping with their ideological perspective of victims of religious persecution and attempted invasion, the corsairs did not see their actions as piratical in the least. On the contrary, they believed themselves to be revered warriors whose raiding activities defended their people and their faith and the economic sustenance and military security of their home ports. The West, however, condemned the corsairs as pirates, for their marauding did not at all conform to European rules of engagement or stipulations for legal commerce raiding.

Corsairs Extend Their Reach

As the raiding intensified over the years, the corsairs' hunting grounds expanded. While they always represented a grave threat to Mediterranean shipping, their attacks were by no means confined there, especially after they acquired the means and equipment to operate European-style sailing ships. Rather, in their quest for Christian quarry, the corsairs regularly prowled the Canary Islands and the African coast, even going as far as the Red Sea region. They also ventured into European waters, cruising along the coasts of Portugal, Spain, and France, and into the northern seas as well, making their way into the waters surrounding the Netherlands,

England, and even around Iceland, which they raided spectacularly on at least one occasion.

After the mid-17th century, the corsairs increasingly took to the seas in large, powerful fleets, each including at least 20 vessels. They attacked ships and coastal settlements, and everywhere they went, the goal was still the same: hunt down Western goods and kidnap Western people.

The Barbary corsairs became infamous for their reputed violence. Regardless of how savage they really were, the perception among early-modern Europeans was that the North Africans were uncivilized and ruthless. Some modern scholars argue that accusations made against the corsairs were borne more out of fear and prejudice than actual circumstances. Moreover, it is important to remember that many practices, which in our eyes are shocking examples of cruel and unusual punishment, were by early modern standards quite normal; all early-modern states—including those of Europe—employed harsh means of corporal and capital punishment.

But the stories are still sobering. Allegedly first-hand accounts written by witnesses and survivors of Barbary captivity describe dreadful places where thousands of pitiful Christian slaves (in 1621, supposedly more than 32,000 in Algiers alone) were, among other things, tortured, worked harshly and ceaselessly; and housed in dark, hot, vermin-infested prisons, where lice and fleas ate at their skin. North African youths jeered and threw stones, urine, and feces at them and burned them alive.

Methods of torture included bludgeonings, setting feet and hair afire, public whippings, impaling on pikes and giant hooks, genital mutilation, burial alive, and even crucifixion. Over the course of their existence, the corsairs captured and enslaved tens of thousands of Christian men, women, and children. Those who were not ransomed successfully could be worked to death and then denied the decency of a proper burial. Instead, early modern sources decried, their corpses were left to rot and be eaten by dogs. Together these texts provide vivid anecdotes testifying to the corsairs' cruelty and rapaciousness.

How Europe Coped

How did Europeans deal with the scourge of the Barbary corsairs? First, enormous effort went into liberating European captives through the payment of ransoms. To this end, liberation societies were born, associations whose sole purpose was to collect funds for the deliverance of Western slaves. In addition, many states and communities imposed a "Turk's rate" tax as a means to amass money for slaves' emancipation. Finally, Western governments sometimes presented the North Africans with gifts and/or monetary remuneration to expedite the process. Officially designated agents drawn from an extensive network of Catholic orders and Jewish merchants acted as middlemen and took the collected funds to North Africa to purchase slaves' freedom.

Second, European governments negotiated diplomatic agreements with the various North African city-states, and even the Ottoman Sultan himself. These treaties were typically uncoordinated efforts, meaning that they represented an agreement solely between one Western nation and one North African settlement. They often involved the payment of special sums of protection money to the sponsoring North African cities, thus avoiding Barbary harassment. (This was a technique employed especially by Western nations that lacked a strong naval presence in the Mediterranean.) Frequent expirations and changeable terms necessitated a constant revisiting of these diplomatic accords. Overall, the efficacy of the treaties ebbed and flowed over the years.

Third, Western navies also patrolled the waters to stamp out the corsair nuisance. Sometimes, these naval forays resulted in concentrated attacks against a particular North African port city, or demonstrations of naval might in a city's harbor to intimidate the city leadership and encourage the release of slaves. Naval missions departed regularly and enjoyed some success, capturing Barbary raiders and either executing them or selling them into slavery. Such fleets typically cruised the Spanish and Portuguese coasts and Mediterranean Sea. If they apprehended a corsair vessel, they liberated any captive Christians, confiscated the weapons, auctioned the goods at the nearest friendly port, and took the enemy crew prisoner for later strategic disposal.

Western governments also pledged handsome rewards to any of their ships that seized a Barbary vessel. Special incentives included bonus wages, equal access to profits earned from the sale of the ship's goods, and for the captain of each conquering naval vessel the right to take the ship's provisions and small weaponry.

Fourth, European trading nations enacted protocols to protect their shipping against Barbary harassment. Directives from the 17th-century Netherlands, for example, included instructions to ship owners regarding the minimum size of vessels, type and quantity of weapons, and size of crews. Dutch ships were also required to convoy with at least one other similar vessel and were forbidden to transport any ordnance or naval stores to North African cities.

Guilty parties were punished with severe fines and even execution. To detect any recalcitrant ship owners, the government developed an inspection system using the local magistrates of the relevant ports. It also created incentives for these local authorities (as well as for fellow mariners) to report ships not in compliance with the rules.

The Secret to the Corsairs' Success

To a degree, these solutions saved Western lives. Still, though, they did not directly undermine any of the five fundamental factors accounting for corsair potency and durability. Consequently, the Barbary menace was impossible to eradicate for some 300 years. Why?

The North African corsairs were effectively organized following Ottoman naval tradition. They were sheltered by secure bases of operations in the form of the North African ports and economically and politically supported by both their sponsoring cities and ultimately, the Ottoman Sultan. And among themselves they were animated by sturdy bonds of ideological solidarity. Even the European renegades converted to Islam.

The West finally suppressed the corsairs, but not until the early decades of the 1800s when they were in a less vigorous state. In a series of confrontations, Western navies were able to forge (sometimes coerce) diplomatic treaties (e.g., the 1796 agreement with the independent Morocco). They also fought the corsairs and their North African sponsors in wars (e.g., the 1801–05 war between Tripoli and the fledgling United States, whence comes the reference to the "shores of Tripoli" in *The Marines' Hymn*). And finally, they were able to vanquish sponsoring cities (e.g., the 1830 French invasion of Algiers, which signaled the definitive end of the Barbary corsairs). All of these Western triumphs were predicated on the use of sufficiently strong navies. But naval power alone did not do the trick.

In addition to navies, other forces were at work and created favorable conditions for Western success. Compared to the glory days of the 17th century, the Ottoman Empire was weaker economically and politically and thus less interested in corsair activities. Its bonds with the North African ports were even more tenuous, if they existed at all. For their part, the North African city-states were less supportive of corsair activities and less impervious to attack than they had been.

Furthermore, with refugees from the Iberian Peninsula long since absorbed and the absence of a steady pool of Western renegades, it was no longer as easy demographically to outfit a fleet of corsair ships. Among the corsairs themselves, ideological motivations still had their power, but less so. Therefore, the corsairs were less passionate about their enterprise and less willing to risk all. By the 19th century, then, superior Western navies were dealing with a weaker phenomenon, and so strong naval action could result in decisive victory.

What About Today's Pirates?

As the rest of the world considers what to do about the increasingly problematic modern Somali pirates, it would behoove us to think beyond superficial and simple naval solutions on the high seas and consider the five factors underlying the long and productive careers of the Mediterranean corsairs. To analyze Somali piracy more deeply and ultimately suppress it, we must ask ourselves these vital questions:

- Who are these Somali pirates?
- Where do they find recruits, and how many of them are available?
- Why do they take up piratical activities?
- Do we know the exact number, character, and location of all of their havens?
- Are these pirates organized, and if so, how are they organized, and is this organization strong and effective?
- Do the Somali pirates enjoy any outside sources of support? states or groups (including terrorist groups) that are providing money, goods, weapons, intelligence, or other help to their cause?
- Do these pirates maintain close bonds between one another with a keen sense of solidarity and cohesion, and if so what is the nature of this solidarity, from where does it come, and is it powerful and abiding?

We know some of the preliminary answers to these questions from intelligence gathered by American agencies. Today's Somali pirates are, in general, trained militia fighters based in the semi-autonomous regions of Puntland and Somaliland. They do not call themselves pirates. Organizationally, the piracy is based on the clan system so influential in Somalia. But it is allegedly controlled by elements within the Somali government as well as businessmen in Puntland.

The pirates are based in camps located adjacent to coastal port villages, and they also deploy previously captured ships as sea-going bases, or mother-ships. We do not know how intense the bonds of solidarity are among these raiders, but one would guess that relations are strong since the piracy overlays the indigenous clan system. At this time, analysts discern few clear links to terrorism, but this possible development is of ongoing concern.

The key to eradicating Somali piracy lies in interrupting the larger, complex system that supports it. It is essential that the pirates be intercepted in action on the high seas, and the United States and its allies should continue to meet this objective. However, the situation is more complicated than that, and the longer the system is permitted to stay in place and grow, the more intractable the piracy problem will become.

Possible courses of action include somehow interrupting the flow of recruits (by introducing alternative economic possibilities, for instance), establishing some sort of compelling alternative to the clan system (an action that would weaken the pirates' organizational structure and feeling of solidarity), and eradicating the base camps. Diligent efforts must also be made to prevent the Somali pirates from acquiring outside sources of sponsorship and support. The danger is that al Qaeda (or some other terrorist group) will seek involvement in the enterprise, especially since Somalia is an Islamic country. Al Qaeda has experience both in international shipping and allegedly the piracy affecting Southeast Asia.

Above all, we must not ignore this contemporary African piracy or underestimate its potential severity simply because we arrogantly assume that pirates in small speedboats (the Somalis' raiding craft of choice) can do little harm. Indeed, one of the vital lessons the history of the golden age of piracy imparts is that pirates can do serious damage with what seem to be unformidable naval assets. As in the case study of the Barbary corsairs, it is ultimately the support system—based on the previously mentioned five fundamental factors—that determines the success of piracy.

All data come from "Piracy and the Horn of Africa," U.S. Central Command Brief, April 2008.

CHAPTER 3

THE REAL THREAT

3.1
Armed Robbery and Piracy in Southeast Asia

JANE CHAN AND JOSHUA HO[1]

While world figures on cases of reported piracy and armed robbery seem to be increasing, figures within the Southeast Asia region continue to suggest that the overall number of attacks in the region is steadily trending downward (refer to Figure 3.1). There were a total of 11 reported armed-robbery and piracy incidents in Southeast Asia during the first quarter of 2008. Of these, six were actual attacks while the remaining five were attempted incidents. The first quarter of 2008 recorded the lowest number of armed-robbery and piracy activities in the region in the last five years. In fact, the number of actual attacks reported was equal to figures of the third quarter of 1998, where only six actual attacks were reported, the lowest number of actual attacks in the last 10 years. However, the same cannot be said of the steady numbers of attempted attacks being reported in the region.

Types of Attacks

Although theft and/or robbery still make up the main type of attacks in the first quarter of 2008, one of the reported attacks turned violent, resulting in three fatalities and two injuries. As four of the six

"Report on Armed Robbery and Piracy in Southeast Asia First Quarter 2008," by Jan Chan and Joshua Ho. Reprinted by permission of the authors.

1. Jane Chan is an Associate Research Fellow and Joshua Ho is a Senior Fellow of the Maritime Security Programme at the S. Rajaratnam School of International Studies, a Graduate School of Nanyang Technological University, Singapore.

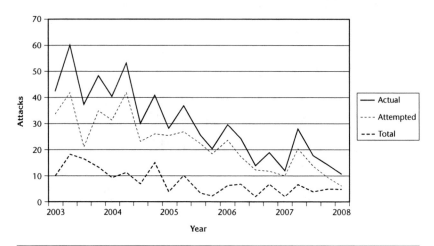

FIGURE 3.1
Regional Trends by Quarters, 2003–2008

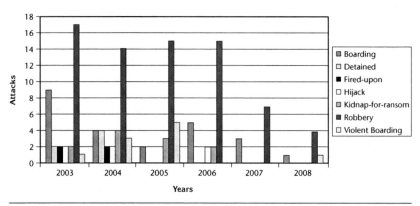

FIGURE 3.2
Types of Actual Attacks, First Quarterly Comparison, 2003–2008

actual attacks reported during the first quarter of 2008 were theft and/or robbery cases, the violent boarding incident served as a harsh reminder of the possible level of violence one can face in an attack at sea. A first-quarterly comparison over the last five years saw a consistent pattern of the types of attacks being perpetrated in the region (see Figure 3.2). Based on previous analyses of the modus operandi common to this region, it was often concluded that such attacks were by and large opportunistic in nature. However, details of recent reports on attempted attacks seem to suggest a rather different trend. All five of the attempted attacks saw two or

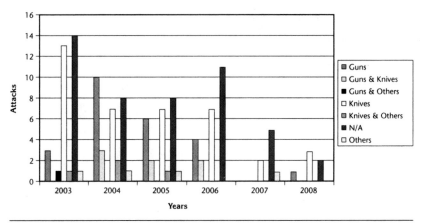

FIGURE 3.3
Types of Weapons, First Quarterly Comparison, 2003–2008

more hostile vessels operating concurrently, suggesting a planned and synchronized operation. Fortunately, all five possible targets were vigilant and engaged appropriate and timely evasive maneuvers to avoid such attacks.

Types of Weapons

Of the six reported actual attacks, three saw the perpetrators armed with knives. Unfortunately, the only reported attack that saw the use of guns resulted in three fatalities and left two others injured. Knives were used in half of the reported incidences during the first quarter of 2008. First-quarterly comparison over the last five years saw a similar gun-knife ratio being used during those quarters (see Figure 3.3). More reports during those selected quarters provide information of the types of weapons being used as opposed to the annual figures where more than half of the reported incidences do not furnish such information. Information on the types of weapons used during attacks is an important gauge of the trend and potential violence that take place in regional waters.

Location of Attacks

The locations of the few reported cases of piracy and armed robbery attacks during the first quarter of 2008 in the Southeast Asia region do not reflect a particular hotspot within regional waters (see

FIGURE 3.4
Location of Actual Attacks in Southeast Asia, First Quarter, 2008

Figure 3.4). Although ports and anchorages were the most commonly targeted areas of attacks in Southeast Asia (where more than two-thirds of the attacks took place while vessels were at anchor and/or at berth), the regional trend seems to suggest that the more serious attacks almost always took place further offshore, targeting steaming vessels on local voyages. The most serious reported attack during the first quarter of 2008 was perpetrated in the body of water between the mainland and Polillo Islands, Philippines. Drawing from the attempted attacks reported during the first quarter of 2008, all cases seem to suggest coordinated attacks targeting steaming vessels further offshore. As all of these reported attempts were successfully evaded, it seems to suggest that crews were in a better position to defend themselves against piracy and armed robbery attacks while at sea.

Types of Vessels

While tankers were the primary targets in Southeast Asia in 2007, vessels targeted during the first quarter of 2008 were varied (see Figure 3.5). As most of the reported actual attacks were theft and robbery cases while the vessels were at anchor or at berth, the targets were most likely those that were engaged in the lowest level of security measures onboard. A passenger boat was the target of the only violent boarding incident during the first quarter of 2008. Most of these attempted attacks were targeted at bulk carriers and

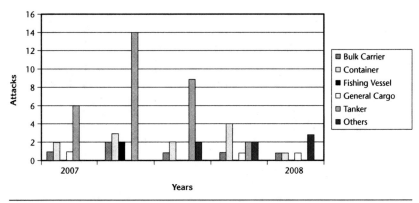

FIGURE 3.5
Actual Attacks by Types of Vessels, 2007–2008

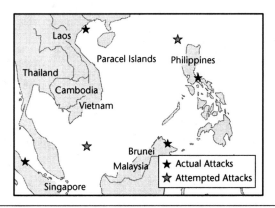

FIGURE 3.6
Location of Attacks in the South China Sea, First Quarter, 2008

tankers of sorts. Fortunately, these targets were vigilant and were able to engage in a high level of security measures to avoid potential attacks.

South China Sea

Figure 3.6 shows the location of actual attacks at or within the vicinity of the South China Sea. There has been no actual piracy or armed-robbery attack being reported in the South China Sea during the first quarter in the last five years (see Figure 3.7). As most of the cases that took place during the first quarter of 2008 were in fact

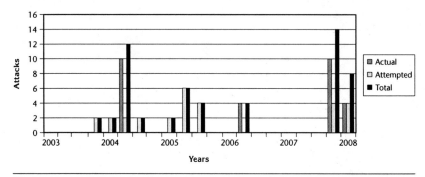

FIGURE 3.7
Types of Actual Attacks in the Vicinity of the South China Sea, 2003–2008

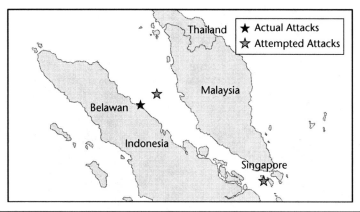

FIGURE 3.8
Location of Attacks in the Malacca and Singapore Straits, First Quarter, 2008

perpetrated within the vicinity of ports and/or anchorages, it shall be highlighted that two of the five attempted attacks in the region took place within the waters of the South China Sea.

Malacca and Singapore Straits

There were only three reported cases of piracy and armed-robbery attacks in the Malacca and Singapore Straits during the first quarter of 2008, and only one was an actual attack (see Figure 3.8). A chemical tanker was boarded at Belawan Port, Indonesia. Similar to

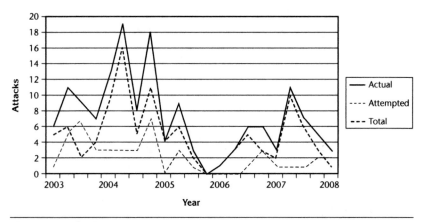

FIGURE 3.9
Quarterly Trend in the Malacca and Singapore Straits, 2003–2008.

the first quarter of 2007, the Malacca and Singapore Straits recorded one of the lowest numbers of piracy and armed-robbery attacks in Southeast Asia during the first quarter of 2008. However, these figures are not reflective of the occasional peak in the number of attacks that often take place during the second quarter of each year (see Figure 3.9).

Indonesia

Half of the total number of actual attacks in the Southeast Asian region took place within Indonesian waters. The first quarter of 2008 recorded three actual attacks being committed within Indonesia's jurisdiction (see Figure 3.10). Despite the figures recorded during the second quarter of 2007, there have been significantly fewer reported cases in the Makassar Strait since the second quarter of 2006. The figures of the first quarter once again highlight that Indonesian ports and anchorages remain the weakest link within a region that is prone to armed-robbery and piracy activities.

Apart from the one reported incident in Belawan Port along the Malacca Strait, Figure 3.11 shows the location of two other actual attacks perpetrated within Indonesian waters. As previously mentioned, the type of vessels targeted in the region varied, and cases reported in Indonesia reflected that trend. A bulk carrier was attacked at the Pulau Laut anchorage while a tug was attacked when it was steaming in the vicinity of the Karimata Strait.

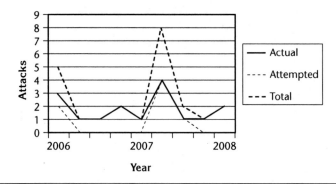

FIGURE 3.10
Trends of Attacks, 2006–2008

FIGURE 3.11
Location of Actual Attacks in Indonesia, First Quarter, 2008

Conclusion

There was one major incidence that ought to be highlighted during the first quarter of 2008. A passenger boat was attacked at gunpoint, resulting in three fatalities and two others wounded. More importantly, the incident did not take place in one of the usual hotspots, highlighting the fact that apart from keeping the ports and sea lines of communications safe, all other regional waters are equally important and equally prone to potential attacks.

Having mentioned the above, regional figures on reported piracy and armed-robbery attacks in recent years have been generally trending downwards. This is despite the occasional hike in reported figures, usually during the second quarter of the year. With reference to the lower number of reported cases during the first quarter of 2008, there is less of a pattern in terms of the specific details useful in the study of the issue. For example, the types of vessels being targeted were varied in contrast to 2006 and 2007, where a specific type of vessel was more prone to attack than others. Generally, vessels with a weak level of security are prone to attacks, regardless of the make. Also, if we look at the location of the attacks, it does not reflect a particular hotspot within the region. Be that as it may, it is also obvious that security in the vicinity of the ports and anchorages within the region leaves much to be desired.

There is no doubt that littoral states, with the support of some user states, have dedicated much effort and resources in trying to overcome the problem. One such recent effort was the launch of a new data-sharing system, the Malacca Strait Patrol Information System (MSP-IS), which allows the sharing of shipping information between the littoral states. Although the number of actual attacks in the region has often been speculated to be under-reported, it is vital to recognize that until there is a system that allows for 100-percent reporting, current published figures remain the only gauge of the problem at hand, and as it stands, it seems to be under control.

References

- IMB Weekly Piracy Report. [Online] Available at *www.icc-ccs.org*

- IMO Reports on Acts of Piracy and Armed Robbery Against Ships. [Online] Available at *www.imo.org*

- Lloyd's List Bulletin. [Online] Available at *www.lloydslist.com/viewbulletin*

- Maritime Security Council's News Alerts

- ONI Worldwide Threat to Shipping Report. [Online] Available at *www.nga.mil/portal/site/maritime*

- ReCAAP Information Sharing Centre Report. [Online] Available at *www.recaap.org*

3.2
Terrorism's Effect on Maritime Shipping

ROGER L. TOMBERLIN

Abstract

In the first years of the nineteenth century, Mediterranean pirates, with the support of the Barbary States of northern Africa, would capture merchant ships, terrorize their crews, and hold the ship for ransom. In response, the United States launched the Barbary wars, the first successful effort by the young republic to protect its citizens from a ruthless, unconventional enemy by fighting a protracted struggle overseas. Today, the international community fails to realize that sea piracy still has not been eliminated. Not only has piracy never been eradicated, but the number of pirate attacks on ships off the coasts of Somalia, Nigeria, and the Malaccan straights has tripled in the past decade elevating piracy to its highest level in history. And contrary to the stereotype, intelligence has revealed that today's pirates are often trained fighters aboard speedboats equipped with satellite phones and global positioning systems and armed with automatic weapons, antitank missiles, and grenades. Many of these so called pirates have ties to their regional terrorist organizations.

Most disturbingly, the scourges of piracy and terrorism are increasingly intertwined: piracy on the high seas is becoming a key tactic of terrorist groups. Unlike the pirates of old, whose sole objective was quick commercial gain, many of today's pirates are maritime terrorists with an ideological bent and a broad political agenda. This nexus of piracy and terrorism is especially dangerous for energy markets: most of the world's oil and gas is shipped through the world's most piracy-infested waters. As the world's need for oil, natural gas and goods swell in today's economy, the need for intelligence concerning the pirates and their home base of operations becomes ever inerrably important. Terrorist incidents have an adverse impact on Maritime shipping throughout the world.

Maritime Terrorism

Terrorism on the other hand is relatively easy and simple to define. In the context terrorism can be defined as:

> [the] unlawful use or threatened use of force or violence against people or property to coerce or intimidate governments or societies, often to achieve political, religious, or ideological objectives.[1]

Many Western Intelligence Agencies have reported that certain Islamic terrorist groups have declared that they are intent on bringing down the economies of the West in order to further their own religious aims. These statements infer that these terrorist groups will utilize piracy as an instrument to damage the World economy. The raisons d'etre for these attacks are to inflict economic damage. The result is that it is easy to detect the indirect benefit piracy can have to terrorist groups. Valuable shipping lanes such as the Suez, Strait of Hormuz, or the Malacca Strait, could be targeted by Terrorist groups by sinking a vessel in a maritime chokepoint, and although terrorist groups would undoubtedly claim responsibility, their method of attack would probably be similar to that of a pirate attack. Western Intelligent Services still do not have any evidence to suggest that terrorists are actively pursuing piracy as a deliberate method of conflict. There is no evidence that the attack on the USS Cole and MV Limburg was an act of piracy but rather the results of the following investigation indicate that it was a terrorist attack. These were specific terrorist attacks aimed at specific targets, both military and economic (Homeland Security, 2005).

In 1985, the Palestine Liberation Front's (PLF) seized the passenger ship Achille Lauro, and the taking of its crew (331), and passengers (120 of 754), as hostages. The initial aim of the hijacking

---

1. Terrorism definition is from the United States Department of Defense. There are many other agency definitions however the DOD encompasses all the points.

was to seize the vessel and use it to conduct a terrorist attack on an Israeli oil terminal in the port of Ashdod, but when that attack was thwarted the hijackers, pirates, or terrorists (using whichever terminology you wish) opted to demand the release of Palestinian prisoners. The aftermath of the Achille Lauro incident saw a significant downturn in the cruise liner industry, with a resulting economic effect on the countries frequented by cruise ships. That the incident has not been repeated, owes much to luck rather than increased security such as the utilization of the Long-Range Acoustic Device (LRAD) defensive weapons. The PLF did not intend for any economic downturn to occur, but as previously said, certain terrorist groups could actively seek to put pressure on some fragile Western economies. An attack now, some twenty years after this event, could not only have an adverse effect on the cruise industry, but could also contribute to any downturn in the global economy. It could be argued that the attack on the Achille Lauro was not an act of piracy, and was purely an act of terrorism, and the perpetrators had a political motive, rather than a private agenda.

Is there a Nexus Between Piracy and Terrorism?

Terrorist groups could see their aims furthered by pirate activity, and some have used techniques similar to those that have been used by pirates during attacks. However, the previously mentioned terrorist attacks have been quite specific in their targets, whereas pirate attacks appear to be random and uncoordinated. It is extremely doubtful that terrorist groups would form an alliance with any external groups including one with pirates. Terrorist groups are very closely knit, suspicious of outsiders or those who arc unknown to them, especially if they do not share the same ideology. It is probable that terrorists would conduct their own piracy campaign rather than using any criminal group. The Abu Sayyaf Group (ASG), which is based in the Southern Philippines, has been linked to hijacking and kidnapping for ransom, including raids from the sea on holiday resorts. International reporting has indicated that the line between piracy and terrorism is narrow and that the group is believed to have moved from being an Islamic separatist group to a criminal enterprise. If that is the case, then the group is moving from political ends to private ends in its criminal enterprises. This does not suggest that the ASG has moved away from terrorism. ASG claimed responsibility for the attack on the Superferry 14 in early 2004. This suggests that the group will continue to engage in acts of terrorism, while engaging in piracy to raise funds to continue to conduct a campaign of terror.

Another Southeast Asian group that has been linked to piracy is the Free Aceh Movement (Gerakan Aceh Merdeka; GAM). GAM seeks the removal of Indonesian government structures and forces from the Aceh region of Sumatra. The Indonesian and Malaysian authorities have linked this group to acts of piracy in order to raise funds. The main maritime operating area for this group is within the confines of the Malacca Straits, and it is probable that they are involved in a vast number of the incidents that are reported in the region. It has not been possible to assess the full extent of this activity, as GAM has denied some of the attacks attributed to it. It has been reported that pirate groups in the region have copied CAM's uniforms and tactics, leading to an inflated number of attacks being attributed to GAM. This is supported by reports that GAM funding has mainly come from other sources (International, 2006).

In another piracy hotspot, the Horn of Africa, the indigenous terrorist organization Al Ittihad Al Islamiya (AIAI) may be involved in piracy. AIAI is a very loose arrangement of individuals, whose tribal loyalties, and shifting external alliances, produce a wide spectrum of terrorist and criminal acts, from banditry to piracy and seajacking. AIM seeks to establish an Islamic nation in the Horn of Africa (HOA). There have been reports that suggest that they have engaged in acts of piracy in order to raise funds. The majority of reported incidents in the HOA, however, have been conducted by armed gangs, whose loyalty is clan based rather than linked specifically to AIAI. These gangs are heavily armed and, in the true sense of the word, pirates, not terrorists. In recent months, piracy in the HOA has escalated: ships attempting to bring food aid into the region have been taken, along with their crews, and have been held hostage by armed militia—sometimes for several weeks, even months. In order to reduce the likelihood of an attack, and under the instructions from the IMO, ships not bound for HOA destinations have been navigating further and further from the coast. Though this may prevent attacks in coastal waters, it may subsequently drive the pirates farther out to sea as well (Luft & Korin, 2004).

In West Africa the Ijaw militias are conducting a civil war and are also involved in intertribal conflicts in the Niger Delta region of Nigeria. Over the last two years, there have been increasing reports of piracy in the region, including attacks against oil-support vessels and off shore installations. This has helped turning the region into one of the most reported in terms of piracy, second only to the Malacca Straits. The attacks have been accompanied by theft and kidnapping for ransom, and those involved have become more violent in their methods. Because of the level of corruption in the region, the amount of money that the oil industry is making has enabled criminal gangs to move into what was hitherto thought to be a political conflict against the government. Those attacks attributable to the Ijaw militia are possibly being committed in order to raise funds in order to support their continued attacks on the Nigerian government and the country's oil industry. However, it is likely that many of the attacks reported are criminal, and motivated much by political corruption. The remainder of the incidents is acts of petty theft and have little to do with piracy in its general description.

There has been much speculation about the role that Al Qaeda have had in the incidents of piracy and terrorism. In the immediate post-9/11 analysis of the maritime domain, government agencies reporting, coupled with a plethora of press reports, identified Al Qaeda (AQ) as having a fleet of ships that were ready to attack ships and ports throughout the world. The organization undoubtedly has links to the maritime industry, but that is through ship owners and operators who are sympathetic to Islamic rather than terrorist aims. There is little evidence to suggest that a fleet of hundreds of vessels and phantom ships is anything more than speculative. Evidence in the trial of Wadi Al Hage, who was convicted of involvement in the embassy bombings in East Africa, identified that a vessel had been used for logistics purposes, MV Sky 1. Intelligence agencies targeted the holding companies and vessels linked to them, which provided a framework of suspect vessels considered to be linked to terrorism. In the years that followed, none of these suspect vessels have been linked to terrorist acts, and just a few have been linked to illicit activity such as human trafficking and contraband smuggling. Al Qaeda operators have obviously been linked to the bombings of the USS Cole and MV Limburg, but they have to date, never been linked to any act of piracy (Johnston, 2005).

There are two terrorist organizations who have known maritime links, and those are the Liberation Tigers of Tamil Elam (LTTE) and the Lebanese group Hezbollah. LTTE has an established maritime arm, the "Sea Tigers," which has been linked to acts of piracy against foreign-owned commercial vessels. It has recently been reported that LTTE no longer requires funding from illegal activities such as piracy, but there remains a determination to conduct maritime terrorist acts. Hezbollah are known to operate in the Eastern Mediterranean, but they are not linked to piracy and they have not been involved in any terrorist attacks on Western shipping interests in the region. There is no doubt that they have the capacity and the expertise to conduct such terrorist attacks and may well be predisposed to do so (Molyneux, 2003).

Attacks in South East Asia are almost always attributed to terrorism, rather than piracy. In March 2003, the MV Dewi Madrim, a chemical tanker was boarded by pirates while underway, and it has been speculated by many that these pirates were in fact terrorists. Reports were circulated that suggested that they had not been after "booty," but had boarded the vessel to gain experience in ship handling, prior to conducting an attack using a similar vessel against U.S. naval vessels in port. There were also reports that suggested that certain members of the crew were taken as hostages in order to teach the terrorists ship-handling techniques. In the aftermath there has been much speculation by alleged maritime-security experts that this was a terrorist attack, but there is little evidence to support this view. It was probable that the pirates had sufficient skill to steer the ship anyway, and had reduced speed to a minimum in order to maintain steerage way, and to enable the pirates' own vessel to stay alongside. The pirates had left the vessel after approximately one hour taking cash, personal property, and ship's equipment with them, when they absconded (Luft & Korin, 2004).

Trends

The total number of incidents reported in 2007 indicates an overall increase in the number of attacks as compared to 2006. Compared to 2006, there has been an approximate 10% increase in the total number of attacks reported to the Piracy Reporting Centre. The significant increase in the incidents can be directly related to the increase in the reported incidents in Nigeria (42) and Somalia (31) as compared to the attacks reported in Nigeria (12) and Somalia (10) in 2006. This rise can be attributed to the increased ability of the pirates to attack vessels further out at sea as well as being better armed, organized and last but not least the lack of proper law enforcement.

Nigeria has recorded the second highest reported incidents in 2007 with the highest number of vessels boarded (35). The attacks and kidnappings are all being justified under the umbrella of political change. From the shipping industries point of view this is nothing short of being criminal. Somalia has seen the highest hostages taken (154) in eleven hijackings. The recent intervention of the international community and the coalition forces may prove to be the only way forward in curbing the enthusiasm of the pirates who have until now shown complete disregard for the law. On the brighter side, there has been a steady decrease in incidents reported in SE Asia (See Figure 2.12).

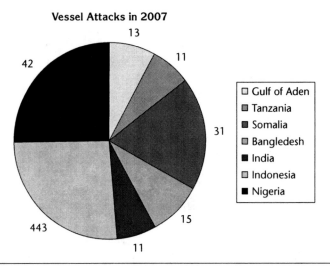

FIGURE 2.12
Vessel Attacks in 2007

Over the last five years, there has been a significant drop in the incidents reported in Indonesia, where in 2003, there were 121 reported incidents and in 2007, there have been only 43 incidents. Malaysia, Malacca Straits and Singapore Straits have also seen steady decrease in reported incidents. This welcomed reduction has been the cumulative result of increased vigilance and patrolling by the littoral states and the continued precautionary measures on board the ships. Authorities in Bangladesh have to be commended for their efforts in reducing the reported incidents from 47 in 2006 to only 15 in 2007. This should however, not be taken as an indication that the threat has ceased to exist. Masters are advised to maintain strict anti piracy watches especially while approaching the anchorage and while anchored. The nature of the attacks indicates that the pirates/robbers boarding the vessels are better armed and they have shown no hesitation in assaulting and injuring the crew. The total incidents in which guns have been used are 72. The total number of crew assaulted and injured is 64 as compared to 17 in 2006 (Morgan O'Rourke, 2005).

This rise in the incidents indicates a breakdown in the capability of certain countries to address the problem. The IMB strongly believes that unless continuous worldwide pressure on the law enforcement agencies and governments is exerted the governments will not give this crime the priority that it requires. Piracy not only affects the crew on board the vessels, traders and governments but also, at the grass route the common man who may probably be deprived of much needed aid being shipped.

The IMB therefore strongly urges all ship Masters, Owners, shipping industry and the respective flag states to report all incidents of actual and attempted piracy and armed robbery to the IMB Piracy Reporting Centre. These reports are extremely important to indicate to the law enforcement agencies and the governments the severity of the problem in their waters hence urging them to take appropriate action. The IMB is aware that a number of incidents go unreported each year due to various problems (Morgan, 2007).

Ship Board Defenses

Piracy is a crime and is not something that can be eradicated by the private sector. It will take the strong determination of all nations to work together and assist each state to bring a close to this horrific crime spree. The private sector may help prevent piracy in some of the following ways:

Convoys

As in the days of the North Atlantic in World War II, the merchant marine vessel had to defend itself from German U-boats by the use of convoys. Safety in numbers is a key aspect of anti-piracy practice. Vessels traveling in a convoy present as a much harder target for pirate vessels. One problem with this solution is that convoying is costly to smaller in the terms of burning extra fuel to maintain uniform speed.

Variance

As with the avoidance of crime, it is important to vary routines as much as possible to avoid piracy. Unfortunately, many vessels are unable to vary their schedule due to strict deadlines or lack of feasible alternative routes. However, even the appearance of variance may be beneficial should your vessel be the target of a planned attack. One example would be the removal of exact time and date information from online cruise line itineraries, easily accessible by all Internet users (Turbiville, 2005).

Shifting Cargo

Some companies have kept routes but have either cut down on the number of runs or have changed the cargo aboard their vessels to items less attractive to pirates. In Nigeria, one bank with branches on islands only accessible by boat had experienced a rash of cash-in-transit robberies on the waterways between their main location and their branches. Bank management decided to maintain only electronic transactions at their branches, allowing them to stay in business; electronic transactions meant no cash was necessary, and all cash-in-transit deliveries were rendered obsolete.

Offensive Measures

Many vessels are now equipped with various measures of combating maritime attacks that are already underway. The highest profile of these measures is currently the Long-Range Acoustic Device (LRAD) that was deployed by the *Spirit* in November, 2007. The LRAD produces high frequency sirens that force pirates without auditory protection to retreat, and in the case of the *Spirit,* the LRAD afforded the cruise ship enough time to gain speed and outrun its assailants. The effectiveness of both devices diminishes with both distance from the ship and the use of ear protection. The use of sophisticated ear protection will significantly decrease the effectiveness of both LRAD and MRAD by blocking the frequency that would temporarily or otherwise disable any potential attacker while still enabling the attacker to hear nearby voice commands.

Inventus UAV

The Inventus UAV (unmanned aerial vehicle) is a state-of-the-art reconnaissance system packaged in a highly efficient, highly stable flying wing form. Outfitted with cameras, the Inventus flies and covers a large ocean area and relays a real-time data link back to the ground station. This link provides real-time aerial surveillance and early warning of suspect or unauthorized craft movements to the coastal or law enforcement authority. Inventus is fully autonomous and can be launched and recovered even from a seagoing or patrol vessel. There are gas and electric formats and both fly in all weather conditions.

Secure-Ship

Secure-Ship is the most recent and effective innovation in the fight against piracy. It is a non-lethal, electrifying fence surrounding the whole ship, which has been specially adapted for maritime use. The fence uses 9,000-volt pulse to deter hoarding attempts. An intruder coming in contact with the fence will receive an unpleasant non-lethal shock that will result in the intruder abandoning the attempted boarding (Luft & Korin, 2004).

Conclusion

Maritime terrorism is without doubt a major problem, and reporting suggests that an attack by terrorists in the Malacca Straits, Nigeria or the Horn of Africa is inevitable. But before jumping to conclusions, is the increase in piracy linked to terrorism? There are some who would say that there is no link between the two. Piracy is not known to be linked to terrorism and vice-versa. I am certain that it is not, but there is no evidence to support this; conversely, there is no evidence to refute it either. The major Western navies are spending large sums of money in combating maritime terrorism, while piracy goes unchecked and thrives. We equip our law-enforcement agencies to combat organized crime in our cities, but do little to combat organized crime on the high seas. The sea, and the waterways that the merchant fleet use, are largely unregulated in developing countries, while in the North European maritime domain, they are relatively well administered, and the maritime industry does much of its own policing.

All the major navies and law enforcement entities need to have a specific policy on dealing with, and taking action against, pirates. Rules of Engagement should allow for vessels to take strong and decisive action. The regional navies and law enforcement agencies should be equipped for what they need to do, and advised accordingly.

References

Homeland Security. (2005). The National Strategy for Maritime Security. In M. Markham (Ed.), *Bullentin* (Report No. 4, pp. 1–5). Washington, United States: U.S. Department of Homeland Security.

International Chamber of Commerce. (2006, Winter 12). *Piracy and Armed Robbery Against Ships* (2006-1). United Kingdom, UK: International Maritime Bureau.

Johnston, Tim. (2005, June 27). Shipping industry's response to piracy is all at sea Mallacca Strait. *Financial Times,* p. 4.

Lull, Gal, & Korin, Anne. (2004). Terrorism Goes to Sea. *Foreign Affairs,* 83(6), 61.

Molyneux, J. (2003). [Indonesian Terrorist Organizations]. Unpublished raw data.

Morgan, J. (2007). International: Blood and Oil; Nigeria. *The Economist, 382*(8520), 71.

Morgan O'Rourke. (2005). Piracy on the High Seas. *Risk Management, 52*(9), 8.

Turbiville, Graham. (2005). Singapore forms maritime special-operations unit. *Special Warfare, 17*(3), 43.

3.3
The Overstated Threat

COMMANDER JOHN PATCH, U.S. NAVY
(RETIRED)

It Is Too Easy to Confuse Piracy with Water-borne Terrorist Acts. Don't Believe the Hype and Consider the Source

Modern pirates bear little resemblance to popular romantic Hollywood characters. Increasingly violent and greedy, their actions seem an affront to the very ideals of Western civilization. Armchair admirals and politicians are quick to shake their fists, avowing, "Something must be done." Maritime industry is quick to follow, with unsettling incident accounts and dire financial projections. Yet, more informed analysis of piracy reveals that the impact in blood and treasure is altogether minimal.

Indeed, common misperceptions abound. While maritime piracy incidents capture media attention and generate international calls for action, the piracy threat is in fact overstated. It is nothing more than high-seas criminal activity, better addressed by law enforcement agencies than warships. As a localized nuisance, it should not serve to shape maritime force structure or strategy.

The distinction between piracy and terrorism is neither semantic nor academic. If piracy, the responsibility lies with local law enforcement officials, not the military. But maritime terrorism means scrambling the Navy.

"The Overstated Threat," by Commander John Patch, U.S. Navy (Retired). Reprinted from *Proceedings,* December 2008, Vol. 134, No. 12, with permission; Copyright © 2008 U. S. Naval Institute/*www.usni.org.*

No Link, No Evidence

A critical contemporary myth to debunk is the alleged nexus between piracy and international terrorism. Serious scholars and analysts view with circumspection any assertions of this linkage. For instance, a recent International Institute of Strategic Studies (IISS) forum revealed that there is "no evidence terrorists are gaining any benefit from piracy"—the real threat being organized criminal activity, not terrorism.[1] The institute cites a study emphasizing the importance of not exaggerating the extent of either threat. Piracy, it maintains, is essentially a localized problem: "It is a nasty headache where it occurs, but its real effects on world trade and the movement of people are negligible." The study concludes there is no great risk of terrorists posing as pirates or adopting their methods either to seize a ship for hostages or to use the vessel itself as a weapon by igniting volatile cargo. To be sure, maritime terrorism is clearly a proven method of al Qaeda and other terrorist groups, but piracy cannot be plausibly conflated with it.

A 2008 RAND study reached similar conclusions. It detailed the causes for piracy in the last decade: local corruption, increased maritime traffic, small arms proliferation, lax coastal/port security, increasingly difficult maritime surveillance, lingering effects of the Asian financial crisis, and the denser traffic through congested choke points. RAND did not list terrorism, because "the presumed convergence between maritime terrorism and piracy remains highly questionable. . . . To date, there has been no credible evidence to support speculation about such a nexus emerging."[2] RAND further assessed that the objectives of the two actors remained entirely distinct. A recent piracy incident seems to support this: during the September 2008 hijacking of a Ukrainian freighter—the *Faina*—off Somalia, the pirate leader admitted via phone to a *New York Times* reporter that the group wanted "just money."[3]

---

1. Martin N. Murphy, "Contemporary Piracy and Maritime Terrorism: The threat to international security," interview with Dr. Patrick Cronin, International Institute of Strategic Studies.
2. Peter Chalk, "The Maritime Dimension of International Security: Terrorism, Piracy, and Challenges for the United States," RAND Corporation, 2008, xiv. Graham Ong makes similar conclusions in "Ships Can Be Dangerous Too" *Institute of Southeast Asian Studies working paper,* 2004.
3. Jeffrey Gettleman, "Somali Pirates Tell Their Side: They Want Only Money," *New York Times,* 30 September 2008.

Marginal Impact

Piracy of course has costs, both human and economic. Crews are kidnapped, injured, and occasionally murdered. Time is money in international shipping; delayed or stolen cargoes, waylaid vessels, and idle crews all mean lost profits and possible liabilities. Second-order effects in markets affected by piracy also have uncounted costs. Similarly, the potential consequences of an environmental disaster from mishandled or abandoned vessels with hazardous cargo could be severe. While impossible to quantify, the positive reinforcement that highly visible piracy successes have on would-be criminals is also a factor. Yet, the most significant systemic costs come from increases in vessel and cargo insurance premiums—especially for marine business in high-risk regions.

Overall, however, the consequences to maritime commerce are surprisingly minimal, though precise figures on the losses in commercial shipping are not available. The Center for Strategic and International Studies estimated that in 2001, piracy cost the industry $16 billion, but some analysts dispute this figure and it pales beside larger estimates of total global maritime trade, regardless.[4] A 2006 assessment of the risks of piracy indicated shipping industry losses were relatively small in relation to the total volume of ocean transports.[5] The study IISS cites above asserted "truth be told, losses are so low that there is little incentive for the shipping industries even to make a serious collective effort to tackle it."[6] So why all the hand wringing over piracy?

Widely Held Misperceptions

Even as the facts fail to support allegations of terrorist linkages or dire economic consequences, governments, pundits, and the media continue to hype the "threat." For instance, the U.S. *National Strategy for Maritime Security* relates that pirate groups could employ capabilities to board and commandeer large underway ves-

---

4. John J. Brandon, "Piracy on High Seas is Big Business," Pacific Forum, CSIS, 30 March 2001. $16 billion likely represents less than .1 percent of the annual global value of maritime cargo, vessels, and insurance.
5. Munich Re Group, *Piracy—Threat at Sea: A Risk Analysis,* September 2006, p. 7.
6. David Osler, "Lloyd's List—Sharp perspective on clear and present danger," The International Institute for Strategic Studies, 17 August 2007.

sels to facilitate terrorist acts.[7] This seems a poor basis for guiding decisions on how America is to address piracy. Regrettably, many apply similar logic to organized drug smugglers, with the apparent intent of exaggerating the threat. The U.S. Coast Guard's recent adoption of a risk-based threat assessment process that includes analyzing the likelihood of specific terrorist methods, targets, and attack consequences appears to be a sounder decision-support model, easily applied to piracy.

Notwithstanding the lack of any clear evidence, government officials and respected journals continue to make spurious claims. British maritime authorities in 2006 dismissed allegations of a piracy-terrorism nexus in a House of Commons report, responding that the report's conclusions were "not based on informed and corroborated intelligence."[8] A recent *Foreign Affairs* article claimed "the scourges of piracy and terrorism are increasingly intertwined: piracy on the high seas is becoming a key tactic of terrorists."[9] Office of Naval Intelligence (ONI) piracy expert Charles Dragonette roundly disputed the article as "uncritically repeating myths, half truths, and unsupportable assertions of an alleged nexus of piracy and terrorism."[10] The result, however, is a persistent blurring of the line between piracy and terrorism.

Another factor contributing to the confusion and ignorance surrounding piracy is the lack of a standard and comprehensive piracy definition, especially as it applies to high seas and territorial waters. Any act of maritime crime occurring within a sovereign state's 12-nautical-mile limit (the vast majority of reported incidents) simply is not piracy. As such, no state except the sovereign has any legal authority to address criminal acts against shipping in its waters. The resultant muddying of piracy and maritime crime reduces the accuracy of available piracy statistics.

The International Chamber of Commerce's non-profit International Maritime Bureau (IMB) Piracy Reporting Center also has a relatively loose definition that allows incidents both within and

---

7. U.S. Government, *National Strategy for Maritime Security,* September 2005, p. 5.
8. United Kingdom, House of Commons—Transport Committee—Piracy. 8th Report of Session 2005–2006, London, The Stationery Office Ltd., 2006 and the separate "Government Response."
9. Gal Luft and Anne Korin, "Terrorism Goes to Sea," *Foreign Affairs,* November/December 2004.
10. Charles Dragonette, "Lost at Sea," Letter to the Editor, *Foreign Affairs,* March/April 2005.

outside 12 nautical miles to qualify as piracy.[11] For instance, the IMB records reports of perceived small boat shadowing in high-threat areas as attempted pirate attacks, even though incident specifics are almost never confirmed. Similarly, an attempt by Greenpeace to board or thwart legal maritime activity also falls under the IMB piracy definition. Piracy data over different periods can also appear to support differing conclusions. Statistics for the past decade show a relatively consistent number of incidents per year, suggesting no increase, but a regional spike in one area can be hidden by a drop in another—Somalia versus the Strait of Malacca, for example.[12] Prudent maritime analysts should scrutinize piracy reporting, data, and statistics; claims that piracy is "spiraling" are usually unsubstantiated.

A second concern with IMB reporting is possible bias. Its Piracy Reporting Center seeks to raise awareness of hotspots, detail specific attacks and consequences, and investigate piracy incidents and armed robbery at sea and in port. While a noble cause endorsed by the United Nations, the center's *raison d'etre* is trumpeting the "piracy threat." Just as well-intentioned humanitarian aid groups occasionally exaggerate the scope or intensity of a crisis for effect—to draw more international attention and resources—so, too, is the IMB vulnerable to bias. Further, the bureau is almost exclusively funded by maritime shipping companies and insurers, with vested interests in keeping piracy in the headlines.[13] Profit-oriented businesses loathe implementing costly preventive measures, naturally preferring that international organizations, national law enforcement agencies, and armed forces take care of the problem instead.

The international shipping industry thus has a specific interest in exaggerating the global threat of piracy. Apparently capitalizing on the heightened 2008 media attention on Somali piracy, shipping organizations from all sides of the industry issued in September what they described as "a crisis call" to the International Maritime Organization and the UN to take "real and immediate action" to

---

11. Major Frederick Chew, Singapore-Navy, "Piracy, Maritime Terrorism and Regional Interests," Australian Command and Staff College Geddes Papers, 2005, p. 74.
12. International Maritime Organization, "Reports on Acts of Piracy and Armed Robbery against Ships," Annex 5, 13 April 2007.
13. ICC IMB, "Piracy and Armed Robbery against Ships: 2007 Annual Report," January 2008.

tackle piracy in Somalia, urging more nations to commit naval vessels to the area to deal with the threat.[14]

Only the Symptoms

Gray hulls bristling with weapons and sensors designed for conventional war are simply ill equipped to handle piracy—and are better assigned elsewhere. The recent situation off Somalia is a telling example. By late October 2008, the month-long saga of the pirated Belize-flagged motor vessel *Faina,* loaded with T-72 tanks, showed no signs of resolution, though six warships monitored the situation from the horizon. Astoundingly, this equates to roughly one destroyer or cruiser per pirate, but no appreciable ability to resolve the crisis. The presence of Russian crewmembers on the *Faina* prompted Moscow to send the frigate *Neustrashimy* with marine commandos at best speed from the distant Baltic Sea. NATO, the European Union, and India all promised to also send warships to help U.S. Navy ships patrolling the Horn of Africa region—potentially the largest anti-piracy flotilla in recent history.[15] On 12 November, British and Russian naval forces halted a pirate attack in the Gulf of Aden. British sailors killed two pirates in a firefight before the pirates on boad a dhow surrendered.

Five-inch guns and Harpoon missiles, however, are simply not the right weapons to confront pirates holding dangerous cargo or hostages. Even with an exceedingly rare UN ruling to allow foreign warships to take actions within a sovereign's territorial waters, the group of powerful warships near the *Faina* could do little to influence events. In the few instances when maritime force has been effectively applied, such as the 2008 commando operation rescuing French citizens or the 2007 U.S. Navy destruction of pirate skiffs, these strictly military actions rarely address the cause of piracy itself. A notable exception was the 2006 U.S. Navy operation involving American and Kenyan law enforcement officers, including a detailed forensic investigation resulting in the detention and subsequent sentencing of Somali pirates in a Kenyan court.

---

14. David Osler and Sandra Tsui, "Shipping unites in crisis call" to Mitropoulos for piracy action," Lloyd's List, 18 September 2008.
15. Jamey Keaten, "8 EU States Mull Anti-piracy Force," *Associated Press,* 2 October 2008. Belgium, Cyprus, France, Germany, Lithuania, the Netherlands, Spain, and Sweden volunteered ships. Like the United States, UK forces were already over-assigned and unavailable.

In recent months, the disadvantages of keeping expensive warships occupied with marginal-gain low-end missions such as piracy became apparent. The U.S. commander of Naval Forces Central Command (NAVCENT) stated in September that the international shipping industry must take on more responsibility to protect vessels against pirate attacks rather than rely on the U.S. Navy.[16] This likely reflects the appreciation that maritime powers do not have the resources to handle both conventional naval requirements and what is essentially a law enforcement mission. NAVCENT also seemed to signal its limitations, admitting that despite the presence of Coalition warships, "criminals still successfully targeted several vessels in the region." Notably, the Middle East Royal Navy commander commenting on the September NAVCENT statement emphasized, "we do what we can, but the solution to this problem is clearly not at sea, but ashore in Somalia."

Source of Piracy is Ashore

Pirate cells, especially more organized groups, require a network of support on land. Logistics, communications, weapons, money exchange, and marketing of stolen goods are all requirements managed ashore. Pirate groups usually exploit local villages or communities, but sometimes—as in Somalia—these provide the support network itself, or at least benefit significantly. Yet, targeting pirate infrastructure inland is no easy task: sovereignty, laws of armed conflict, and rules of engagement typically prevent unilateral actions. This is especially frustrating off Somalia, as no national police or armed forces exist. Some argue the piracy-terrorism nexus justifies more liberal military action in Somalia, but as noted earlier, such logic is both faulty and dangerous.

Informed analyses all similarly conclude that a holistic strategy to address piracy requires both sea- and land-based measures. Studies consistently show that the combined effects of regional economic crises and inadequate legal and security systems cause regional growth trends in piracy. A natural corollary is that law enforcement and intelligence services operating on land can more effectively identify and target piracy infrastructure ashore.[17] Yet,

---

16. "Navy Calls on Industry to Tackle Piracy," *Associated Press,* 23 September 2008.
17. Dr. Rohan Gunaratna, "The Threat to the Maritime Domain: How Real Is the Terrorist Threat?" *Economics and Maritime Strategy: Implications for the 21st Century,* U.S. Naval War College, National Security Economic Papers No. 2, 8 November 2006, p. 88.

these studies conclude that because of the inherent tension between securing shipping lanes and respecting state sovereignty, most anti-piracy initiatives are ad hoc.[18]

The Somalia example again illustrates the inefficacy of solely sea-based anti-piracy efforts. The Officer of Naval Intelligence reported in 2006 that Somalia's Union of Islamic Courts (UIC) seized control of Harardhere, the coastal village at the center of piracy. The courts' spokesmen asserted they were in full control of the village, the era of banditry and piracy was over, and the actions of pirates were unlawful, unacceptable, and un-Islamic.[19] After locals were threatened with swift administration of Sharia law, piracy abruptly ceased off Harardhere—until Ethiopian forces pushed UIC elements from the region. It is ironic that Ethiopian military operations designed to oust the radical Islamist threat reintroduced an era of significant Somali piracy.

A Recognized Structure

The International Maritime Organization (IMO) remains the recognized international body with the mandate to establish a global anti-piracy plan. The organization provides an accepted, common framework for action and represents the best hope for establishing and sustaining an international regime to eliminate piracy. Existing international conventions that support anti-piracy measures, such as the Law of the Seas, Safety of Maritime Navigation, International Ship and Port Facility Security Code, and the Safety of Life at Sea Convention, are initiatives born out of the organization's forum. Regional initiatives, such as the ASEAN Regional Forum, can work through the IMO to ensure localized multinational efforts contribute to a global anti-piracy effort. Benefits include increased capacity building, law enforcement interoperability, standard reporting procedures, global maritime information center support, and improved cooperation among coast guards. Since these efforts inherently involve law enforcement and regulatory agencies, however, they are usually inappropriate for armed forces. In fact, the Coast Guard (with its law enforcement responsibilities unique to the armed forces) is the lead maritime agency in the U.S. delegation to the IMO.

---

18. Nathanial Gronewold, "Soaring prices spur worries about piracy, marine terror," IISS, June 2008.
19. David Pearl and Charles Dragonette, "Worldwide Threat to Shipping Mariner Warning Information," Office of Naval Intelligence, 16 August 2006.

While law enforcement agencies are inherently more prepared to deal with maritime crime, naval forces still have a role in supporting them. Most states simply do not have the wherewithal to provide for persistent territorial or exclusive economic zone (EEZ) patrols. Regional multination initiatives, such as Coalition Task Force 150, bolster nearby state efforts in piracy hotspots with presence and response forces. Such multinational maritime forces also reinforce international regimes, especially when participating navies enter into local agreements with law enforcement to eliminate the perceived sanctuary of territorial waters. One method periodically used is to embark law enforcement detachments (LEDETs) from both flag and host nations to support local law enforcement operations (including forensics, detainee handling, evidence chain of custody, etc.). U.S. Navy warships periodically host U.S. Coast Guard LEDETs during counterdrug and embargo enforcement operations. The importance of the onboard capability to conduct the full scale of law enforcement operations—that ultimately address the source of piracy ashore—cannot be overstated.

Commercial Sector Has a Role

Multinational shipping corporations, insurers, and vessel masters must all bear some of the burden of responsibility to deter and hinder pirates. Indeed, the commercial sector enjoys huge profits facilitated by maritime security; it also has the means to act against piracy. The IMO promulgates standard, proven anti-piracy practices. Yet vessels and shippers routinely ignore them. For example, ONI makes periodic unclassified threat assessments that the State Department and IMB incorporate into special warnings to mariners. In the Somali case, ONI urged mariners to avoid the piracy-prone areas by at least 200 nautical miles as early as 2005. Considering that numerous pirated vessels were well within the 200 miles when seized, it seems clear some masters chose to ignore the warnings at their peril (presumably to avoid excess fuel costs of indirect routes).

Evidence indicates ship owners are clearly not doing enough to protect their vessels and crew and must invest in anti-piracy systems, such as ship-wide alarm and surveillance systems, anti-boarding devices (electric fences, interior-locking armored doors, long-range acoustic devices, water cannons, etc.), and even armed guards in high risk areas. Recent press reports indicates that private security contractor Blackwater USA is offering services to protect shipping off of Somalia. Of course, these measures are expensive, thus often not implemented. Somalia again offers a patent lesson, as ONI reports that foreign-controlled (usually Asian) fishing vessels continue to operate freely in Somalia's unregulated EEZ, taking advantage of the failed state's lack of regulation. These vessels are easy targets; Somali pirates, as well as quasi-official regional authorities, occasionally seize them. ONI reports that in several cases, hijacked fishing vessels served as pirate mother ships to conduct additional attacks.[20]

Rigorous flag-state enforcement of maritime security regulations is one method to compel commercial anti-piracy measure compliance. Companies often choose flags of convenience, however, for low cost and lax enforcement. Still, the 2005 piracy attempt against U.S.-flagged *Seabourn Spirit* serves as a testament to anti-piracy best practices. The cruise liner, carrying several hundred vacationers, escaped hijacking by Somali pirates. The attack failed because the captain reacted to the approaching vessels immediately, heading out to open sea at full speed, and conducting evasive maneuvers to prevent a boarding. The pirates gave chase, fired rocket-propelled grenades and automatic weapons at the liner, and did not break off until the *Seabourn Spirit* employed a long-range acoustic device, which generates focused, painful noise. In theory, if mariners heed warnings and regulations and implement prudent anti-piracy measures, this could eliminate the market for Somali pirates, making the practice unprofitable.

Piracy Threat in Context

In its current form and scope, piracy threatens no vital U.S. national security interests. It is in no way comparable to legacy threats that shape national strategy, such as terrorism or weapons of mass destruction proliferation. Hence, it is inherently disingenuous to inflate the piracy "threat" to justify either force structure or maritime strategic underpinnings.

As such, maritime policy and strategy deliberations and crisis course of action planning efforts should consider this reality. In this context, more U.S. anti-piracy options emerge—including no military response at all. America has long championed freedom of the seas, but it is perchance time that the many flag states and private companies enjoying the benefits of the global maritime commons

---

20. Pearl, "Worldwide Threat to Shipping Mariner Warning Information," Office of Naval Intelligence, 13 February 2008.

contribute to the costs of keeping it secure. Because the U.S. Navy lacks the resources to effectively accomplish even a fraction of its assigned missions, treating piracy for what it is—criminal activity—should lessen the demands on an already overtaxed American Fleet.

3.4
The Threat to the Maritime Domain: How Real Is the Terrorist Threat?[1]

DR. ROHAN GUNARATNA

Introduction

Armed groups seek to attack aviation, maritime, and land transportation targets. In the class of threats, the terrorist intentions and capabilities to strike transportation infrastructure have grown dramatically since September 11, 2001. Although land transportation remains more vulnerable to attack, aviation remains the preferred target of multiple threat groups. Since Al Qaeda used commercial aircraft to attack America's iconic targets, multiple attempts to target aviation have been detected and disrupted by security, intelligence, and law enforcement. The UK authorities disrupted an elaborate plot in August 2006 to attack a dozen aircraft from London bound for the United States. The threat has been sustained.[2] Similarly, the successful attacks on land transportation targets in

---

1. I would like to thank Professor Rich Lloyd, The William B. Ruger Chair of National Security Economics at the Naval War College, and Professor Jeff Norwitz, The John N. Brown Academic Chair of Counterterrorism at the Naval War College, for their invitation to speak at the Economics and Maritime Strategy Ruger Chair Workshop, November 7–8, 2006, and to write this paper.
2. On December 22, 2001, Richard Reid, wearing a TATP-laden operational shoe bomb, boarded a Paris-to-Miami-bound American Airline flight. In Operation Snagged, an identical shoe bomb was recovered from 44 St. James Street, Barton, on November 27, 2003. In Operation Dover Port, Andrew Rowe was arrested at a port in France on October 26, 2003. He was planning to attack Heathrow. On September 15, 2004, a fully operational shoe bomb

77

Madrid on March 11, 2004; in London on July 7, 2006; and Mumbai on July 11, 2006; demonstrate both the dispersed and enduring nature of the threat. The failed attack in London on July 21, 2006, and several attempts in continental Europe and elsewhere, demonstrate that the threat is recurrent.

To assess the current and emerging threat, it is necessary to understand how armed groups exploit the maritime domain. The lack of understanding of the guerrilla and terrorist interface with the maritime environment has led to a hyping of the threat. This has led the commercial and naval community to invest billions of dollars in protecting and securing maritime assets. What is the real threat to onshore and offshore maritime infrastructure from sea, land, and air? This paper will examine the development of maritime terrorist and guerrilla capabilities and how guerrilla and terrorist groups have penetrated the maritime domain both to support their operations and to mount attacks.

Understanding the Maritime Domain

A study of maritime-capable groups worldwide demonstrates that only a few armed groups have developed the capabilities to mount attacks on maritime targets. Most groups exploit the maritime environment to transport goods and personnel.[3] The attacks in the aviation domain are not restricted to aircraft. Armed groups seek to attack fiat only aircraft, ships, and land transportation but also airports, ports, and land transportation hubs. Attacking an airport could have the same effect as attacking an aircraft. Similarly, an attack on a railway station could have the same effect as attacking a train. Likewise, an attack on a port will have the same effect—or a greater effect—than an attack on a ship. Unlike the aviation and land transportation domains, the maritime domain naturally does

---

mailed from Thailand to California was detected at the Carson mail facility in California. In 2005, an Algerian terrorist prosecuted in Northern Ireland had a manual advising the bomber to detonate his shoe bomb in the aircraft toilet. Global Pathfinder Database, International Centre for Political Violence and Terrorism Research, Nanyang Technological University, Singapore, accessed November 11, 2006.

3. It is very much like the terrorist and the extremist use of the Internet. Instead of mounting attacks on information infrastructure, terrorist and guerrilla groups use the Internet to disseminate propaganda, raise funds, train, rehearse, and coordinate operations. Likewise, the maritime domain is primarily a medium to support operations and not to mount attacks.

not constitute an attractive domain to attack. The terrorist preference is to attack a high-profile national symbol. In a globalized
world, an attack on an aircraft in any part of the highly visible aviation arena will have global implications. In contrast to damaging a
ship on the sea surface, bombing an airliner in the skies or an international airport will draw extensive publicity and generate fear. As
such, the threat to aviation and airports is very high compared to
the threat to the maritime and land domains.

It has been argued that hardening aviation and airport targets
has shifted the threat to maritime targets. Certainly threat displacement has taken place, but still, due to the potential for high publicity, the terrorist preference is to attack hardened targets. After 9-11,
more than a dozen plots to attack airlines, both in the sky and on
the ground, have been foiled or aborted. This demonstrates that
contemporary terrorists are keen to identify the gaps and loopholes
in security and penetrate the aviation domain rather than strike the
maritime domain.

In most cases, guerrilla and terrorist groups will attack a maritime target only if it is attractive or profitable. Attacking a ship on
the high seas is like a tree falling in the forest. Guerrilla and terrorist groups seek to mount low-cost, high-impact attacks. As armed
groups seek publicity, their preference is to attack a target near the
waterfront or in port. Furthermore, most groups do not have access
to large boats or ships that can operate outside territorial waters.
Except to steal cargo or kidnap personnel and passengers, the guerrillas and terrorists prefer to attack targets not far away from shore.
As such, guerrilla and terrorist target choices reduce the threat to
maritime infrastructure. By nature, most guerrillas and terrorists are
landlubbers.

Understanding the Maritime Threat

Maritime guerrilla and terrorist capabilities are an extension of the
land capabilities. However, maritime intentions are different from
maritime capabilities. Translating intentions into capabilities
requires significant human expertise (experience and training) and
resources. If a guerrilla and terrorist group can develop its understanding and knowledge of the maritime environment, it will begin
to exploit that domain. In the early phases, most groups use the
maritime environment to support land operations and, second, to
mount attacks.

At this point in time, only a few groups have the domain expertise. Even fewer groups have developed the capacities to operate

out at sea. If they are to operate in a sustained manner, they must possess or have access to a fleet of craft, usually fishing craft, and seafarers. The overall terrorist and guerrilla know-how and understanding of operating in the maritime domain are limited. The body of knowledge and understanding is growing by direct transfer and by emulation. More armed groups are likely to mount guerrilla and terrorist tactics in the maritime domain in the future.

Among the contemporary terrorist and guerrilla groups, only half a dozen groups have developed maritime attack capabilities. The most prominent among them are the Palestinian Flamas, the Lebanese Hezbollah, the Abu Sayyaf Group (ASG), the Free Aceh Movement, the Moro Islamic Liberation Front, Al Qaeda, and the Liberation Tigers of Tamil Eelam (LTTE). We consider two case studies: Al Qaeda and the LTTE. Of these two groups, the LTTE has built a state-of-the-art blue-, brown-, and green-water capability, both for support and attack operations. To penetrate the maritime domain, the LTTE operations serve as a model for other terrorist and guerrilla groups.

The LTTE Maritime Structure

The LTTE maritime organizational structure provides insight into the future capabilities of terrorist and guerrilla groups seeking to operate in the maritime environment.

1. Sea battle regiments
2. Underwater demolition teams
3. Sea Tiger strike groups
4. Marine engineering and boat-building unit
5. Radar and telecom unit
6. Marine weapons armory and dump group
7. Maritime school and academy
8. Recruiting section
9. Political, financial, and propaganda section
10. EEZ-marine logistics support team
11. Reconnaissance team and intelligence section
12. Welfare and registry.

The LTTE was able to build a robust maritime infrastructure because of the initial assistance it received from India's foreign intelligence service, Research and Analysis Wing (RAW). In 1986–87, RAW trained LTTE members in Vishakapatnam, a seaport in Andhara Pradesh, and facilitated the LTTE's construction of a blue-water fleet. After the LTTE declared war on the government of India in 1987, the LTTE maritime capabilities suffered extensively. After the LTTE support structures moved out of India's sphere of influence, the LITE built up a state-of-the-art shipping and procurement network in Europe to procure and ship dual-user technologies and weapons. For instance, the LTTE procured 60 tonnes of high explosives from the Ukraine and transported it onboard MV *Baris* (previously MV *Illiyana,* and thereafter MV *Tara 1* and MV *Venus*) during the peace talks in 1994. After the shipping network in Europe was disrupted under Indian pressure, the LTTE strengthened its existing financial, procurement, and shipping network in Southeast Asia. The LTTE used its commercial presence in Southeast Asia to build operational bases, primarily using Myanmar's island of Twante and, thereafter, Thailand's Pukhet. The LTTE boatyard in Pukhet was building a minisubmarine.

After the Thai authorities shut down the boatyard, the LTTE moved its boat-building activities to New Zealand. Boat designs procured in Australia and built in New Zealand were used in maritime suicide attacks in Sri Lanka.

As the LTTE is not an Islamist group, it is not perceived as a threat by most foreign governments. Thus, the LTTE continues to operate both in Sri Lanka and globally through front, cover, and sympathetic organizations. They include trading and commercial firms, especially fertilizer and shipping companies.

Al Qaeda's Maritime Structure

In contrast to the LTTE, Al Qaeda does not possess a permanent and robust infrastructure dedicated to maritime operations. Unlike the LTTE, Al Qaeda has neither a blue- nor a brown-water fleet. Although two dozen ships linked with Al Qaeda members, supporters, and families have been identified by the intelligence community, to date no ship has been intercepted transporting weapons.

However, Al Qaeda mounted a number of terrorist attacks, successfully and unsuccessfully. Al Qaeda leadership tasked its operations leader in the Arabian Peninsula[4]—Abd al Rahim al Nashiri, alias Abu Bilal, alias Mullah Bilal, alias the Prince of the Sea, a specialist in explosives—to mount maritime attacks in 1999. Osama bin Laden specifically instructed al Nashiri to attack oil supertankers. A Saudi of Yemeni roots, al Nashiri operated largely out of Yemen, both with Al Qaeda and with other Islamist groups. He had links with individuals and groups in the Arabian Peninsula and North Africa.

As there was no dedicated maritime component in Al Qaeda, the rest of the organization assisted al Nashiri. For instance, Tawfiq bin Attash alias Khallad, deputy of Khalid Sheikh Mohamed (9-11 mastermind), visited with al Nashiri and his associates to support his operations both in the Middle East and in Southeast Asia. By watching videos of Al Qaeda recordings of LTTE maritime attack on international television channels,[5] Al Qaeda copied LTTE maritime tactics as well as developed their own repertoire of tactics. They included blowing up explosives-laden vessels near naval, merchant, and cruise ships; blowing up explosives-laden vessels at seaports; using big ships, including tankers, to crash into smaller vessels; diving aircraft into ships, including into an aircraft carrier; using underwater demolition teams to destroy ships; and sinking ships in narrow channels. Responsible for attacking the USS *Cole* and MV *Limburg,* al Nashiri succeeded in blowing up explosives-laden boats near naval and merchant ships.

Even in the conduct of maritime operations, Al Qaeda had no problem with working with like-minded individuals and other groups. As a result, Al Qaeda traces were found in maritime opera-

---

4. Al Nashiri, the first head of the Al Qaeda organization in the Arabian peninsula, was succeeded by Yousef al Aiyyari. After al Aiyyeri was killed by Saudi security forces in May 2003, Abu Hazim al Shair al Yemeni, a former bodyguard of Osama and a poet, was appointed. Abu Hazim at Shair recruited pilots to attack Heathrow. Abu Hazim al Shair was succeeded by Abdu Aziz at Mukrin. After al Mukrin was killed, he was succeeded by Salih Sufi. There has been a very high attrition rate of the Al Qaeda leadership in the Arabian peninsula. As the bulk of the recruits and finance for Al Qaeda originated in the Arabian peninsula, Osama handpicked the leaders of the Arabian peninsula. While most of them were former bodyguards of Osama bin Laden, they had long-standing contact with Khalid Sheikh Mohamed and Tawfiq bin Attash, also a former bodyguard of the al Qaeda leader.
5. CNN's Nic Robertson recovered about 200 tapes from the Al Qaeda registry in Afghanistan. There were few clips of LTTE maritime attacks.

tions mounted by other groups. Al Qaeda trained in Iraq and funded an operational cell in Turkey that was planning and preparing to strike an Israeli cruise ship. Other leaders and members of Al Qaeda and its associated groups attempted a number of other maritime attacks. In Singapore, working with Al Qaeda, Jemaah Islamiyah (JI) members mounted surveillance on U.S. warships. Video footage of U.S. ships was recovered both in the residence of a JI member in Singapore and in the bombed residence of Abu Hafs in Afghanistan. In Malaysia, Al Qaeda associate group Kumpulan Militan Malaysia (KMM) planned to kill U.S. sailors but, fearing retaliation, aborted the operation. Tawfiq bin Attash flew to Malaysia and planned to attack U.S. vessels in Port Kiang in Malaysia. Al Qaeda's senior representative in Southeast Asia, Omar al Farouq, an Iraqi-Kuwaiti, and Ghalib, a Somali, planned a suicide attack on U.S. vessels exercising off Surabaya, Indonesia.

Al Qaeda Maritime Operation

Qaeda's road to maritime attacks developed the same way most other threat groups graduate from support to attack operations. Al Qaeda used trawlers and other vessels to transport arms, ammunition, and explosives from Yemen to neighboring countries. In fishing vessels, Al Qaeda also transported explosives into Kenya for the East Africa attack in August 1998. An Al Qaeda cell in Yemen began planning to hit USS *The Sullivans* in the spring of 1999 and made preparations in the summer of 1999. Al Qaeda began recruiting Saudis of Yemeni background and Yemeni residents, including those who wished to be suicide operatives. Al Qaeda preparations included leasing a safe house for six months, installing a gate, procuring a truck, and procuring and modifying a boat to accommodate more explosives. On January 3, 2000, when USS *The Sullivans* arrived in port, the explosives-laden suicide boat was launched from a nearby beach. From weight, the boat sank almost immediately. USS *The Sullivans* departed unaware of the attempt. The boat and explosives were recovered the next day for use in the USS *Cole* attack. As Al Qaeda in Yemen needed financing to execute the next attack, they decided to meet with Tawfiq bin Attash in Singapore. As there were visa requirements for Singapore, they shifted the venue of the meeting to Thailand. Two Al Qaeda members, Nibras and Quso, departed for Bangkok, where they met with Khallad, who gave them the money. After returning to Yemen, they made preparations in the spring and summer of 2000 to attack the USS *Cole*.

In preparation for the USS *Cole* attack, Al Qaeda built a much more extensive land infrastructure. A metal fence was built around the house they rented in an Aden suburb to keep their activities hidden from neighbors. In addition to renting a new safe house and adding a higher fence, Al Qaeda rented another apartment with a harbor view. This safe house functioned as the perfect observation post. Al Qaeda modified the boat, painted it, laid a red carpet, and refitted the insulation. Although the neighbors reported the noise of construction and power outages, the authorities failed to investigate. Compared to the USS *The Sullivans* attack, the investment Al Qaeda made to ensure the success of the attack on USS *Cole* was significant. Learning from the USS *The Sullivans* failure, Al Qaeda rehearsed the operation. To ensure that the boat had the right quantity of explosives, Al Qaeda conducted a dry run. Al Qaeda even tested the explosives. One month before the attack, in keeping with the standard operating procedure for Al Qaeda leaders, al Nashiri departed for Afghanistan.

The USS *Cole,* a guided-missile destroyer (DDG), had a crew of 346. The 154-m-long and 21-m-wide ship had a displacement of 8422 tons. The ship had a maximum speed of 33 knots. Its armaments included antiaircraft missiles, antiship missiles, torpedoes, a 5-inch gun, and Phalanx CIWS. The sequence of events was:

0849 local—USS *Cole* moors for refueling in Aden Harbor

1115 local—Ship is approached by small boat; two adult males aboard

1122 local—Boat comes along port side of USS *Cole*

Detonation immediately afterward

The execution phase of the attack was less than 30 minutes; the attack phase was 7 minutes. The sneak attack killed 17 and injured 42, mostly sailors gathering at the galley area for lunch. The repairing of the ship cost US$250 million. The one-billion-dollar ship was out of commission for two years. The U.S. government did not retaliate against Al Qaeda. In the eyes of the jihadists, USS *Cole* was America's state-of-the-art warship. In retaliation for the attacks on the U.S. embassies in East Africa in August 1998, USS *Cole* had fired cruise missiles at the Al Qaeda camps in Afghanistan. As such, the attack against USS *Cole* was considered a huge victory. Al Qaeda wanted to exploit the publicity to recruit and generate support. Al Qaeda leadership had instructed Quso to videotape the attack, based on a pager code, but he overslept on the day of the attack. Osama bin Laden was keen to screen the USS *Cole* attack video at his son's wedding in early 2001. Osama authorized US$5,000 to buy the camera equipment and videotape the attack. Thus, Quso did not endear himself to Osama. Although the failure to videotape the attack was a disappointment personally for Osama, the attack itself was a significant victory for Al Qaeda.

Two years after the attack on USS *Cole,* Al Qaeda reconstituted its personnel and resources to mount a second attack in Yemen. The next visiting U.S. warship was to be the next target. But when the naval ship failed to turn up, Al Qaeda attacked MV *Limburg,* a target of opportunity. A Very Large Crude Carrier (VLCC), the 25-crew MV *Limburg* was Belgian-owned and French-flagged. The 332-m-long and 58-m-wide ship has a displacement of 300,000 tons. MV *Limburg* has a capacity for 2.16 million barrels, but the cargo at the time of the attack was 397,000 barrels. Early morning on October 6, 2002, when *Limburg* was within visual range of shore (~3 nm), an attack boat rammed the starboard (seaward) side. The oil tanker was moving slowly toward the terminal, and a pilot boat was coming along the port side. While one crew member was killed, 90,000 barrels of oil spilled. As in the USS *Cole* attack, a safe house was used with a walled courtyard, and the boat was transported to a launch site just before the attack. Directed by al Nashiri, two suicide bombers in an explosives-laden boat attacked the near-stationary vessel. Unlike in the case of the USS *Cole,* Al Qaeda targeted an oil tanker instead of a warship. Furthermore, Al Qaeda leveraged an existing indigenous extremist network. It consisted of former members and supporters of the Islamic Army of the Abyan, a group that was dismantled by the Yemeni authorities two years earlier. The Al Qaeda plan was for the attack on MV *Limburg* to coincide with a simultaneous land-based attack. Although the Al Qaeda leadership had mentioned economic targets, the attack shocked the maritime community. The Yemeni authorities briefly held the ship owner, thinking that an accident on board the *Limburg* had caused the oil to spill.

Within a month of the attack on MV *Limburg,* al Nashiri was tracked down and captured. Al Nashiri was escaping from Yemen to Malaysia. He was planning and preparing several maritime operations. When al Nashiri was arrested in November 2002, a 180-page dossier of targets was recovered from his laptop. An operation al Nashiri was planning against U.S. and UK ships in the Strait of Gibraltar, off the northern coast of Morocco, was disrupted in June 2002. Three Saudi Al Qaeda members with Moroccan wives pretending to be businessmen constituted the attack team. They had received US$5,000 and direction from Nashiri to mount reconnaissance on both land and maritime targets. When the Al

Qaeda reconnaissance cell was disrupted in June 2002, no explosives were found. NATO maritime forces responded by boarding high-risk and suspicious ships, and German naval ships escorted tankers through the Strait of Gibraltar.

Maritime Attack Capabilities

Most terrorist and guerrilla groups can build maritime support capabilities by chartering ships or leasing boats. But to mount sustained attacks, they must build their own fleet and personnel. Unlike the LTTE, Al Qaeda failed to harness its existing expertise to operate in the maritime domain. Al Qaeda failed to build a dedicated maritime infrastructure of personnel and resources to attack maritime assets. Although Al Qaeda had experts who understood the maritime domain and operational infrastructure, it failed to grow its expertise. It was largely because the group's capabilities were scattered and had no permanent safe haven near the sea.

After the attack on USS *The Sullivans* failed, Al Qaeda explosives expert Abdul Rahman al Mohajir al Masri designed a shaped charge. A trainer at al Farook in Mes Aynak, southeast of Kabul (before the camp moved in 2000 to Kandahar), Abdul Rahman al Mohajir served under Abu Mohamed al Masri and later Hamza al Rabbiyah, the successive heads of training.[6] His reputation as the successful designer of the USS *Cole* attack was such that the leader of Al Qaeda in Iraq, Abu Musab al Zarqawi, requested the then head of Al Qaeda's external operations, Faraj al Libi, to dispatch Abdul Rahman al Mohajir to Iraq.[7] Instead, the Al Qaeda leadership on the Pakistan-Afghanistan border offered Hamza al Rabbiyah, but

---

6. After Al Qaeda was dislodged from Afghanistan, Abdul Rahman al Mohajir accompanied Hamza al Rabbiyah to South Waziristan and thereafter to North Waziristan. Under pressure from the Pakistani military, Al Qaeda dismantled its camps in South Waziristan and moved to North Waziristan to establish camps. Only the Chechen, Uigurs, and Central Asian jihadists of the Islamic Movement of Uzbekistan remained in the south. When Abdul Rahmana al Mohazir was killed by Pakistani forces in April 2006, he was head of training in Waziristan.

7. Zarqawi's driver was captured and Zarqawi's computer seized by the United States in February 2005. Correspondence recovered from the computer showed that instead of Abdul Rahman al Mohajir, Faraj al Libi offered Hamza al Rabiyyah. Later Faraj at Libi told CIA interrogators that Zarqawi did not have the skills of Hamza al Rabbiyah and that is why Zarqawi insisted on Abdul Rahman al Mohajir.

Zarqawi preferred Abdul Rahman al Mohajir. Zarqawi, who had mounted one maritime attack, was keen to use his expertise to mount more maritime attacks. Zarqawi also funded an attack to hit an Israeli cruise ship in the Turkish Mediterranean port of Antalya. However, Zarkwai, too, failed to develop a permanent operational infrastructure—both personnel and resources—dedicated to attacking maritime targets.

Immediately after Operation Enduring Freedom began in Afghanistan, Al Qaeda also considered hijacking an aircraft and crashing it onto a U.S. aircraft carrier in the Indian Ocean. The U.S. government released a NOTEM (note to mariners) of the impending threat. Until Al Qaeda operational leaders with the competence to operate in the maritime domain were captured or killed, Al Qaeda's maritime capabilities focused on mounting surface operations. Nonetheless, Al Qaeda was planning to build an underwater diving capability. Recoveries from the residence of Abu Hafs al Masri, alias Mohammed Atef—the Al Qaeda military commander killed in November 2001—included a diving manual. The Al Qaeda documents indicated that the group had recruited a specialist who understood diving, diving medicine, and closed-circuit and semiclosed-circuit gear. As the group needed operational cover, Al Qaeda intended to enlist the support of commercial and recreational divers to build an underwater diving capability. Furthermore, Al Qaeda had plans to establish its own diving schools. When Al Qaeda's infrastructure in Afghanistan was dismantled and its plans disrupted, its associated groups invested in building diving capabilities in Europe and in Asia. Although the Al Qaeda attempt to penetrate a diving school in Holland was detected, its training activities continued uninterrupted in Southeast Asia. With the assistance of Arab diving instructors, the ASG in the Philippines has trained at least 40 of its members in Jolo, Sulu archipelago, Mindanao since 2001.

With the diffusion of Al Qaeda's ideology of global jihad focusing on killing Westerners in large numbers, several of its associated groups are behaving like Al Qaeda. On February 27, 2004, ASG mounted an operation using a member of the Rajah Solaiman Revolutionary Movement. Redento Cain Dellosa, trained by JI, planted an explosives-laden television set in the tourist compartment of Super Ferry 14, plying between Manila and the southern Philippines. Next to the television IED the bomber left a plate of hot food to indicate that he was a passenger who had briefly stepped out of his cabin. The explosion and the subsequent fire killed 118 passengers; it was the worst maritime terrorist attack in history. Several other attempts to bomb ferries, before and after the sinking of Super Ferry 14, were frustrated by the Philippine authorities. However, the threat of terrorist groups planting bombs on ferries is very real, both in Southeast Asia and beyond. Thus, future maritime threats to ships will not only be from surface and underwater attacks but also from carrying a bomb on board a ship.

Lessons Identified

Most guerrilla and terrorist groups learn incrementally. Most groups are not innovative but imitative. Contrary to the prevalent view, they learn both by emulation and technology transfer. More than the direct transfer of technologies, they copy technologies, tactics, and techniques. For instance, Al Qaeda's attack on USS *Cole* was a copycat of LTTE's attack on *Abheetha,* a Sri Lankan navy supply ship. On May 4, 1991, *Abheetha* was anchored 6 miles north of Point Pedro, northern Sri Lanka, when an explosives-laden suicide boat rammed it. The attack caused extensive damage to the ship, and killed six and injured 18 naval personnel. The LTTE maritime suicide wing (Black Sea Tigers) members Captain Sithambaram and Capain Jeyanthan were also killed.

Similarly, it is very likely that one attack inspires another. After the alarm and publicity generated after Al Qaeda's attack on the USS *Cole* on October 12, 2000, many terrorist and guerrilla groups became interested in mounting attacks in the maritime domain. Within a month of the USS *Cole* suicide bombing on October 12, the terrorist "copycat effect" was demonstrated. LTTE suicide stealth boats breached the defenses of Trincomalee, the most protected Sri Lankan naval port, and destroyed a fast personnel carrier on October 23; and a Palestinian Hamas suicide boat attacked an Israeli naval craft on November 7, 2000. As the bomber detonated prematurely, only the skin of the Israeli craft was damaged.

To attack maritime targets, terrorist groups build their support and operational infrastructures on land, not at sea. Thus, the logical starting point in preventing future maritime attacks is to disrupt and degrade the terrorist infrastructure on land. The USS *The Sullivans,* USS *Cole,* MV *Limburg,* and several other case studies demonstrate that both maritime terrorism and piracy should be fought on land. As the terrorist and criminal infrastructure and personnel are based on land, they can be identified and targeted much more effectively by law enforcement and intelligence services operating on land. The failure to detect the planning and preparations of a maritime terrorist or piratical attack on land will lead the terrorist group or the criminal group to successfully launch the maritime attack. In a maritime terrorist or piratical attack, the time the terrorists and pirates spend out at sea is a few minutes. Unless the method, the place, and the exact time of the attack is known, it is not possible to interdict a maritime terrorist or piratical attack out at sea. As such, the maritime police units and navies have a very limited opportunity to successfully respond to maritime terrorism and piracy.

Conclusion

Most threat groups exploit the maritime domain for support, not offensive operations. More groups are interested in developing and expanding their range of maritime capabilities. Over time, most threat groups with access to water move from conducting support operations to guiding surface and underwater attack capabilities. Traditionally maritime terrorist technologies originated in the Middle East, but now they can be seen increasingly in Asia. In the coming years, the Asian threat groups are likely to innovate certain technologies and tactics that Middle Eastern groups are likely to copy.

Compared to the threat to aviation and land transportation, the threat from terrorism to naval ships and commercial shipping is medium to low. While the maritime assets are vulnerable to terrorist attack, the actual threat to maritime assets is medium to low for two reasons. First, very few terrorist groups have the capabilities to attack maritime targets. Second, very few attractive maritime targets could be attacked without expending many resources. Although naval vessels can be protected by enhanced perimeter security, it is neither feasible nor cost-effective to protect every merchant vessel. An effective strategy for consideration by law enforcement and intelligence services should include (a) creating dedicated maritime counterterrorist commands to target terrorist groups with land-based maritime assets, (b) securing waterways used by ships operating in areas where terrorist and criminal groups are active, and (c) protecting cruise liners, oil tankers, LNG and LPG carriers, and other vessels transporting strategic cargo operating in areas where terrorist and criminal groups are known to be active.

The threat of a maritime attack is of low probability. Depending on the target attacked, the consequences can be medium or high. As 95 percent of the world's trade moves by sea, even if ten vessels are attacked in a single day, shipping will continue. Certainly the rising insurance premiums and investment in security will increase the cost of transportation and goods. However, the dependence of nations on the maritime environment percent or trade and commerce is of such paramount consideration that governments and the private sector will not seek alternative modes of transport. If the number of maritime attacks increases, governments and the private sector will invest excessively in securing the maritime domain. As of today, most of the investment to secure the maritime domain is driven by fear, not by an understanding of the threat.

Chapter 4

Interoperability versus Support Systems on Land

4.1
Legal Interoperability Issues in International Cooperation Measures to Secure the Maritime Commons

CRAIG H. ALLEN
CHARLES H. STOCKTON

The life of the law has not been logic, but experience.

—Oliver Wendell Holmes, Jr., *The Common Law*

Introduction

I would first like to say that I much prefer the phrase "securing the commons" to the more provocative and inaccurate "command of the commons." The latter is impossible to objectively assess and, more important to me, a legal oxymoron. The commons are just that: a shared space not subject to any nation's sovereignty or control, and, for that reason, a space where all states have an obligation to promote and enforce the public order necessary to prevent a tragedy in those commons, whether by overuse, abuse, or malevolent misuse. The U.S. approach reflected in the National Strategy for Maritime Security (2005) eschews any pretension to "command" of the maritime commons, calling instead for enhanced maritime domain awareness and an active, layered defense, together with measures to reduce vulnerability and improve consequence management readiness.

In a workshop of distinguished economists, I confess my lack of competency on all matters involving the dismal science and will instead focus my remarks on some of the salient legal issues raised by the title of this panel—more specifically, on legal interoperability issues. On this question I am happy to report that over the past five years or so the law has adapted to our often tragic "experience" (to quote Justice Holmes) in a number of proactive ways, in an effort to anticipate conflicts and eliminate them where possible. However, more work lies ahead.

Combined operations—particularly coalition operations—are one area where more remains to be done. The U.S. Army's *Operational Law Handbook* sets the scene. It explains that

> The United States often chooses to participate in operations alongside other nations. While some of these operations are conducted within an established alliance such as NATO, others are coalition action. Coalition action is multinational action outside the bounds of established alliances, usually for single occasions or longer cooperation in a narrow sector of common interest. Recent examples are Operation Enduring Freedom and Operation Iraqi Freedom. Unlike NATO operations, coalition action by its nature does not have a predetermined structure or decision-making process.
>
> [One] disadvantage of coalition action is that it often raises significant interoperability issues that need to be resolved to ensure success of the operation.
>
> Interoperability issues arise for a number of reasons. First, the coalition partner may have different legal obligations, such as being signatory to a treaty to which the United States is not a party and which the United States does not consider customary international law. Second, the United States and the coalition partner may both be legally bound by a provision of international law, by treaty or custom, but may interpret their obligations differently. Finally some differences may not result from law at all, but from the application of domestic policy.[1]

Planning for multinational operations in the maritime commons may take one of several forms. In established alliances, such as NATO, planners can address interoperability issues through prior agreements, such as the Allied Publication series and the NATO standardization agreements (STANAGs). In what is sometimes referred to as proactive, "Phase Zero" planning, the geographic combatant commanders prepare theater security cooperation plans

---

1. U.S. Army Judge Advocate General's Legal Center and School, *Operational Law Handbook* (Charlottesville, Va.: U.S. Army Judge Advocate General's Legal Center and School, 2006), at pp. 527–30.

for their areas of responsibility. Those plans typically call for military-military exchanges and other relationship-building measures with other forces in the theater, to improve military capabilities and interoperability. Finally, there is the ad hoc planning approach, hopefully drawing on planning models and templates.

Actual maritime security operations within the various theaters may be carried out unilaterally, by established alliances, such as NATO, or by coalition actions, such as the Commander Task Force 150 operations in the far western Indian Ocean and Red Sea approaches off the Horn of Africa. Other recent, and nongeographically specific, partnering initiatives include the Proliferation Security Initiative and the 1,000-ship navy concept—now called the Global Maritime Partnership.[2]

At-sea maritime operations take a variety of names, including maritime security operations (mentioned above),[3] or more specific labels, such as maritime interception operations,[4] maritime interdiction operations,[5] or maritime law enforcement operations.[6] In

---

2. The U.S. Navy CNO has called the 1,000-ship navy "a network of international navies, coast guards, maritime forces, port operators, commercial shippers and local law enforcement, all working together."

3. Maritime security operation missions include ensuring freedom of navigation, the flow of commerce, and the protection of ocean resources, and securing the maritime domain from nation-state threats, terrorism, drug trafficking, and other forms of transnational crime, piracy, environmental destruction and illegal seaborne immigration. Chief of Naval Operations and Commandant of the Marine Corps, *Naval Operations Concept* (2006).

4. U.S. Navy, *Maritime Interception Operations,* NTTP 3-07.11/CGP 3-07.11 (2003) (defining "interception" as the "legitimate action of denying suspect vessels access to specific ports for import or export of prohibited goods to or from a specified nation or nations, for purposes of peacekeeping or to enforce imposed sanctions."). "Expanded" MIO refers to interception operations in the absence of a collective security measure.

5. See Chairman, Joint Chiefs of Staff, *Doctrine for Joint Interdiction Operations,* Jt. Pub. 3-03 (1997), which defines interdiction as "an action to divert, disrupt, delay or destroy the enemy's surface military potential before it can be used effectively against friendly forces." Within the U.S. *National Strategy for Maritime Security* framework, interdiction is described as "actions taken to divert, delay, intercept, board, detain, or destroy, as appropriate, suspect vessels, people, and cargo." "Interdiction" is the favored term in most NATO countries. It is also used in the Proliferation Security Initiative "Statement of Interdiction Principles." On the other hand, it is disfavored by some states, particularly China.

6. Maritime law enforcement operations refer to activities by officials with the legal authority to detect crimes, apprehend violators, and gather the evidence necessary to support prosecution.

some cases the legal basis for the maritime operation comes from a UN Security Council resolution or a right of individual or collective self-defense, but in many of the boardings the legal basis for the "end game" ultimately lies in the extraterritorial application of some nation's domestic law. Regardless of the form of the cooperative arrangement, the participating states often come to the table with divergent rule sets (legal authorities and restrictions).[7] Despite the pressure of globalization to harmonize the law and make it more uniform, differences continue to exist, whether on matters of trade, immigration, maritime crime, security cooperation, disclosure of intelligence, or the interpretation or application of law of the sea or law of armed conflict issues. As a result, the participating states must confront several recurring legal interoperability issues. For this synopsis, several issues are highlighted for possible discussion:

- Rules of Engagement
- Rules regarding the right to exercise self-defense
- Targeting issues (i.e., what is a "military objective"; pro-portionality issues)
- Use of certain means and methods (landmines, chemical riot control agents)
- Status and treatment of detainees
- Status of armed forces (SOFAs, VFAs, Article 98 agreements)
- Access to information and intelligence.

Theater security cooperation plans can help avoid or mitigate some of the common legal interoperability problems, but they have never received the funding needed to reach their full potential. In some cases, the divergent rule sets can in fact be harmonized into "com-bined forces" rules, as in the case of Combined Rules of Engagement (CROE). Another commonly used approach to work through or around such issues calls for the participating states to collectively prepare a "legal matrix" that displays the key elements of their respective rule sets and reveals any variations. The difference in the two approaches is an important one: in the first, the relevant rules are in fact harmonized (often, however, by reducing the rules to the least common denominator); in the latter, national differences are main-tained, but once collected into the matrix by the operational com-mander they are at least *available* for communication to the

---

7. For the lawyer, legal interoperability questions are typically analyzed under the "conflict of laws" framework. Proactive lawyers seek to avoid conflicts by, for example, working to unify and/or harmonize the laws, or at least being clear about which law will apply to a given transaction, through insertion of a choice of law clause.

participating units, though classification issues and other objections might impede the full realization of that goal.

The U.S. Naval War College, with the support of its International Law Department and the affiliated Naval Reserve components, has taken the initiative to address a number of these recurring issues, by, for example, sponsoring flag- and general-officer-level courses for Combined Forces Maritime Component Commanders, where interoperability issues can be analyzed and minimized as much as possible; and by its work on drafting model CROE and on collecting and clarifying the discordant laws governing maritime exclusionary zones. One subject where additional efforts to promote legal interoperability are needed is in intelligence matters.[8]

Legal Interoperability on Intelligence Matters

It has become commonplace to criticize the intelligence community for its secretive, stove-piped approach, which, as famously described by the U.S. 9/11 Commission, impedes their ability to "connect the dots." While such criticism might be politically popular, it reveals a shameful disregard for the underlying legal and policy issues, to say nothing of the practical limitations that militate against wider disclosure of some classified information. Nevertheless, a number of recent studies, presidential directives, statutes, and international agreements have called for greater intelligence-sharing. Not surprisingly, the 9/11 Commission was among the first. Congress soon followed, demanding greater intelligence-sharing in the 2004 Intelligence Reform and Terrorism Prevention Act. The new catch-phrase admonishes that the old "need-to-know" restriction must give way to a "need-to-share" approach, an approach that's increasingly facilitated by the policy directing members of the intelligence community to "write for release."[9] In 2003, the states participating in the

---

8. The author is indebted to Captain Santiago R. Neville, USN, the RADM Edwin Layton Chair in Intelligence at the Naval War College, and to Captain Maureen Neville, USN, Officer-in-Charge of the Office of Naval Intelligence Detachment at NWC, for their helpful suggestions on intelligence interoperability issues.

9. *See,* e.g., Director of Central Intelligence, Directive 8/1 (June 4, 2004) (defining "write to release" as: "A general approach whereby intelligence reports are written in such a way that sources and methods are disguised so that the report can be distributed to customers or intelligence partners at lower security levels. In essence, write-to-release is proactive sanitization that makes intelligence more readily available to a more diverse set of customers. The term encompasses a number of specific implementation approaches, including sanitized leads and Tearline reporting.").

Proliferation Security Initiative agreed to a Statement of Interdiction Principles that provides a framework for intelligence-sharing in counterproliferation operations. In 2004, the G-8 states entered into an agreement that called upon the member states to pass legislation if necessary to ensure that terrorism information can be shared internally with police and prosecutors and externally with other countries. The G-8 agreement also recommended that each state ensure it can legally use a variety of "special investigative techniques," such as wiretaps, audio and visual surveillance, and interception of electronic communications.

The call for greater intelligence-sharing in some areas of common concern and concerted action carried over into the National Strategy for Maritime Security and its eight supporting plans. One of those supporting plans lays out the means to achieve greater Maritime Domain Awareness (MDA); another provides the framework for Global Maritime Intelligence Integration. But any discussion of sharing must give careful consideration to the applicable legal limits on doing so. It is almost certainly the case that some components of the MDA system, or information in the MDA system, will not be disclosable to foreign nations under existing law. Doing so may reveal sources and methods in a way that may cost the lives of the former and the long-term effectiveness of the latter. Within the United States, we must also grapple with the legal restrictions on providing proprietary information and information obtained through intelligence channels to law enforcement agencies—a question only partly addressed by the Foreign Intelligence Surveillance Act, USA PATRIOT Act, and Maritime Operational Threat Response plan. This is not the forum to explore these technical and partly classified interoperability issues. Let me just say that more work might be needed, either to clarify the restrictions or to at least avoid unreasonable expectations on the part of coalition partners.

Let me close with a short list of some of the recurring intelligence- and law-related interoperability issues that coalition commanders and operators and their intelligence officers and lawyers should be prepared to address and respond to (I would be happy to discuss any of these with the distinguished panelists):

- A request to disclose the factual basis for invoking the right of self-defense (i.e., proof of an imminent threat) to the UN Security Council, a regional security body, or a coalition partner.
- A request by a partner state to disclose the basis for concluding that a potential target constitutes a "military objective," or that striking that target would not violate the prohibition on "disproportionate" use of force.

- A request by a partner state (or flag state) to disclose the basis for a boarding, search, seizure, or arrest, where the governing legal standard is "reasonable basis to believe," "probable cause to believe," or something similar.
- A request from a partner state (or an international criminal tribunal) to disclose intelligence for use in a criminal prosecution. In U.S. prosecutions, this issue is addressed in the less-than-pellucid or -predictable Classified Information Procedures Act.

Conclusion

In a workshop of legal experts from around the world, held in this same room last week, 94 percent of the experts stated that they believe future U.S. Navy operations will be "more combined." Assuming they are right, the effectiveness of future international cooperation in securing the maritime commons will require us to continue to work toward resolving legal interoperability questions. Experience has shown that information-sharing not only serves to improve security-related decision making, it can also be an effective trust-building measure. Although there are plainly good reasons to facilitate timely and effective information-sharing in many cases, it is important not to lose sight of the fact that increased disclosure might come at the expense of the long-term effectiveness of the intelligence community. The solution to legal interoperability issues is not to eliminate every national restriction, but rather to carefully review the disclosure laws and policies, to ensure any unnecessary restrictions on disclosure are removed, to follow the write-for-release policy when drafting intelligence products as much as possible, and then to ensure that our maritime security partners understand the remaining restrictions on disclosure and the reasons for them.

4.2
International Cooperation in Securing the Maritime Commons

A Food for Thought Paper Based on Practical Experience in International Cooperation

VICE ADMIRAL LUTZ FELDT

Introduction

It is of utmost importance to define the political aim that should be achieved by the anticipated international cooperation. The already elaborated twin goals economic prosperity and security are providing excellent guidance on the so-important operational level. But what we need, too, is an overarching object for our efforts. That is due to the recognition that we are dealing with a process-orientated matter.

Globalization is an economic phenomenon—but with numerous various aspects. Taking these aspects seriously, we need a broader approach, as given by the above-mentioned twin goals. So my suggestion is to use "Freedom of the Seas" as the political aim. Maritime power—for example, the 1000-ship navy—is the operational level. In accordance with Alfred Thayer Mahan, the three pillars of maritime power are naval power, a powerful merchant navy, including the ability and capability for sea exploitation and environmental protection, and, as the third pillar, the control of strategic points, today called "choke points" or "hot spots." Mahan came to the conclusion that these are the preconditions of the maritime power of one single nation. I think they are valid in international operation as well.

Factors Creating the Framework for Cooperation

First of all, we are dealing simultaneously with national states and independent international institutions and networks.

Secondly, the exploitation of the whole richness of the sea is already an important process on the maritime agenda. It includes trade and industrial and scientific activities. It will increase in importance.

Thirdly, the environmental point of view is already a valuable cause for international cooperation. It will increase its influence on all kinds of international activities, mostly in the field of economic development. I think we should give this factor a lot of attention.

Last but not least, it is very valuable to take the cultural and/or intellectual dimension into account. There are various approaches possible. I want to put my focus upon two of them: firstly, the fact that the free movement of people and ideas is playing an active part in the development of the hearts and minds of people; and secondly, that different mentalities are playing a major role in all kinds of international cooperation. This difference has to be accepted and to be taken as a given. As an example, I want to underline the different ways of executing leadership on board our ships and in our staffs.

As a summary it is very obvious that three out of the four factors are directly or indirectly related to economic prosperity as the major driving force of our global world.

The fourth one is what I call the "software" of any kind of international cooperation. It is creating a possible link between various mentalities—ways of thinking and solving tasks.

So it is not all about money; it is about people as well.

Practical Experience

Thinking about where we, the military, come from, we know that international cooperation has been happening in some parts of the world for decades. And this cooperation is still ongoing as we are discussing our way ahead.

NATO was established in 1949 as the North Atlantic Treaty Organisation, as an organisation focused on the Atlantic Ocean. Since the end of the Cold War, it has been executing land operations. With the diminishing of SACLANT, the navy's guardian in Norfolk, Virginia, there is only limited promotion for the maritime origin of the alliance. But it is still the only and most developed organisation for international cooperation in the maritime commons. NATO units of all sizes had been a "fleet in being" during the Cold War and are now "fleets in operation," opposing the threat caused by terrorists. Almost 60 years of cooperation have developed a high standard of common understanding, common procedures, and a high degree of standardisation. It is a true story of success.

But at the same time areas of concern have become apparent, too: the technical gap, the diminishing influence of the smaller nations (navies), the still-existing different leadership policies and the perception of a lot of nations, inside and outside of NATO, that the alliance is a purely U.S.-led organisation. This makes some initiatives for more and deeper international cooperation more difficult than they should be.

The experience of NATO can and should be used as a tool for shaping international cooperation.

Another example is the Partnership for Peace program. Established in the early 1990s, colocated but separate from NATO Headquarters, it offered a very comprehensive training schedule. This schedule has been shaped to the different demands of the participating nations (navies) and worked for cooperation as well as for integration. It has worked well in the region of northern Europe. It cannot be used as a blueprint for other regions, but it is offering a lot of very successful advice for our way ahead.

The Mediterranean Dialogue is another way to establish links for a closer cooperation. The situation is different from that in northern Europe, and it needs more patience and preparation to reach the goal. Some of the basic work has been done by NATO's Southern Command in Naples. This has been further taken by the regional seapower symposium hosted by the Italian navy every second year. The focus was on regional cooperation to produce a white shipping plot. Another topic was the coordination and cooperation inside the territorial waters of the different North African nations in order to achieve a better picture of the situation.

Even a real-world operation such as "Enduring Freedom" is a proof of the willingness and ability for cooperation in a certain region in order to achieve a common goal.

My experience in maritime-related matters from the EU's perspective is very limited. But this is due to the fact that the EU has not been focused on maritime matters, and still is not in securing the maritime commons. The "Green Paper" published in June 2006 about "The Future Maritime Policy: Taking Stock of the Process" is a very encouraging approach and offers the opportunity to include naval options to the concept. A quotation from a speech given by a member of the European Commission responsible for fishery and maritime affairs, Mr. Joe Borg, presents an inside look into the commission's activities:

> A new holistic maritime policy is needed, because globalization is fast increasing its pace and magnitude, generating more trade and economic interactions between the different regions of the world. In these circumstances, Europe will depend even more on its seaports and its merchant fleet, its shipyards, the marine equipment, and its logistics. This is why the commission in its strategic objectives for the current mandate has recognised the need, within the context of the Lisbon Strategy for growth and jobs, of a thriving maritime economy.

Meetings like the Combined Forces Maritime Component Commanders Course for flag-level officers, which took place here at the Naval War College in September this year, are unique facilitators for increasing cooperation. Continuing with this region-oriented approach and keeping in mind the different national interests is the first step in creating the global awareness that is needed for the realisation of the twin goals. In addition to what I have laid down above, there are a lot of international security agreements, bilateral as well as multilateral, that can be used to promote the vision of the 1000-ship navy and bring it to reality.

When I look at my catalogue of questions guiding me through my practical experience, I want to add some information of a different kind than the above-mentioned.

It is always a very crucial and sensitive task to manage the decision of who will be in the lead of any kind of international operation, seminar, or training. In our anticipated cooperation, it is not always appropriate to link the overall responsibility together with the effort made by the individual participating nation. A well-balanced method is required and must be decided at one of the flag-level courses.

Funding is a crucial issue in all kinds of international cooperation. The participation or nonparticipation of a nation is not alone a question of willingness or of political approval but often a question of resources available. But common training is a prerequisite for achieving the goal and developing a mutual understanding in operating together.

For the time being, the U.S. command structure is sufficient for the organisation and the necessary administration. In addition to this, the already-existing seapower symposia will be used as important places for discussions and decisions. And there is an urgent need to establish seapower symposia in all regions of the world. The International Seapower Symposium taking place here at the Naval War College should be seen as the forum to deal with all matters that are related to the step-by-step realisation of the 1000-ship navy.

Conclusion

A strong motivation to participate in this international effort is needed. A precondition for participation is a common assessment, based upon trust and confidence, about the threat on one hand and information management on the other hand.

Including representatives from international and national organisations dealing with the sea, with emphasis on coastguard-like organisations, the merchant navy, and international maritime law, will serve the idea of a broader approach.

And last but not least: tasking a professional company to develop a media campaign to work for the different regional seapower symposia will enhance acceptance and understanding inside and outside the military.

Economics and maritime strategy are very much related to each other. In the discussion about what is the important factor of our globalization process, economics are, in the perception of the peoples, the only factor.

In international cooperation at sea, answering the question how we can achieve our goal is a lot about trust and confidence. And it is about the willingness and ability of the big actors in the actual maritime commons to create a situation where, on one hand, a strong leadership is provided, but on the other hand the smaller actors have a fair chance to bring their ideas and abilities, including responsibility and leadership, into the process of establishing the 1000-ship navy.

4.3
Feral Cities—Pirate Havens

LIEUTENANT COMMANDER
MATTHEW M. FRICK

Throughout History, Support Systems in Place on Land Have Been Lifelines for Pirates

For modern seafarers, the names Strait of Malacca, Horn of Africa, or Caribbean Sea provoke a sense of fear in some, caution in others, and concern in all. The reason for these reactions is piracy. From coastal fishing vessels and tug boats to plush cruise liners, virtually every sector of maritime trade and commerce has been affected by pirates to some extent.

Pirates, however, do not commit piracy for piracy's sake. Whether looking to collect a ransom for a captured vessel and crew, instilling fear in others to protect local fishing grounds, or merely robbing the ship's purser, pirates always return to dry land to enjoy the spoils of their efforts: a "feral city." As defined by Dr. Richard J. Norton in the *Naval War College Review*, a feral city is one in which the state government "has lost the ability to maintain the rule of law within the city's boundaries yet remains a functioning actor in the greater international system."[1] The typical city itself, while marked by a lack of any real social services, heightened levels of disease

"Feral Cities—Pirate Havens," by Lieutenant Commander Matthew M. Frick, U.S. Navy. Reprinted from *Proceedings*, December 2008, Vol. MSP 134, No. 12, with permission; Copyright © 2008 U.S. Naval Institute/*www.usni.org*.

1. Richard J. Norton, "Feral Cities," *Naval War College Review* 56, no. 4 (Autumn 2003), p. 98.

and pollution, and little to no individual security, is not a bastion of complete anarchy. In fact, some semblance of hierarchical order governs the city and international economic activity, despite the varying degrees of corruption and oppression that may be present.

While the emergence of a feral city with a population that exceeds one million, according to Dr. Norton, may seem far-fetched in today's modern age of globalization, reality begs to differ.[2] Mogadishu, the capital of Somalia, is a prime example. And places like Mexico City, Johannesburg, and Sao Paulo are either well on their way to becoming feral cities, or they already exhibit pockets of feral characteristics. The near-autonomous nature of a feral city, when coupled with a geographic position accessible to the world's oceans, makes for a perfect sanctuary from which to conduct acts of piracy.

The concept of a pirate haven is not new. Mogadishu and Aceh in Sumatra are merely the latest examples in a history of feral places turned pirate bases that spans both the globe and the ages. A brief look back in time offers several examples of locales where piracy has flourished. Common to nearly all of them is the existence of a city beyond the control of any legitimate, recognized government where pirates called the shots and business was conducted on their terms. New Providence, Port Royal, Canton, Petit Goave, Madagascar, and Barataria were merely precursors to the lawless pirate strongholds of today and provide a glimpse into what may be in store for the future.

Port Royal, Jamaica

In the 17th century, Port Royal, was the most notorious outpost for pirates operating in the Atlantic Ocean and the Caribbean. A British colony, Jamaica was ideally situated close to the Spanish colonies along the trade routes of the Caribbean and South America known as the Spanish Main. Far from the eyes of the King, pirates took to the island and virtually infested the bustling city, attracting merchants and other economic enterprises thirsty to profit from the pirates' labors. So important was the presence of the pirates in Port Royal to the Jamaican economy that colonial officials around 1665 protested the move to establish plantations on the island. In fact, Jamaica Governor Thomas Modyford feared the loss of the pirate trade so much he rejoiced when the winds of yet another war with

2. Ibid.

Spain came blowing.[3] At the time, England tolerated pirates, issuing many of them letters of marque, officially sanctioning seagoing freebooters to act as privateers, essentially committing piracy against any Spanish-flagged vessels. At the end of the war, the letters of marque expired or were revoked, yet piracy continued, just not under the King's colors.

By the early 18th century, pirates continued to rule Port Royal. Colonial attitudes, however, changed significantly. Pirates out of Port Royal had moved beyond targeting only Spanish treasure ships and captured approximately 30 vessels trading with Jamaica in the first three months of 1718 alone. When Nicholas Lawes was appointed governor in April 1718, he brought with him several English warships to deal with the piracy issue once and for all. Unfortunately for him, the pirates were so embedded in Port Royal and were so successful, a large number of the Royal Navy's captains decided it was more in England's interest to foster trade with Spain than to spend time and risk lives hunting down pirates.[4]

As Jamaica and Port Royal continued to gain economic prosperity over this period, more and more local inhabitants became fed up with the pirates running rampant in their city and the surrounding waters, as well as England's apparent inability to do anything about it. This is not to say that many of Port Royal's citizens did not support the pirates. On the contrary, it was precisely these merchants, ship owners, and colonial officials who enabled the pirates to operate and kept piracy a lucrative business. When Governor Lawes brought ships of the Royal Navy with him to Jamaica—the errant captains mentioned above notwithstanding—the local pirate supporters often provided the freebooters with intelligence on the locations and dispositions of these warships.[5]

Pirates continued to rule Port Royal until around 1720 when the combination of increased Royal Navy presence and the executions of Charles Vane and "Calico" Jack Rackham all but ended the presence of pirates in Jamaica.[6] With the loss of Port Royal as a pirate

---

3. Anne Perotin-Dumon, "The Pirate and the Emperor: Power and the Law on the Seas, 1450–1850," in C. R. Pennell, ed., *Bandits at Sea* (New York: New York University Press, 2001), p. 43.
4. Marcus Rediker, *Villains of All Nations: Atlantic Pirates in the Golden Age* (Boston: Beacon Press, 2004), pp. 15–16.
5. Cyrus H. Karraker, *Piracy Was a Business* (Rindge, NH: Richard R. Smith Publisher, Inc., 1953), p. 203.
6. Ibid., p. 208.

haven and the death of Edward "Blackbeard" Teach at Ocracoke, North Carolina, the Golden Age of Piracy effectively came to an end.

Ranter Bay, Madagascar

Before the demise of the pirates at Port Royal, another pirate base was operating halfway around the world on the East African island of Madagascar. In Captain Charles Johnson's 1724 fictional account, *A General History of the Robberies and Murders of the Most Notorious Pirates,* the pirates named the city there Libertalia and widely considered it a paradise for their chosen profession. There, pirates lived under the same quasi-governmental structure that existed at sea. With elected leadership and a few basic laws enforced by everyone, this early form of true democracy came to represent the nature of pirate thoughts on justice, equality, and self-rule.

A pretty pirate picture, to be sure, the grand life in Libertalia as recorded by Captain Johnson is actually contrived. While pirates did operate in and around Madagascar out of a port city they named Ranter Bay, and historic documents offer proof of the democratic, libertarian form of self-imposed government on board many pirate ships, the carry-over of this "hydrarchy" on shore to the extent that Johnson tells it is not likely.[7] Regardless of the social commentary behind the story of Libertalia, the fact remains that Madagascar, specifically Ranter Bay, was an autonomous pirate stronghold and trading center that flourished for much of the early 18th century.

Canton, China

Much farther east, and almost a century after the purge of piracy from Port Royal, another city gave life to perhaps the largest—at least numerically—pirate fleets in history. In Canton (Guangzhou), China, at the turn of the 19th century, a former prostitute named Shih Yang married the leader of a local band of pirates named Cheng I. Now known as Cheng I Sao (wife of Cheng I), Shih Yang

---

7. Marcus Rediker, "Hydrarchy and Libertalia: The Utopian Dimensions of Atlantic Piracy in the Early Eighteenth Century," in *Pirates and Privateers: New Perspectives on the War on Trade in the Eighteenth and Nineteenth Centuries,* ed. David J. Starkey et al. (Exeter, England: University of Exeter Press, 1997), pp. 30–31.

helped her husband form a confederation with other groups of pirates, and by 1805 they had amassed a fleet of more than 400 junks and as many as 60,000 pirates. The pirates of Canton controlled not only the South China Sea, but also the many internal waterways throughout coastal China.

The pirate confederacy was not without its squabbles, however, and the group eventually formed seven separate, smaller fleets each named for the color banner that represented it. Despite this division, the pirate leaders knew the benefits of maintaining their Canton-based alliance and continued to work together. When Cheng I died in 1807, Cheng I Sao, or Madame Cheng as she became known, inherited the leadership of the Red Flag Fleet. For three more years the pirates continued to control life in Canton and along much of the South China coast until Cantonese officials entered into a series of negotiations with Cheng I Sao and the other pirate leaders in 1810. The pirates of the confederation in effect surrendered, but under terms of their own choosing. In fact, many of the former pirates were subsequently offered positions in the imperial military.[8]

Barataria, Louisiana

While Madame Cheng's Red Flag Fleet terrorized the South China Sea, another pirate was busy making a name for himself in the fledgling United States of America. Jean Lafitte gathered around him a group of freebooters to rival the smugglers already a part of the New Orleans landscape. His audacious exploits and colorful character are well-known to American school children, particularly in the South. From the story of countering the governor of Louisiana's bounty for Lafitte's head by offering a reward of his own for the governor's head, to aiding Andrew Jackson against the British during the War of 1812, Lafitte succeeded in securing his place in the annals of American history.

Almost as famous, or infamous, as the name of Jean Lafitte is the name of the place where he and his pirates lived and operated from: Barataria. Lafitte's home on Grand Terre in the swamps and marshes around New Orleans was the ideal place to establish a base of operations. Populated by trappers and fishermen, Grand Terre was also the home of a large number of New Orleans' busiest smugglers who were in no hurry to call attention to their practices

8. Dian Murray, "Cheng I Sao in Fact and Fiction," in C. R. Pennell, ed., *Bandits at Sea*, pp. 258–260.

and have the state and federal governments encroaching on their business.

Lafitte's pirates were men from various nations who sailed under an even greater variety of foreign flags in war as they did in their exploits as buccaneers. They worked together under Lafitte's dynamic leadership in the relative safety of Barataria, their makeshift village established around Laffite's home. Despite the long-standing practice and acceptance of smuggling as a legitimate occupation, the presence of Lafitte's self-titled corsairs was difficult for many residents on Grand Terre to stomach.[9] War and piracy had taught these men that life was short, and thus they placed a low value on it. Their willing cruelty and disdain for anyone but themselves ensured that the people on Grand Terre left them alone. The governor of Louisiana was both incapable militarily and unwilling constitutionally to do anything about them. Thus, Barataria remained a virtually untouchable pirate haven for many years, and Lafitte continued to disrupt seagoing trade unabated throughout the Gulf of Mexico.

The Same, But Different

The pirate havens described here have many of the same characteristics as feral cities, or more precisely, feral sections of cities. This observation highlights an important lesson for present and future feral cities-turned-pirate havens: pirates may be able to control a portion of a city or area, but they are not likely to rule over much land the farther one moves away from the beach. Nevertheless, even a small portion of a coastal city that tolerates the existence of pirates among its citizens, willingly or not, presents pirates the right conditions to establish a toe-hold on land that will spread cancer-like to the water surrounding it.

The similarities between pirate havens of history and the feral cities of today or the future primarily concern the issues of economic and individual security. The first, economic, is at the heart of piracy. For the predator to survive there must be, by definition, some form of prey. Without vulnerable commercial shipping and maritime commerce, piracy would not exist; certainly not on any significant scale. Pirates do not openly attack warships, nor are they likely to pursue a vessel whose crew puts up a significant armed resistance that hampers any chance of a successful attack.

---

9. Lyle Saxon, *Lafitte the Pirate* (Gretna, LA: Pelican Publishing Company, Inc., 1989), pp. 40–43.

When the pirates are dissuaded from targeting a certain seaway or type of vessel, insurance rates drop and more trade is funneled back to that area. This often reduces operating costs for ship owners in terms of time and money spent avoiding pirate-infested waters. In addition, nearly all pirates commit their crimes for economic reasons. Whether for ransom or theft, the pirate is ultimately looking for monetary gain, with few exceptions. This was as true in the 18th century as it is today.

Money, however, is not an end unto itself. It must be spent for its worth to be realized. Pirate havens, both then and now, play a major role in the ability of pirates to use their ill-gotten gains, no matter how great or how small the value. During the Golden Age of Piracy, pirates often sought wealth for wealth's sake. They either wanted to better the living conditions that drove them to go on the account in the first place, or be free to spend their money living out their lives in a condition of blissful debauchery.

No Buried Treasure

The tales of buried treasure popularized in fiction throughout the years are precisely that: fiction.[10] Pirates knew their days were numbered when they chose their profession, and they wanted to spend other people's money until their time was up. Those who were not hanged more often than not died penniless. Today, many pirates use their monetary gains simply to survive and provide basic necessities for their families. In all cases, one man's gain is another man's loss, and the impact is felt more in terms of economic cost than anything else.

The second, more obvious issue common to piracy through the ages is individual security. From the red flag flown from the mast of an 18th-century pirate vessel—signaling to the pirates' intended victims that no quarter would be given and everyone on board would be killed—to the small go-fast boats of today carrying men armed with automatic rifles and rocket-propelled grenades, the business of piracy was and is a bloody one. Even British warships shied away from pirate waters when their captains felt the risk to life and limb too great.[11] Today, the International Maritime Bureau has issued warnings to mariners to remain outside 200 nautical miles

---

10. David Cordingly, *Under the Black Flag: The Romance and Reality of Life Among the Pirates* (New York, NY: Random House, 1995), p. 179.
11. Rediker, *Villains of All Nations*, pp. 15–16.

from the coast of Somalia to mitigate the chances of being attacked.[12]

The violent activities of pirates at sea translate directly to their behavior on land. For this reason a pirate haven, once established, often becomes a scene of fear and lawlessness controlled to one extent or another by the pirates who inhabit it. The local populace and even the state or national government have few options for dealing with the freebooters on land when a large number of pirates have set up camp. Those locals who would like to resist the pirate infestation are too afraid for their lives to do anything about it, while others are content to allow business as usual to continue if they are making a profit. Governments are perpetually at odds on how to expel the pirates from their land bases without the risk of excessive collateral damage and loss of innocent life. Many are not willing to take that risk, and so piracy continues, as it did in Port Royal almost 300 years ago.

Lesson Learned?

A feral city turned pirate haven never was, nor will it ever be, easy to tame. History has given several examples of pirate havens, and each eventually found its demise for its own reasons. The hopeful lesson here is that pirate havens come and go. However, the reasons men turned to piracy are even more varied than the pirate cities themselves, making it difficult to decipher a method for dealing with piracy today. By looking at the pirate havens of old, however, it is evident that the most successful way of stopping pirates, and one that is the most likely to be successful today, is to face the pirates directly, on the waters in which they operate.

While certainly not an easy task, the only real way to eradicate piracy is to catch them away from the safety of the feral cities that sponsor them. A concerted effort on the part of the world's navies and coast guards to turn the tables on the pirates is required. The risk for pirates must be far, far greater than the potential reward. This means more patrols, liberal rules of engagement, and a willingness to accept some losses in an effort to rid the oceans of piracy. The red flag must fly from every mast, signaling to each pirate, "no quarter given."

---

12. Peter Lehr and Hendrick Lehmann, "Somalia—Pirates' New Paradise," in Peter Lohr, ed., *Violence at Sea: Piracy in the Age of Global Terrorism* (New York: Routledge, 2007), p. 6.

CHAPTER 5

LEGAL AND POLICY CHALLENGES

5.1
Piracy, Policy, and Law

COMMANDER JAMES KRASKA
CAPTAIN BRIAN WILSON

Capturing the Bad Guys May Be the Easy Part

At 0530 on a quiet Saturday morning, 5 November 2005, a hail of automatic weapons fire rained down on the *Seabourn Spirit.* Piercing the hull, a rocket-propelled grenade crashed into a cabin of the luxury cruise ship. For the 302 passengers and crew, there was no police or coast guard to provide immediate assistance. They were under attack by pirates in international waters and far from help. Despite the damage, the ship was able to evade her pursuers.

Less than a year later, a dhow plying the ancient trade route between India and Africa was taken over in international waters by ten Somali pirates armed with rocket-propelled grenades and AK-47 assault rifles. Fortunately for the 16 Indians on board, there was a U.S. warship nearby. When the USS *Winston S. Churchill* (DDG-81) encountered the besieged dhow, her immediate mission was clear: gain control of the vessel and detain the pirates.

Once the pirates were in custody, the way ahead became less clear as the destroyer's commanding officer, and more broadly, the American government and the international community confronted the myriad diplomatic and legal challenges of piracy suppression in the 21st century. Who would investigate and prosecute the case? Where would the pirates be held, and by whom? What about the Indian crew members, all of them witnesses to the crime, and what would happen to their ship and cargo?

"Piracy, Policy, and Law," by Commander James Kraska, JAGC, U.S. Navy, and Captain Brian Wilson, JAGC, U.S. Navy. Reprinted from *Proceedings,* December 2008, Vol. 134, No. 12, with permission; Copyright © 2008 U.S. Naval Institute/*www.usni.org.*

The successful interdiction by the *Churchill* sparked a global effort to develop a modern playbook for confronting piracy. In the United States, the Bush administration began to develop a policy consistent with national maritime strategy, which culminated in a comprehensive piracy policy governing diplomatic and legal action and signed by President George W. Bush in 2007. This establishes a framework for warships that encounter or interrupt acts of maritime piracy and armed robbery at sea, as well as for agencies charged with facilitating the prosecution of perpetrators and the repatriation of victims and witnesses. But because much of the ocean's surface is beyond state jurisdiction, effective piracy repression demands international action and coordination.

The Response

Since 2006, the United Nations and its agency for maritime matters, the International Maritime Organization (IMO), have aggressively confronted piracy. This action could not be more timely: a disturbing spike in piracy is occurring off the Somali coast with an intensity and frequency unmatched since the era of Caribbean buccaneers of the early 19th century.[1] As this was written in late October, about 100 crew members were being held hostage and so far in 2008 more than $30 million in ransom money has been funneled to organized criminal gangs in Somalia.[2] This is not just a regional issue. Global energy markets are affected because 30 percent of the world's daily oil supply is carried on tankers through the Gulf of Aden on their way to the Suez Canal.[3] Sea lines running between Yemen and Somalia constitute the main link between Europe and Asia.

Piracy's devastating effects extend beyond the immediate threat to ships, people, and property. It endangers sea lines of communication, disrupts freedom of navigation and the free flow of commerce, and undermines regional stability. Nations as diverse as France, Malaysia, and Russia are sending warships to respond. The private defense contractor Blackwater has fitted out a helicopter-carrying security escort ship—the *MacArthur*—and offered her services to commercial ships transiting the Gulf of Aden. The United

---

1. Ellen Knickeyer, "100 Hostages Held by Somali Pirates," 12 September 2008, *The Washington Post,* A11.
2. Ibid.
3. "America, Russia and Terrorists of the Seas," *International Herald Tribune,* 2 October 2008.

States and other countries participate in Combined Task Force 150, a multinational coalition that coordinates with the U.S. Fifth Fleet off the Horn of Africa. Ten European Union countries have agreed to contribute to an anti-piracy task force headed for the region.[4] The policy and legal efforts that support these operations are essential to effective piracy repression. It is especially important to ensure that all nations converging on the region to address piracy are operating within the same set of rules.

Defining Piracy

Generally, piracy is any illegal act of violence, detention, or depredation committed outside territorial waters for private (rather than political) ends by crew or passengers of a private ship or aircraft against another ship, persons, or crew. Inside territorial waters such crimes constitute armed robbery at sea and are the responsibility of the state. These definitions emerged from customary international law, the 1958 Convention on the High Seas, and the 1982 United Nations Convention on the Law of the Sea (UNCLOS), which has become the de facto constitution for the world's oceans.

The UNCLOS, the UN Charter, and more broadly, customary international law, provide authority that may be invoked for seizing a pirate ship, boarding a ship on the high seas, conducting hot pursuit, and taking action in furtherance of the inherent right of individual and collective self-defense. On the high seas or in any other place outside the jurisdiction of a state, any nation may seize a pirated ship, arrest the pirates, and seize the property on board and submit the matter to its civil and criminal courts. Only warships and military aircraft or vessels in government service, however, may exercise this authority.

Boarding may be conducted under a variety of legal rationales, including the consent of the flag state under Articles 92 and 94 of UNCLOS, the exercise of the right of self-defense under Article 51 of the UN Charter, the right of visit a vessel under Article 110 of UNCLOS if there are reasonable grounds to believe it is engaged in piracy, and in some cases, the extension of port state control measures. Some nations, including the United States, also accept that the master of a vessel can consent to a boarding. If a seizure of a

---

4. Jenny Booth, "Europe to Send Warships to Defeat Somali Pirates," *The TimesOnline* (UK), 2 October 2008; and Michael Evans, Rob Crilly, and David Charter, "Euro Task Force Declares War on Somali Pirates," The *TimesOnline* (UK), 3 October 2008.

suspected pirate ship is determined to be without adequate grounds, however, the state making the seizure could be liable to the flag state for any loss or damage.

Further, in 1988, IMO member states approved a maritime anti-terrorism and criminal law treaty in the wake of the 1985 *Achille Lauro* hijacking. The treaty is directed at acts that endanger the safe navigation of ships, and it was amended in 2005 to include a legal framework for combating the proliferation of weapons of mass destruction and their delivery systems Whether the focus is on piracy in the Baltic in the 14th century or in the Indian Ocean in the 21st century, nothing is as inimical to piracy as regional stability and the rule of law. In an important exception to the norm of flag state jurisdiction, all states may take action against piracy, which is a violation of international law and a universal crime.

Decisive U.S. Action

The wide-ranging policy signed by President Bush—the broadest presidential articulation of U.S. policy toward international piracy since the time of the Barbary pirates—was developed through the National Security Council by Navy judge advocates in the Office of the Under Secretary of Defense for Policy and Strategic Plans and Policy, Joint Staff. It establishes seven goals, each an important component for addressing piracy.

Prevention

One of the most ambitious initiatives is the International Shipping and Port Facility Security (ISPS) Code. The code tightens security throughout the world's commercial fleets and ports by obligating operators of ships and port facilities that handle ships of more than 500 gross registered tonnage to develop, implement, and evaluate security plans. The United States was a leader in crafting the code, which was adopted in 2002, and the U.S. Coast Guard certifies as compliant foreign ports that are departure points for vessels bound for the United States. Because of the major infrastructure changes required, parties to the International Convention for the Safety of Life at Sea (SOLAS) were given two years before compliance became mandatory.

Deterrence

Coastal and maritime states leverage the deterrent value of presence at sea and in ports in the same way that a street cop walks through a neighborhood. Piracy tends to surge when it is ignored and recede when it is addressed by the international community. Several international initiatives in the straits of Malacca and Singapore have, for example, dramatically reduced the incidence of piracy.

Reduce the Maritime Domain's Vulnerability

The complex and ambiguous nature of contemporary maritime threats places a premium on collection and dissemination of actionable information. To anticipate and counter threats requires situational awareness that depends on the ability to monitor activities so that trends can be identified and anomalies differentiated. One of the most important tools in this effort is the Automatic Identification System (AIS), which is required on all ships over 300 gross tons or that carry 12 or more passengers on international voyages. The system broadcasts a signal, which provides pertinent information about the ship and its movement. In the Mediterranean and Gulf of Guinea, the Navy is working with partner nations to promote an advanced system that fuses AIS information in an Internet-based exchange portal.

A global satellite-based vessel identification system that is more secure than AIS—Long Range Identification and Tracking—was introduced in 2006. Once fully operational in December 2008, it will provide global surveillance of maritime traffic for the purposes of detecting, identifying, and classifying vessels and will be key to reducing vulnerability in the maritime domain.

Hold Pirates Accountable

The present policy is an extension of 200 years of experience in prosecuting piracy. From 1815–23, for example, piracy cases—which are federal crimes under Title 18 of the U.S. Code—were among the most numerous reviewed by the U.S. Supreme Court.[5] In the 2006 case of the Indian dhow, the pirates were transferred to Mombasa and later convicted in a Kenyan court and sentenced to seven years imprisonment. Local action is particularly beneficial

---

5. G. Edward White, "The Marshall Court and International Law: The Piracy Cases," 83 *American Journal of International Law 727* (October 1989).

because it demonstrates responsible governments maintaining order and stability in their maritime neighborhood.

Presere Freedom of the Seas

Freedom of navigation underpins global prosperity, peace, and security. Throughout world history the foremost powers achieved and maintained their position of leadership through preeminent seapower and reliance on freedom of the seas.

Historically, the United States has actively defended this freedom. Piracy was the catalyst for George Washington to launch the Navy by building six frigates to operate against the Barbary pirates while European governments paid tribute to transit the Mediterranean. Freedom of the seas was a feature of President Woodrow Wilson's Fourteen Points in World War I, and one of the aims of the Atlantic Charter during World War II. By including freedom of the seas as a major component of its piracy policy, the United States acknowledges that pirates work to deny the international community the exercise of a long-established freedom and well-recognized right.

Protect Sea Lines of Communication

The initial rise of the global economy can be attributed in large part to unimpeded ocean transit. There is an interlocking and reinforcing quality to open sea lines of communication, as freedom and safety in the maritime domain generate stability and prosperity on land. Free trade and international investment help socialize non-democratic nations into an interdependent liberal world system. Today, shipping is the heart of the global economy with more than 80 percent of the world's trade traveling by sea.

Lead and Support International Efforts

One promising means of achieving greater cooperation is the Global Maritime Partnership. The concept embraces a figurative 1,000-ship navy, representing the idea that no nation can do it alone. This approach is central to that adopted in *A Cooperative Strategy for 21st Century Seapower* and is key to expanding maritime security cooperation.

All nations have a common interest in taking action against piracy because all benefit from a stable maritime security environment. In the Indian Ocean, for example, the United States and India both desire freedom of navigation, the free flow of commerce, and protection of the sea lines. When the two countries reached agreement on civilian nuclear cooperation in 2006, they also affirmed their commitment to address piracy and armed robbery at sea with the signing of the Indo-U.S. Framework for Maritime Security Cooperation.

Beyond the Policy

In addition to the formal U.S. piracy policy, a working group principally composed of the Departments of Defense, Justice, and Homeland Security developed complementary disposition and logistics guidance for managing suspected pirates, victims, and witnesses taken into custody by warships during counter-piracy operations. The guidance is valuable to on-scene responders and includes recommendations for recording, among other points, accurate identification of vessels involved, identification of victims and witnesses and persons-under-control (PUCs), and information collection checklists.

Piracy and armed robbery at sea are global concerns, and the International Maritime Organization in particular has been a remarkably effective forum advancing issues of maritime security and the most active multilateral institution in combating piracy. The organization first addressed the problem in 1983 after Sweden expressed alarm to the Maritime Safety Committee over the high incidence of piracy. Later, the IMO produced a draft text that became the basis for Resolution A.545(13), which set measures to prevent acts of piracy and armed robbery against ships. Three years later the organization approved Circular 443, "Measures to Prevent Unlawful Acts Against Passengers and Crew On Board Ships," which applied to passenger ships on voyages of 24 hours or more, and the port facilities that service those vessels. In November 2001, the IMO assembly adopted a code of practice for investigating piracy and armed robbery against ships.[6]

A multi-layered regional approach to piracy in the Straits of Malacca and Singapore has led to a dramatic reduction in incidents on those waterways. Under Japanese leadership in 2004, Asian nations signed the Regional Cooperation Agreement on Combating Piracy and Armed Robbery against Ships in Asia (ReCAAP), the first treaty dedicated solely to combating piracy. The pact, which

---

6. IMO Doc. A.922(22), "Code of Practice For The Investigation Of The Crimes Of Piracy And Armed Robbery Against Ships," 2001.

entered into force in 2006, established the Information Sharing Centre in Singapore to share piracy-related information among member states. The IMO sponsored meetings in Tanzania and Yemen seeking a treaty against piracy in the western Indian Ocean. Just as the ReCAAP agreement was its model, this action could serve as a framework for regions—such as the Gulf of Guinea and the Caribbean—affected by piracy but are struggling to develop the capacity to address the problem.

The IMO has sponsored other multilateral efforts. In 2005, more than 25 shipping nations, the littoral states of Malaysia, Indonesia, and Singapore, the international shipping industry, and non-governmental organizations met in Jakarta to develop a framework for improving maritime safety, security, and environmental protection in the Straits of Malacca and Singapore. The negotiations continued in Kuala Lumpur in 2006 and Singapore in 2007. In Singapore, states signed the *Cooperative Mechanism,* which provides for shipping nations to help littoral states develop maritime security capacity for the straits. The mechanism marks the first time that littoral and maritime states have worked together to ensure the safety and security of an international strait, as envisaged in Article 43 of UNCLOS. It provides a forum for regular dialogue, a committee to coordinate and manage projects, and a fund to manage contributions from shipping states.

The successes of ReCAAP and the *Cooperative Mechanism* show that building partnerships is a prerequisite for developing greater coordination for maritime security.

Dramatic Action

Perhaps most significant, the UN Security Council took historic action against maritime piracy this past summer. Resolution 1816, which was decided under Chapter VII of the UN Charter and therefore legally binding on all states, called on them to cooperate in counterpiracy actions off the coast of Somalia. The resolution authorizes operations inside Somalia's territorial waters to deny that area as a safe haven for pirates who operate outside the 12-mile limit. It also provides for disposition and logistics of persons-under-control detained as a result of counterpiracy operations.

The resolution encourages states to increase and coordinate their efforts to deter acts of piracy in conjunction with the Transitional Federal Government of Somalia, a weak ruling authority inside the fractured state. It also calls on states, the IMO, and other international organizations to build a partnership to ensure regional coastal and maritime security, and is designed to bring together flag, port, and coastal states, and other states with jurisdiction under national and international law. They will cooperate in determining criminal jurisdiction for acts of piracy, in its investigation and prosecution, and in rendering disposition and logistics assistance to victims, witnesses, and persons detained.

Although decided under Chapter VII, the resolution does not compel any state to take PUCs from U.S. warships, but it does provide a valuable umbrella of political cover to states, making it easier to achieve PUC disposition and logistics. The Security Council recently adopted Resolution 1838, which condemns acts of piracy in the region around Somalia and, under Chapter VII, called on states to take part in actively fighting piracy by deploying naval vessels and aircraft. The Security Council also reaffirmed the Law of the Sea Convention's rules applicable to countering piracy and armed robbery at sea.

While piracy has varied in scope, location, sophistication, and lethality over the past 2,000 years, there is one constant: maritime piracy will always exist. Enhanced worldwide repression efforts have resulted in unprecedented development in the legal authorities and level of cooperation to combat the scourge. Effectively responding to this threat requires a comprehensive approach that encompasses political, military, financial, and legal support for operations, logistics, investigations, and prosecutions. More important, there must be the will to move anti-piracy efforts to the forefront.

Looking forward, it is fair to ask how success will be measured. Will the new policy and legal authorities be effectively employed? Will success be solely linked to numbers, data, and trends on a flowchart? Such measurements would only tell part of the story because they cannot account for increased maritime security capacity building, which generates positive benefits beyond piracy. And those numbers do not take into account how these efforts have better prepared states to individually and collectively respond to this international crime.

5.2
Drawing Lines in the Sea

LIEUTENANT TIMOTHY A. MARTIN

The Laws That Govern Traffic on the World's Oceans Can Be as Difficult to Shape as Water

Crimes committed at sea often affect more than one country, which increases the complexity of law enforcement and makes pursuit and apprehension of suspects challenging. Whether dealing with weapons or narcotics smuggling, or violent crimes such as piracy against ships, some form of agreement or level of cooperation among maritime states is necessary. Increasingly, however, there is regional consensus on the thorny issue of maritime law enforcement and interdiction of vessels where international waters meet territorial seas, which indicates that a shift in perceptions is occurring about how regional ocean security is managed.

The U.S. Naval War College, in an introduction to its Winter 2008 *Review,* described the ocean as a "vast maneuver space, where the presence of maritime forces can be adjusted as conditions dictate to enable flexible approaches to escalation, de-escalation, and deterrence of conflicts."

Fluid Boundaries, Shifting Laws

Maritime security plays a dynamic role in international relations. Enforcing international law at sea remains a politically delicate task.

"Drawing Lines in the Sea," by Lieutenant Timothy A. Martin, Royal Australian Navy Reserve. Reprinted from *Proceedings,* December 2008, Vol. 134, No. 12, with permission; Copyright © 2008 U.S. Naval Institute/*www.usni.org.*

U.S. Navy Staff Judge Advocate Michael Bahar, in a 2007 article, writes that states may have common threats, but in all likelihood any changes to international laws to deal with them that threaten territorial sovereignty will fail. Bahar noted in the conclusion to his 2007 treatise on naval deterrence and anti-piracy that, "since, and perhaps because of, the demise of the Soviet Union, asymmetric and law enforcement type threats have dominated the strategic landscape."[1]

However, as small states have changed their allegiances from international superpowers to regional, order-based systems of states, protecting their sovereignty is increasingly sought through international law.

Flag states are responsible for protecting seafarers, migrants, and refugees against abuse, and preventing weapons smuggling. Interdiction has traditionally referred to the strategic operations of naval forces when denying access or transit through a specified maritime region during times of war. Since World War II, however, the term has increasingly referred to law enforcement operations, as a means to enforce trade sanctions, to prevent the movement of weapons of mass destruction (WMDs), and particularly in the Caribbean Sea, to prevent the smuggling of illicit drugs.

The phrase, "crimes at sea" refers to acts of violence, theft, the transport of illicit drugs, and violence resulting in death. Attacks against ships in Southeast Asia, and increasingly off the coast of Somalia, directly affect professional seafarers who have variously been robbed, assaulted, taken hostage, and murdered. In the Caribbean Sea, illicit drug trafficking increases the prevalence of illegal arms, which has been shown to increase violence and murder rates, especially in micro-states.

Piracy is universally accepted to be a criminal act. Illegally boarding a vessel for the purpose of committing robbery, hijacking, or violence against a vessel and its crew is a crime, regardless of what you call it. Bahar points out that enforcing law presents no problem if the coastal states have municipal laws prohibiting such acts, have the political will to enforce them, and have the capacity to do so. However, when crimes are committed on international waters, border regions, or international transit zones, enforcing law at sea becomes trickier.

---

1. Michael Bahar, "Attaining Optimal Deterrence At Sea: A Legal And Strategic Theory For Naval Anti-Piracy Operations," *Vanderbilt Journal Of Transnational Law,* vol. 40 (2007).

The World's Oceans since 9/11

The United States-led Proliferation Security Initiative (PSI) and the International Ship and Port Facility Security (ISPS) Code were responses to the potential threat of the spread of WMDs and thus were a direct outcome of the 9/11 attacks. PSI is a cooperative although informal arrangement, without a formal treaty. All states party to this arrangement agreed to the 2003 Statement of Interdiction Principles (SIP), which gives guidance on the interception of vessels under accepted international law as laid out in the 1982 United Nations Convention on Law of the Sea (UNCLOS). Participating states agree to abide by these principles, but the SIP does not authorize states to conduct interdictions at sea. According to the U.S. Department of Defense (DOD), PSI provides a framework of cooperation for further activities.

Enforcing international law at sea can place authorities in a tenuous legal position, requiring special response mechanisms and procedures. For instance, determining what cargo is "reasonably suspected" is likely to be contestable, as many states reserve the right to ship military, nuclear, and other materiel by sea, and there is nothing in UNCLOS that specifically prohibits the transport of WMDs through international waters. While the ISPS Code stipulates how and when interdiction should be conducted, deciding which states can carry out interdiction, and which state's vessels may be targets of interdiction, may in time prove to be contentious if it is not applied universally, regardless of which flag a ship flies.

However, both the SIP and ISPS Code are ambiguous on the issue of how a threat will be determined and by whom. Such ambiguity should allow flexibility when deciding whom should be targeted, as well as allowing states with veto powers in the UN Security Council, which may legitimately ship nuclear weapons and materials, to avoid being targeted as long as they do not export WMDs to rogue states or non-state groups or individuals.[2]

The ISPS Code was created under the auspices of the International Maritime Organization (IMO) and is part of the 1974 Safety of Life at Sea Convention (SOLAS) concerning the safety of merchant ships. All 148 signatory countries to SOLAS are expected to comply with the ISPS Code. However, the IMO maintains that it does not issue blacklists of states or ports that do not comply with the code.

---

2. Mark R. Shulman, "The Proliferation Security Initiative and the Evolution of the Law on the Use of Force," *Houston Journal Of International Law,* vol. 28 (2006) part 1.

Interdiction of the *So San:*
Piracy or Law Enforcement?

On 9 December 2002 the Spanish frigate *Navarra* was patrolling the Arabian Sea as part of Operation Enduring Freedom. It boarded a small Cambodian-registered vessel, the *So San,* which displayed no flag or markings and had refused to heave to after several requests. The vessel later turned out to belong to the Democratic People's Republic of Korea (DPRK) and was manned by North Korean nationals bound for Yemen, carrying a concealed cargo of 151 short-range SCUD missiles armed with conventional warheads, along with other materials for making explosives not listed on the ship manifest. The Navarra seized the vessel and escorted it to the U.S. base at Diego Garcia, which ignited protests from the Yemeni government and later claims by the DPRK that this was an act of "unpardonable piracy."

The *So San*'s interdiction and her subsequent release demonstrates how complicated it is to apply interdiction in international waters. Interestingly, while the ISPS Code is an international means to prevent WMDs from being shipped to U.S. ports, thus protecting American interests and security needs, the code has also allowed supplementary inspections of containers around the world, resulting in increasing detection of narcotics and other illegally smuggled goods. The ISPS Code additionally offers greater enforcement of laws in international waters and in territorial seas in areas that UNCLOS does not provide. While UNCLOS arguably provides guidance for peaceful use of the sea, indicated by its limited reference to war, still it does provide for the enforcement of law at sea.

However, the Caribbean Regional Maritime Agreement (CRA) uses the 1988 Drugs Convention as its basis. Drafted in November 2003, its title was, "Agreement Concerning Cooperation in Suppressing Illicit Maritime and Air Trafficking in Narcotic Drugs and Psychotropic Substances in the Caribbean Area." Initial negotiations were co-chaired by Costa Rica, the Netherlands, and the Caribbean Community, and were supported by regional governments. The CRA creates a juridical structure for multilateral cooperation and coordination with regard to maritime law enforcement operations. It forms the basis for further agreements and sets out modern operational procedures to confirm the nationality of suspected vessels and aircraft. The CRA covers ship-boarding, ship-riding, pursuit, entry to investigate, over-flight, and the relaying of orders and instructions to aircraft.

The agreement, when it is fully operational, could serve as one of the most comprehensive regional (as opposed to ISPS Code's international focus) agreements concentrating on law enforcement interdiction at sea.

The Threat Depends on Point of View

Pursuing suspects at sea requires that authorities operate within the accepted law of the sea principle. Naval and policing forces may not respond to terrorism in the same way, as it's likely they will regard the threat from their own differing perspectives. Bahar writes that terrorism on the high seas may equate to the crime of piracy against shipping under international law, but it is also considered an act of war, an aspect of law currently being questioned in some quarters. International law itself, which in its maritime sense refers to codified conventions and treaties, is not bound to the same obligations or penalties that one is accustomed to in state-based, municipal law. Sovereign states are not obligated to comply with international law, beyond the boundaries of territorial jurisdiction, whether in outer space or on the oceans of the world.[3]

Furthermore, beyond the limits of territorial jurisdiction, pursuing law enforcement authorities may or may not be bound by other security agreements that may exist between other coastal states, but the pursuing authority must still respect the international legal regime, the "principles, norms, rules and decision-making procedures" which have been codified in UNCLOS.[4] To determine acceptable measures for law enforcement and interdiction in international waters requires that common perceptions exist regarding the level of threat, and that the national interests of states have been considered.

Blue-water law enforcement authorities who are required to work within international maritime conventions, codes, and agreements must understand domestic laws and bilateral agreements among neighboring states. Worldwide maritime policing by naval forces and coast guards (especially the U.S. Coast Guard) are the only state-based authorities permitted to police outside of the territorial sea. UNCLOS defines and provides legal guidance on the territorial sea, the contiguous zone, and the exclusive economic zone. Vessels registered or flagged to a particular state retain that state's

---

3. H.L.A. Hart, *The Concept Of Law,* Clarendon Press, Oxford (1961) pp. 208–231.
4. Stephen Krasner (ed.) *International Regimes,* Cornell University Press, Ithaca (1983) p. 2.

sovereign protection. So when authorities interdict a suspicious vessel, they must pay attention to these limitations, or risk being accused either of violating a foreign state's territorial jurisdiction, or breaching international conventions on freedom of the seas.

Enforcing international law at sea therefore requires cooperation among coastal states. Although agreed guidelines can be complicated by geopolitics, principles of cooperative actions are often reduced to acceptable common denominators. How? One means is through adapting existing international maritime law through various mechanisms. Prevention and suppression of threats to maritime security are given authority by:

- The Charter of the United Nations;
- UNCLOS;
- Bilateral agreements and arrangements, and
- National Measures.[5]

International agreements greatly accelerate the process by which law enforcement officials from one state can board suspect vessels flying the flag of another, especially when the flag state is unable to exercise control over the vessel due to its location or other factors, or maintain contact with suspect vessels entering national waters and airspace.

Whether open sea or the high-traffic sea lanes surrounding archipelagos, maritime areas are vast and comparatively less policed than those of dry land, and therefore beyond the reach of land-based police patrols. This makes crimes difficult to detect or prevent. Crimes that occur at sea often go unreported by shipping companies so that crime trend analysis is less certain.

Policing isolated maritime areas is also costly, often under-resourced, and complicated by the rules and agreements that apply to maritime zones. The location of the crime and its geopolitical ramifications often determine the extent to which it can be solved or prosecuted.

Seas Apart, the Same Obstacles

Despite their geographical and cultural differences, Southeast Asia and the Caribbean Sea share similar problems when it comes to policing the seas. They work cooperatively to prevent maritime law

---

5. *www.un.org/Depts/los/convention_agreements/convention_25years/ 07unitar_doalos_2007*.pdf

enforcement from getting bogged down by the regulations and codes of practice provided through UNCLOS. Given the extent of the seas and straits and the numbers of vessels available to patrol them, maintaining a continuous policing presence is difficult. In the Caribbean, coastal radars and USCG aerial patrols are used; in Southeast Asia, the "Eyes in the Skies" program extends the range of patrol, but all are subject to strict regulation when flying over territorial seas.

There are also similarities in the incidence of sea crimes in the Caribbean and Southeast Asia. Typically, crimes occur relatively close to coastal state territories. Increasing numbers of violent sea-crimes and illicit drug and small arms smuggling have indicated a corresponding increase in crimes ashore. Crimes documented by the International Maritime Bureau, the IMO, and other maritime security watchdogs have occurred at sea where theft or kidnapping was the objective. Politically inspired insurgency has also been a suspected motive, even before President Bush declared a war on terrorism, although incidents of maritime insurgency are not easily linked to other crimes that occur on the high seas.

Despite setbacks to international intentions to secure Southeast Asia against lawlessness at sea, and despite official rhetoric from coastal state governments, there remains some resistance to what is considered foreign interference. Nevertheless, financial incentives and resource assistance of those states with vested interests in securing the seaways, including from the United States, Japan, India, and China, continues to influence the way that maritime law enforcement is managed. Agreements are not even close to being codified in Southeast Asia, but similarities with the CRA model suggest this may not be unattainable.

The CRA is an example of a cooperative approach that has the potential to improve capabilities of Caribbean micro-states to address drug trafficking. It could broaden strategic influence and increase financial investment and potential military aid. By agreeing also to adopt the ISPS Code, many smaller states may accrue beneficial attention from the United States in the future. Larger and smaller states derive benefits from multilateralism but cultural, political, or historical issues may prevent an easy association with one or more states in a multilateral proposal. Therefore, a proposal for multilateral agreement must identify core common denominators, in this case the common maritime security issues. The question stands, will these form the basis for a successful formal agreement?

5.3
The Law of Piracy in Popular Culture

JONATHAN M. GUTOFF

Introduction

One longstanding advertising campaign for a popular brand of spiced rum shows various well-dressed, happy men and women, one of whom has a mustache and goatee drawn over his or her face. The caption tells the reader, "The Captain Was Here." In the background, we see a bottle of Captain Morgan's Spiced Rum and a man, presumably the Captain himself, in a bright red frock coat with lots of lace, sporting a lengthy set of Charles II curls and a mustache and goatee, grinning mischievously at the scene. He is obviously the fun-loving sort of guy who could liven up any party of young professionals:[1]

That Captain Morgan (who tortured the inhabitants of Panama City and Portobelo to get them to turn over their riches) and various other sea robbers have been romanticized is no surprise; pirates have been a staple of fiction from antiquity. The subject of this article, however, is not the romanticization of pirates and piracy in popular culture, a task that has already been undertaken by others,[2] but the role of the law of piracy in popular culture.

"The Law of Piracy in Popular Culture," by Jonathan M. Gutoff, *Journal of Maritime Law & Commerce*, Vol. 31, No. 4 (October 2000). Copyright © 2000 by Jefferson Law Book Company. Reproduced with permission of Jefferson Law Book Company in the format Textbook via Copyright Clearance Center.

1. While the advertising campaign may be directed at young professionals, the Captain Morgan's Spiced Rum Web site (*http://www.rum.com*), which features interviews with and pictures of "Morganettes of the Month," comely young women who serve as spokespersons for the product, appears to be aimed at teenage boys.
2. See, e.g., W. Bonner, *Pirate Laureate: The Life and Legends of Captain Kidd* (1947).

135

It should be noted at the outset that I have not attempted to examine the entire range of popular culture and piracy. That would be impossible, as pirates continue to appear in all sorts of cultural artifacts, from Halloween costumes to comic strips to the names of sports teams. Pirates and piracy also are used by all sorts of businesses (in addition to the manufacturers of rum) to indicate that a rollicking good time awaits patrons. Moreover, piracy continues to be the basis of much romantic literature.[3]

What I do attempt here is to look at how the legal regime that has governed piracy is reflected in current works of popular culture. After briefly reviewing the background of pirate literature from the 17th to the 20th centuries, I pay special attention to contemporary times and limit my discussion to films and television. Even within these limitations, I do not claim to have seen everything, although I have seen a lot.[4] While there is not much of an awareness of law in pirate movies, there is some, and an understanding of it may, perhaps, add to the enjoyment of watching pirate movies.

Background:
From the 17th to the 20th Century

The earliest writing on piracy in the modern period is Alexander O. Exquemelin's *The Buccaneers of America*, which appeared in Amsterdam in 1678 (under the title *De Americanensche Zeerovers*) and in England in 1684.

Exquemelin's book was followed in England by Charles Johnson's *A General History of the Robberies & Murders of the Most*

---

3. See, e.g., S. Jeffries, *The Pirate Lord* (1998) (in which a ship full of women falls into hands of a pirate band on a tropical island). While one *Amazon.com* customer claimed it was the "best book [she] had ever read," I cannot recommend it.

4. I have not looked at movies that deal with piracy before the age of the buccaneers in the late 17th century. Thus, anything having to do with Julius Caesar's suppression of piracy in the Mediterranean through the exploits of Drake and Hawkins is ignored deliberately. Similarly, non-European piracy has not been included, thereby leaving out anything having to do with the Barbary pirates.

Also, works of fantasy and science fiction are outside my review. Thus, pure fantasy, like Rob Reiner's *The Princess Bride* (1987), and science fiction, like Stewart Raffill's *The Ice Pirates* (1984), and most importantly, the various versions of Peter Pan, are not considered. I can, however, assure the reader that a knowledge of the law is not at all helpful in viewing any of these movies.

Norotious Pirates (1724).[5] Johnson's work details the lives of such famous pirates as William Kidd, Edward Teach (better known as Blackbeard), and the women pirates Anne Bonny and Mary Read. It also was the basis for the fictional pirates later created by Sir Walter Scott, Robert Louis Stevenson, and J.M. Barrie.

While it makes for highly entertaining reading, Johnson's book is also replete with legal detail. He quotes from royal proclamations and describes charges to grand juries, including one dealing with the history and jurisdiction of the admiralty and the nature of the crime of piracy. In addition, Johnson discusses Kidd's trial (complete with summaries of the testimony). For those readers who still have not had enough law, Johnson also provides, "An abstract of the civil law and statute law now in force in relation to piracy," which is exceptionally detailed.

Although fictional works in the 18th and 19th centuries did not include any legal reference materials, the 19th century did see the publication of an American update of Johnson's work called *The Pirates Own Book or Authentic Narratives of the Lives, Exploits, and Executions of the Most Celebrated Sea Robbers* (1837).[6] This too included a legal appendix, much of it cribbed from Johnson, but updated to include some recent innovations, such as categorizing the transatlantic slave trade as piracy.

Unfortunately, this tradition of legally-informed historical narrative did not last into the 20th century. Today, most treatments of piracy, fictional as well as historical, tend to focus on "cannon, cutlass, gore and decks awash in blood."[7]

Screen (Big and Small) Pirates

To paraphrase Errol Flynn's Peter Blood in *Captain Blood* (1935), 20th century film and television productions that deal with piracy are "entirely ignorant" of the law and procedure surrounding the crime. To be sure, Quinn Harris (Harrison Ford) correctly says in

---

5. As a result of J. Moore, *Defoe in the Pillory and Other Studies* (1939), it was long supposed that "Captain Charles Johnson" was a pseudonym for Daniel Defoe. This view was challenged in P. Furbank & W. Owens, *The Canonization of Daniel Defoe* (1988) and, as a result, leading historians of piracy now generally agree that Defoe was not Johnson.

6. While the author was anonymous, the *Marine Research Society's* 1924 edition identifies him as Charles Ellms.

7. B. Burg, *Sodomy and the Pirate Tradition: English Sea Rovers in the Seventeenth-Century Caribbean* xvi (1984).

response to Robin Monroe's (Anne Heche) query about pirates in *Six Days, Seven Nights* (1998), "they steal ships." Nevertheless, one is sure to learn a lot more about the law of search and seizure from watching the average police show than most of the movies discussed below will teach about the law of piracy.

Egalitarianism

One characteristic common to most pirate movies is the seemingly democratic nature of the pirate bands. This is not a recent invention, but apparent in films from the 1930s to the 1990s. Peter Blood, for example, obtains the agreement of the entire crew concerning the articles under which they will ship, including a promise not to harm any woman. In *Treasure Island* (1950), the men being led by Long John Silver (Robert Newton) assert the right to retire into common council to decide whether to continue to follow him. And in *Cutthroat Island* (1995), Morgan Adams (Geena Davis) assumes the captaincy of her father's ship not by inheritance, as one might expect, but by election of the crew.

The foregoing is one aspect of real piracy that movies convey, if not well, then at least not badly. Moreover, for film makers, the appeal of the egalitarian nature of pirate society is obvious: it makes the pirates sympathetic to democratically-inclined audiences.

Sentence

Those convicted of piracy in London were hanged at "Execution Dock," near Wapping, on the north bank of the Thames, to set an example for that neighborhood's large population of maritime workers. Outside London, those found guilty of piracy generally were hanged at prominent dockside locations. To make sure that the example set for mariners also would serve others who might be tempted to "go upon the account," the bodies of pirates were often wrapped in chains where all could witness, and perhaps contemplate, the wages of sin. (The chaining, it should be noted, was done not as a sign of humiliation but to hold the bodies together during the inevitable decomposition). After the trial and execution of William Kidd in 1701, his body was set out in chains in the Thames River at Tilbury Point.

The actual punishments of pirates have proved, for the most part, too gruesome to serve as entertainment for modern audiences. As a result, Hollywood has only hinted at the end of sea robbers. Long John Silver worries about going to Execution Dock but does not end up there. Similarly, in *Captain Kidd* (1945), the movie's protagonist is condemned, but the character (played by

Charles Laughton) is not seen swinging from a gibbet or bobbing up and down in the tide.

Recently, however, there has been some change. In Cutthroat Island, the waterfront of Port Royal, Jamaica is decorated with a variety of realistic corpses hanging in chains and cages in various states of decomposition. These are banged about with much abandon in an otherwise dull chase scene. If gore sells, the punishment of piracy offers numerous chances to make a killing.

Summary Punishment

In many pirate movies, there is talk about pirates being strung up from the yard arm, and in *Cutthroat Island* the character William Shaw (Matthew Modine) is rescued from a summary hanging aboard ship after being declared guilty of piracy. Can this be right? What about the courts? What about due process of law?

Surprisingly, it *is* right. As one well-known 18th century legal dictionary explained: A Piracy attempted on the Ocean, if the Pirates are overcome, the Takers may immediately inflict a Punishment by hanging them up at the Main-yard End; though this is understood where no legal judgment may be obtained; And hence it is, that if a Ship shall be on a Voyage to any Part of America, or the Plantations there, or a Discovery of the Parts; and in her Way is attacked by a Pirate, but in the attempt the Pirate is overcome, the Pirates may forthwith be executed without any Solemnity of Condemnation, by the Marine Law.[8]

Thus, to the extent that cinematic pirates are caught on the high seas, they may be, to the delight of audiences, strung up from the yard-arm.

Jurisdiction

In a January 2000 episode of *The Simpsons* entitled "The Mansion Family," Mr. Burns, the local industrialist, checks into the Mayo Clinic. Before leaving, he asks his hapless employee, Homer Simpson, to house sit. Homer decides to throw a party aboard *Gone Fission*, Mr. Burns' yacht, and pilots her to outside the 12-mile limit so as to be able to buy beer in the morning, contrary to state law.

Once on the high seas, there is total debauchery. On one vessel, a man and a cow are married. On another vessel, a major league baseball game is rebroadcast with only implied oral consent (rather than the required "express written consent"). Meanwhile, on

---

8. G. Jacob, *A New Law Dictionary,* at "Pirates" (8th ed. 1762).

the *Gone Fission,* Homer and his friends start to drink and taunt the Coast Guard, which, it is explained, cannot go out past 12 miles. Much to Homer's frustration, however, when the yacht is later attacked by pirates, the Coast Guard refuses to come to his aid.

To be sure, the problem of jurisdiction of piratical vessels is a real one in many parts of the world. It arises, however, out of the need to pursue pirate vessels from the waters of one sovereign to the waters of another. In contrast, there is nothing that prevents a United States vessel from boarding a vessel engaged in piracy on the high seas. In other words, the Coast Guard could have come to Homer's aid.

Conclusion

Pirates and piracy have a firm place in popular culture. They entertain either through their romance or their violence. The law of piracy, however, has played only a marginal role in these stories, and arises only in aid of the entertainment. Technical issues are avoided or, if necessary, as in the case of *The Simpsons,* misrepresented.

There is nothing particularly disturbing in all of this. After all, few people—even among this journal's readership—want to go to the movies, rent a video, or turn on their television and be instructed in maritime law. Knowledge of the law, however, does tend to increase the appreciation of the fare being offered.

5.4
Fighting Piracy

International Coordination is Key to Countering Modern-Day Freebooters

COMMANDER JAMES KRASKA
CAPTAIN BRIAN WILSON

Maritime piracy is experiencing a renaissance not seen since the period of the Barbary pirates. Last year, 111 ships were attacked off the dangerous waters of Somalia: 42 were hijacked, 815 mariners were taken hostage and the ransom paid for the release of some vessels fetched several million dollars. In response, a combination of coalition naval power and statecraft is creating new international authorities to address piracy, but after the talking is over, concrete steps must be taken to implement and sustain the new initiatives.

A banner year for maritime piracy, the number of attacks in the waters off the Horn of Africa doubled in 2008 compared with 2007. Instability from Somali piracy is reverberating throughout the global supply chain, which already was reeling from the worldwide economic slowdown. The resurgence is occurring along critical sea lines of communication. Each year, 20,000 ships pass through the Gulf of Aden, a vital shipping route for international trade that connects the Middle East to Europe and North and South America. In response to the threat to shipping, warships from the United Kingdom, Denmark, the Netherlands, France, Pakistan, India, Iran, Russia and other countries operate in the area. The European Union (EU) deployed naval forces to the Gulf of Aden under Operation Atalanta to conduct counterpiracy patrols, the first EU operational

"Fighting Piracy," by Cmdr. James Kraska & Capt. Brian Wilson, *Armed Forces Journal*, February 2009, pp. 10–17, 37. Reprinted by permission of Army Times Publishing Company.

naval deployment outside Europe. China sent two destroyers and a supply ship 4,000 miles to fight Somali piracy, the first operational out-of-area deployment in the history of the PLA Navy. New Zealand and Australia also have joined the effort, South Korea is on the cusp of doing so and during the last week of January, Tokyo approved a deployment by the Japanese Maritime Self-Defense Force (JMSDF) as a "police action" to patrol as early as March.

On Jan. 8, the Combined Maritime Forces (CMF) in Bahrain created Combined Task Force 151, a multinational counterpiracy naval force of more than 20 nations. Previously, coalition efforts against piracy included ships and aircraft from CTF-150, which was established at the outset of Operation Enduring Freedom to conduct Maritime Security Operations (MSO) in the Gulf of Aden, the Gulf of Oman, the Arabian Sea, Red Sea and the Indian Ocean.

"Some navies in [CTF-150] did not have the authority to conduct counter-piracy missions," CMF commander Vice Adm. William Gortney said. "The establishment of CTF-151 will allow those nations to operate under the auspices of CTF-150, while allowing other nations to join CTF-151 to support our goal of deterring, disrupting and eventually bringing to justice the maritime criminals involved in piracy events."

These patrols have had some success. During the fall of 2008 the U.S., Russia, Britain and India separately thwarted multiple piracy attacks. On Christmas day, the German frigate FDS Karlsruhe, one of the four vessels patrolling with the EU, assisted a 65,000-ton Egyptian bulk carrier in fighting off a pirate attack. In January, EU naval forces intercepted an attempted pirate attack against the Greek-flagged crude oil tanker Kriti as it was sailing in the Gulf of Aden, and on Jan. 13, a helicopter from a Russian frigate disrupted an attempted piracy hijacking of the container ship Nedlloyd Barentsz. The Russian helicopter opened fire on the pirates as the container ship fled. The pace of piracy attacks slowed in January, but that may be due more to the onset of the monsoon season that restricts pirates to the shores than the increasing naval presence.

Merchant shipping firms are taking additional steps to protect vessels and crews. Many slower vessels with lower freeboard, such as heavily laden tankers, are avoiding the area altogether, choosing instead to make the longer trip around the Cape of Good Hope. After the supertanker Sirius Star was seized in November, Denmark's A.P. Moller-Maersk decided to divert some of its 50 oil tankers around the cape instead of using the more convenient route through the Suez Canal in order to steer clear of the Gulf of Aden. Norway's Frontline, which carries much of the oil from the Middle

East to world markets, is considering doing the same, and the additional cost amounts to $1 million per transit. Diverting vessels around South Africa may not make them safer, and the trip increases both the cost of shipping and the time of transit, driving up the price of manufactured goods and commodities. The global shipping industry is especially vulnerable now, dealing with the attacks at the same time that it faces volatile fuel costs, plummeting freight rates, containership surpluses and increased insurance premiums for transits through the pirate-infested western Indian Ocean.

Some vessels, such as retail banks, are increasing passive and nonlethal security measures to foil armed robberies. Instead of using dye packs and silent alarms, ships are ringing lifelines with concertina wire, employing fire hoses to repel boarders, running underway with bright lights to increase visibility and spot trouble earlier, and they are entering convoy protection, when it is available. One nonlethal system, the Long-Range Acoustic Device (LRAD), already is on board some commercial vessels. The system can clearly broadcast at uncomfortably high levels of volume prerecorded warnings in Somali or Arabic, and a new model of LRAD contains laser dazzlers to temporarily confuse attackers. Another system, known as the Active Denial System (ADS) or "pain ray," emits a directional high-powered, 6-foot wide millimeter-wave beam of energy that creates an unbearable sensation of burning on the skin. Vessels are employing navigational tactics as well, including, for higher-speed vessels, evasive rudder steering to throw up a larger wake in the path of inbound piracy speedboats. Mariners and some naval officials express some concern that a more robust defense or greater resistance on the part of merchant ships might lead to more aggressive tactics by pirates. Private defense contractor Blackwater has deployed a security escort ship that includes a helicopter to the Gulf of Aden. The primary benefit of such an asset, however, is using the helicopter for over-the-horizon scouting to avoid trouble, not to pick a firefight.

But more than one-third of attempted ship hijackings in the Gulf of Aden are successful, illustrating that passive defense and patrols by naval forces have been unable to deter or disrupt many attacks. Moreover, once pirates successfully board and hijack a ship, they take the crew hostage and threaten to sink the vessel, limiting options by on-scene warship commanders to rescue the crew and free the ship. Incredibly, 300 seafarers and dozens of ships still are being held for ransom by pirates in the area of Harardhere, Somalia, a situation reminiscent of an earlier era. Confronting criminal acts at sea in an area that stretches 2,000 miles, however, poses significant logistical, operational and political challenges that require us to work smarter, not harder. This means that although there have been calls for expanded naval patrols in the western Indian Ocean, these efforts only will be effective if we change the way we address the problem.

Partnership and Action

The key to solving contemporary Somali piracy builds on the efforts of the U.S., partner nations and international institutions to make the seas safer. In January 2006, the destroyer USS Winston S. Churchill thwarted an attack against the bulk carrier M/V Delta Ranger, which was fired on off the coast of Somalia by pirates wielding AK47s and rocket-propelled grenade launchers. Disrupting the attack, the warship took 10 pirates and freed 16 Indian captives. Eventually, the pirates were transferred to Mombasa, Kenya, and later convicted in court and sentenced to seven years' confinement. This was a noteworthy example of effective maritime constabulary action, and it was the first major anti-piracy operation by the U.S. Navy in 150 years. After the Churchill interdiction, Navy lawyers in the Pentagon conducted a review of maritime and international law and policy, and proposed drafting a new national policy to articulate U.S. interests in combating maritime piracy. The result was a comprehensive policy governing diplomatic and legal action to fight piracy that was signed by the president in summer 2007. The top national goals in the policy include deterrence of piracy through maritime force presence, merchant ship vulnerability assessments, holding pirates accountable through criminal prosecution, preservation of freedom of the seas and a renewed commitment to work with other nations. Perhaps most importantly, the policy emphasized collaborative strategies by maritime and regional states, working in conjunction with the civil maritime sector, to prevent piracy attacks. Annexed to the National Strategy for Maritime Security (NSMS), the policy was used as a basis for the December 2008 National Security Council (NSC) strategy on combating piracy off the Horn of Africa, which sets forth three goals. First, the U.S. seeks to prevent pirate attacks by encouraging merchant ships to update their ship security plans and use the established Maritime Security Patrol Area (MPSA) set up by CMF. Second, the U.S. supports creation of a regional counterpiracy coordination center, an objective that is near fruition. Finally, the U.S. seeks to ensure those who commit acts of piracy are held accountable through negotiation of agreements to formalize custody, extradition and prosecution.

In addition to testing the nation's resolve in dealing with transnational maritime criminal organizations, the U.S. effort against piracy is the first real test of the Cooperative Strategy for 21st Century Seapower, released by the sea services more than one year ago. The strategy emphasizes that no single country can secure the maritime domain, and it places a premium on multilateral action. The goal of the new maritime strategy is to leverage the benefits of working together and capitalize on international law and institutions to facilitate closer collaboration among states. The Global Maritime Partnership, or figurative "1,000-ship navy," embodies these principles in an interagency application, bringing the Coast Guard and the Department of State into the effort. Admirals from Ghana, India, Indonesia, Japan, the Netherlands and Norway, among others, have recognized the potential value of the concept for increasing effective international cooperation. Recently, U.S. Chief of Naval Operations Adm. Gary Roughead re-emphasized the importance of international collaboration in his 2009 guidance, and piracy repression is a fertile area for increased collaboration. So far, however, international cooperation for counterpiracy has unfolded in an ad hoc fashion. New bilateral and regional treaties and a global mandate from the U.N. Security Council are untangling the diplomatic and logistical knots. The essential element for multilateral cooperation is ensuring all the players agree upon a common rule set, which is why international law and law of the sea have become the principal force multipliers in the new fight against piracy.

The Problem of PUCS

The main problem maritime powers now face with piracy is not a lack of operational resources to counter the threat, but what to do with the perpetrators when they are caught. Once pirates are detained and become so-called "persons under control" (PUCs), there are few good options. Additionally, what should be done with victims and witnesses, some of whom may be injured? Determining which state should prosecute pirates detained at sea is particularly vexing. It is typical of the vessels attacked by Somali pirates that the ship is registered in one state, such as Malta, owned by a corporation located in another state, such as the United Arab Emirates, and operated by a crew composed of nationals of several additional states, such as the Philippines and Pakistan. Furthermore, the vessel is likely to be transporting either containerized cargo or bulk commodities owned by companies in yet another country, such as the Sirius Star, which was registered in Liberia but owned by

Aramco, a Saudi corporation. Moreover, a piracy attack may have been interrupted by a warship from yet another state, all of which have different tactics and distinct rules of engagement. On the high seas or in any other place outside the jurisdiction of a state, such as Somalia's ungoverned territorial seas, any nation's warship may take action against piracy. Pirated ships may be boarded, the pirates can be detained and the property on board the vessel can be seized and submitted to admiralty and criminal courts. The registry or "flag" of the attacked vessel, the state of nationality of any of the victims or crew, the nationality of the on-scene warship, and, in some cases, coastal and port states, all have a valid basis for asserting jurisdiction. But it can take weeks or months to sort out these logistics and legal issues, and international agreements can standardize and speed up the process.

Depending on the circumstances, there are a variety of legal rationales that could support a compliant or noncompliant boarding of a hijacked vessel or pirate ship. During armed conflict, merchant vessels may be boarded under the belligerent right of visit and search to determine the neutral character of the goods on board, but that rule of naval warfare does not apply to maritime piracy. In peacetime, boarding a vessel by the naval forces of a state other than the state of registry may be conducted with the consent of the flag state under articles 92 and 94 of the Law of the Sea Convention. The U.S. recognizes that the master of the vessel also may provide consent to a boarding of his vessel. Under article 51 of the U.N. charter and customary international law, all nations may exercise of the right of individual or collective self-defense against a vessel committing a hostile act or demonstrating hostile intent. Naval forces also may board merchant vessels under the right of approach and visit pursuant to article 110 of the Law of the Sea if there are reasonable grounds to suspect the vessel is engaged in piracy. In some cases, the extension of port state control measures may be used by the port state authorities to board a vessel that has declared a nearby port. The Security Council may authorize all states to take action against piracy under chapter VII of the U.N. charter, providing yet another potential authority for boarding pirate vessels.

Collaboration, Not Kinetics

Collaboration and regional partnering, not armed force, is the long-term solution to piracy. Maritime piracy is a violation of international law and a universal crime that imposes a duty on all states to take action. The Law of the Sea Convention, the constitution for the world's oceans, is the essential framework for peacetime maritime security cooperation, and it defines piracy as an illegal act of violence or detention committed for private ends. Maritime piracy is distinguished from maritime terrorism, which is committed for political ends, and efforts to combine the two are not productive. Developing the international law and domestic legal capacities necessary to defeat piracy begins at the International Maritime Organization (IMO) in London. Situated on the Thames, the IMO is the specialized U.N. agency for maritime matters and has 167 member states. Because the organization is a technical rather than a political body, and since it operates under consensus decision-making rules, the IMO has served as an effective, no-nonsense venue for making shipping safer and more secure.

Addressing the problem of piracy off the coast of Somalia in November 2007, the IMO adopted Resolution A.1002(25), which called on regional states in east Africa to conclude a treaty to prevent, deter and suppress piracy. Also at the prompting of the secretary-general of the IMO, in 2008 the Security Council turned its attention toward combating piracy and adopted four key resolutions under chapter VII of the U.N. charter, authorizing "all necessary measures." The Security Council resolutions promote enhanced counterpiracy collaboration among nations, strengthening operational capabilities, removal of piracy sanctuaries in Somalia and support for increased criminal prosecution. Beginning with Resolution 1816 on June 2, the Security Council faced the issue of defeating piracy emanating from a fragile or failed state. For years, pirates in the Horn of Africa eluded capture at sea by fleeing into the jurisdictional protection of Somalia's 12-nautical mile territorial sea. Resolution 1816 authorized naval forces entry into Somali's territorial waters to pursue pirates. Since its adoption, the resolution has been extended to permit operations on the land territory of Somalia. The resolution also emphasized cooperation for logistics and prosecution by calling on states to collectively determine jurisdiction in the investigation and prosecution of persons committing acts of piracy off the coast of Somalia. Finally, the resolution also encouraged states to increase and coordinate their efforts to deter acts of piracy in conjunction with the Transitional Federal Government of Somalia, a ruling authority inside the fractured state. Since Somalia has no maritime law enforcement capability, the resolution also called on states, the IMO and other international organizations to build a partnership to develop coastal security forces.

Next, the Security Council adopted Resolution 1838, expressing its grave concern over the proliferation of acts of piracy and armed robbery at sea against vessels off the coast of Somalia, and the threat it poses to the delivery of World Food Program shipments to

Somalia. The resolution called upon states to take part in actively fighting piracy by deploying naval vessels and aircraft to the Gulf of Aden and surrounding water. The Security Council also reaffirmed that the Law of the Sea Convention embodies the rules applicable to countering piracy and armed robbery at sea. Security Council Resolution 1846 of Dec. 2 broadened the international political support and legal capabilities to combat piracy off the Somali coast. The resolution suggests states consider application of the 1988 Convention on the Suppression of Unlawful Acts against the Safety of Maritime Navigation (SUA) to facilitate the extradition and prosecution of pirates. The SUA Convention arose from the 1985 hijacking of the *Achille Lauro* cruise ship by four heavily armed terrorists from the Palestinian Liberation Organization. After seizing control of the Italian-flagged vessel, the terrorists murdered a disabled American passenger, pushing his wheelchair into the sea. At the time, most states lacked adequate criminal statutes to prosecute vessel hijacking. To fill this void, the IMO brought together member states to develop a maritime criminal law treaty, and SUA emerged from the process. The treaty entered into force in 1992 and has 149 state parties. States that seek to prosecute maritime piracy but do not have current national laws proscribing the crime, such as Japan and Spain, still might be able to prosecute some crimes such as ship hijacking, under legislation implementing SUA. Denmark, Oman and other states have suggested that developing standard rules for arrest, detention and criminal prosecution of pirates is the most pressing issue for suppressing piracy. In most cases, Resolution 1846 and SUA provide a firm legal basis for doing so, and states should ensure their domestic authorities are consistent with the resolution and treaty.

Two weeks later, the Security Council adopted Resolution 1851, authorizing states to take action against piracy safe havens on the shore in Somalia. The authority is likely to be cautiously implemented, however, since major land operations in the country could be perilous. The resolution also invited the states with maritime forces in the area and the regional states to conclude "shiprider" agreements or arrangements so that local law enforcement officials could embark on board foreign warships patrolling the area. The regional countries are particularly important in this regard because they are ideally situated to conclude the endgame—conducting a criminal investigations and criminal trials.

In addition to the four Security Council resolutions, there are three additional breakthroughs in maritime diplomacy that have set the stage for more effectively addressing the threat of Somali piracy.

First, the U.K. signed a counterpiracy cooperation agreement with Kenya in December, agreeing to transfer captured pirates to Mombasa for prosecution. The U.S. and Kenya concluded a similar arrangement on Jan. 29. These agreements will facilitate the handling of PUCs and will benefit the naval forces patrolling the area by ensuring that pirates obtained during counterpiracy operations are quickly removed from warships, freeing the vessel for follow-on tasking. Second, Resolution 1851 encouraged establishment of a multinational Contact Group on Somali Piracy (CGSP), and the inaugural meeting for the group was held at the U.N. on Jan. 14. More than 20 countries, as well as observers from the EU, NATO and the African Union, participated in the discussions. The CGSP formed several working groups to develop collective action against different aspects of the effort against Somali piracy. These groups divided functional lines, with the U.K. leading a group focused on naval operations and information-sharing; another group led by Denmark reviewed the judicial framework and issues associated with PUCs; the U.S. led discussion on strengthening industry awareness and capabilities; and a final group led by Egypt focused on strategic communications and public information. Most importantly, many representatives at the CGSP acknowledged the need for an east African counterpiracy coordination center (CPCC), and Yemen, Djibouti and Kenya each offered to host the center. Third, at an IMO-sponsored meeting in Djibouti on Jan. 29, agreement was reached on a regional arrangement to fight piracy. Based on text that was developed at a previous IMO meeting in Dar Es Salaam, Tanzania, eight coastal states situated on the Gulf of Aden, the Red Sea and the western Indian Ocean, plus Ethiopia, concluded the Djibouti code of conduct to combat acts of piracy against ships, fulfilling the request made by the IMO assembly in 1002(25). The agreement is based on the 16-nation counterpiracy treaty, Regional Cooperation Agreement on Combating Piracy and Armed Robbery against Ships in Asia (ReCAAP), which has been remarkably successful in reducing the number of piracy attacks in East Asia. Just as ReCAAP was the first Asian agreement dedicated to counterpiracy, the Djibouti code of conduct is the first regional agreement between Arab and African countries to address maritime piracy.

The momentum from these global, regional and bilateral diplomatic successes should be maintained. Each development is complementary and promising, but more can be done. Now that there is agreement to share actionable information, cooperate to dismantle maritime criminal gangs and bring their members to criminal trial, the maritime and regional states and largest shipping nations such as Panama and Liberia should ratify the agreements and take the next steps to implement them.

First, the CPCC should be designed to serve as a fusion point for real-time coordination for dealing with PUCs. In the U.S., the inter-agency community resolves difficult national-level maritime issues pursuant to a maritime operational threat response (MOTR) plan that facilitates rapid and real-time communication among the State and Defense departments and the Coast Guard. Each agency is required to operate continuously a tactical watch center that can make agency decisions arising from time-sensitive maritime diplo-matic issues. The MOTR process is used to quickly form adminis-tration positions and courses of action on the full range of maritime exigencies, including interdiction of foreign drug trafficking fast boats and interception of migrants at sea. We need an international MOTR that maintains 24-hour communications among the mar-itime states patrolling offshore, the major flag states and the regional states so that partner nations may quickly coordinate issues regarding on-scene interdiction of vessels hijacked by pirates and pirate "mother ships," and resolve more deliberative questions regarding PUC disposition and logistics.

Second, the maritime states should increase efforts for maritime security capacity-building in the states of the Horn of Africa in order to forge tighter maritime security partnerships with strong regional partners. The states of east Africa are in desperate need of capacity-building assistance to actually implement the Security Council resolutions and new treaties. For example, Kenya has stepped out on many occasions to prosecute PUCs, but it requires greater support. The recently concluded counterpiracy arrange-ments with the U.K. and U.S. can serve as models for similar bilat-eral agreements with other maritime states patrolling the area. But the states in the Horn of Africa require development assistance to be able to more effectively implement their new commitments. Not only do the states in the region lack resources for building naval and coast guard force structure and training maritime law enforcement officers, but they also are in need of greater assistance for develop-ing a mature judicial criminal justice system. The states have insuf-ficient numbers of lawyers and judges, and they sometimes lack essential equipment such as computers and printers.

The Global Train and Equip program under section 1206 of the U.S. National Defense Authorization Act of 2006 is used by the State and Defense departments to methodically assess how to increase the capability of partner nations to solve local problems before they require outside intervention. The program leverages Defense Department funds to train and equip regional forces, mitigating the risk that small problems such as piracy will grow into larger security issues.

One way for the U.S. to develop greater maritime security capacity throughout the Horn of Africa would be to broaden and fully fund Global Train and Equip. About one-third of the program focuses on strengthening maritime security support to regional countries and includes development of coastal surveillance infrastructure, patrol boats and maritime interdiction capabilities. In 2007, for example, Djibouti was awarded $8 million for such purposes. Last year, there were $800 million in requirements, but only $300 million of these were funded. Much like the G-8 has pooled resources to fund Cooperative Threat Reduction for nonproliferation, the major maritime powers should develop and fund a shared and coherent program of maritime security capacity building based upon the Global Train and Equip model. Contributions toward this endeavor can pay off for everyone. In Asia, for example, ReCAAP operates a technologically advanced Information Sharing Center (ISC) in Singapore that serves as secure communications center to coordinate effective multinational operational responses to maritime piracy among member states. But the ISC would not have been possible without generous sponsorship support provided by Japan, and a CPCC for east Africa will not be possible without support from outside the region.

Third, following Kenya's example, regional states should make a greater commitment to accepting PUCs, either temporarily or permanently, and to prosecuting pirates in criminal court. In the past, some pirates were captured, only to be released for lack of a regional country willing to prosecute them. Such action undermines the credibility of the international community and encourages more piracy. For example, the Danish warship on patrol has successfully disrupted numerous piracy attacks, but the media has tended to focus on the one instance they had to release 10 captured suspects because of an inability to prosecute. Toward this end, regional states should conduct a national review of their counterpiracy laws and policies to ensure they can serve a constructive role in the region. Furthermore, the states of east Africa have an opportunity to capitalize on the establishment of a CPCC to broadly develop a more effective maritime security cooperation network in the region. Regional states will be more willing and capable of enforcing the maritime rule of law in their neighborhood if they develop the legal architecture and operational capabilities to deal with piracy—patrol craft and communications systems are needed, as are more lawyers, courtrooms and confinement facilities.

International law has become the most effective force multiplier for developing maritime security, and nowhere is this more evident than in the waters off the Horn of Africa. Naval air and sea operational missions conducted by the world's most capable maritime powers have been unable to arrest Somali piracy because they cannot prosecute the endgame. Piracy flourishes at the seams of globalization because legal jurisdiction is unclear, the costs and time for states to conduct diplomatic transactions are too great, and pirates are able to exploit the inherent isolation of individual vessels and nations. Somalia is a failed state, and the pirates are more powerful than the ruling government. Regional governments have underdeveloped maritime security forces and judicial systems, and suffer from a severe lack of operational, logistical and administrative resources. We need to better connect the capabilities and sea power of the maritime states with the regional expertise, local networks and self-interest of the east African states. In this setting, international law is more important than adding another warship to the equation. In order to "operationalize" the U.N. mandates and international agreements, the CGSP should agree to establish a CPCC at their next meeting in March. The CPCC can serve as the hub for a comprehensive network of states that includes an international MOTR process; command, control and communications for linking major maritime powers, flag states and regional partners; and to coordinate requirements for assistance from outside the region. An international MOTR process would create a network of interested states that could begin to coordinate in real time, working effectively across legal and jurisdictional lines of demarcation to bring collective action against this threat. These initiatives will enhance the capabilities of the states in east Africa to exercise maritime constabulary authority in their own neighborhood, and with that, we will all be better off.

CHAPTER 6

PIRACY AND MARITIME TERRORISM—HOT SPOTS

6.1
Countering Maritime Terrorism in the Caribbean Sea and the Atlantic Ocean

Implications of Possible Maritime Terrorism in the Caribbean

LIEUTENANT COLONEL COLIN L. MITCHELL

This chapter examines the threats to maritime security and addresses the evidence of tactics, techniques, and procedures insurgents at sea use. The chapter also examines the best anti-piracy and counterterrorism practices countries have used over the years to handle large volumes of shipping and handle dangerous cargoes like Liquefied Natural Gas (LNG).

This research is important to the Caribbean and especially the nation of Trinidad and Tobago at this time because the outreach of Islamic fundamentalism and global terrorism has reached the region's shores. This was clearly demonstrated in June 2007, when the authorities arrested two Guyanese nationals and one Trinidad and Tobago citizen for allegedly planning to blow up the JFK Airport. These three persons and another accomplice, who was arrested in New York City, are believed to be part of a new terrorist network that came into being following the outbreak of the U.S. global war on terror. The three individuals who were arrested in Trinidad and Tobago were allegedly trying to establish links with the Jamaat al Muslimeem, a local Sunni Muslim sect that has now become infamous for its 1990 attempt to overthrow the elected government by staging a coup. That attempt was ended on August 1,

---

This Chapter (6.1) is an excerpt from Mitchell's Master Thesis presented to the Faculty of the U.S. Army Command and General Staff College in partial fulfillment of the requirements for the degree of Master of Military Art and Science, Fort Leavenworth, Kansas, 2007.

1990, after seven days, when the Trinidad and Tobago Defense Forces (TTDF), through its quick and decisive action, forced the coup leaders to seek terms of surrender. It is noteworthy that Saddam Hussein invaded Kuwait the following day, August of 1990, having moved his military forces from Baghdad to the border while the world was distracted.

Motives and Modus Operandi of Middle East and Far East Pirates and Terrorists

It is estimated that piracy worldwide is a billion dollar enterprise, and some researchers claim that losses are approximately $16 billion annually.[1] The writers, Gray, Monday, and Stubblefield in their book, *Maritime Terror* support this sum; however, they go further and suggest that even this figure is an understatement, since many ship owners and captains do not report attacks on their vessels because of the delays and "red tape" involved in making these reports.[2] Gal Luft and Anne Korin, senior directors at the Institute for the Analysis of Global Security, wrote that pirate attacks tripled in the decade 1994 to 2004. Their research also revealed that some apparent acts of piracy are in reality terrorist activity since they are not committed for personal gain. Terrorist actions are usually committed in order to make a political statement and strike terror in a populace, as in the attack on the USS *Cole;* to gain the freedom of imprisoned comrades, as in the attack on the Greek passenger ship, *City of Poros,* or to acquire funding for quasi-political causes like the purchase of weapons to be used by freedom fighters. The last reason is the case of the Free Aceh Movement of Indonesia and the Movement for the Emancipation of the Niger Delta. These two groups attack vessels at sea and confiscate the vessels and cargoes for resale or secure both along with the crews for ransom. The two factors, profits for the attackers and the ship owners' reluctance to report attacks, may have contributed to the pirates and terrorists' continuing attraction of attacking ships.

The research found that piracy is a major problem in the regions of Southeast Asia, West Africa, and around the Horn of Africa. Most pirate and maritime terrorist activities occur in the Far East and Middle East regions. In 2003, there were 445 reported pirate attacks worldwide in which ninety-two seafarers died. Of that total, 129 attacks took place in the Far East, seventy-seven in the Indian

---

1. Mann, 2.
2. Gray, Monday, and Stubblefield, 1.

Ocean, and seventy in Africa. The situation in 2006 reflected a similar average with the Far East recording sixty-six attacks, thirty-eight in the Indian Ocean, and forty in Africa, for a total of 173 attacks. Pirates and maritime terrorists engage in the same activities of attacking and seizing ships at sea, but they do so for different reasons. Pirates are waterborne bandits who attack shipping and coastal regions to rob and steal for their own benefit. Terrorists engage in the same acts; however, their ultimate goals go beyond self-interest since their actions are politically motivated. Their purpose is to draw attention to their cause and to strike fear and create confusion in the targeted population.

Sometimes, however, financial gain may be vital to achieving political ends; therefore, some terrorist organizations use piracy to fund their agendas.[3] The Free Aceh Movement funds it operations from the proceeds of piracy and averages $100,000 per ship in ransom payments. The success of this type of piracy has inspired groups in other regions of the world, notably Africa. The Movement for the Emancipation of the Niger Delta (MEND) that operates in the Niger Delta of Nigeria is a case in point. The MEND use piracy and kidnapping for ransom to gain funds needed to finance their struggle for greater autonomy in the oil-rich Niger Delta. The MEND acquired the means to range far into the Atlantic Ocean in order to attack ships and kidnap crew members for ransom.

Terrorists have attacked ships in the past to deadly effect and they are likely to continue to do so when opportunities arise. Pirates, whose motivation is mainly profit, will attack all types of ships, especially high-value targets like tankers; however, terrorist attacks to date have been mainly against passenger ships; notwithstanding that the USS *Cole* was a U.S. Navy destroyer. While maritime security for passenger ships improves, terrorists will continue to seek out targets of opportunity, and their focus may extend to include targeting other regions around the world where maritime security may appear to be less stringent.

The research revealed that modern pirates cum terrorists are usually well-armed with rocket-propelled grenades and modern heavy machine guns that are mounted on their boats. They are likely equipped with GPS devices and wireless communications. Some even employ military-type tactics in their ship attacks. This is the case of the Free Aceh Movement that operates in the Straits of Malacca region in Southeast Asia, where this organization is fighting to gain independence from Indonesia. The Free Aceh Movement's combatants actually operate in military-style uniforms

---

3. Luft and Karin, 1.

in the belief that this will provide some recognition to the organization. This in turn is supposed to legitimize their actions, since their acts of piracy are not an end in itself, but a means to an end: the acquisition of funds to maintain their struggle for independence. It was found that many have had prior military service and, therefore, they are able to apply this military training and discipline to the training of new recruits and the pursuit of what they now perceive as their legitimate agenda. These pirates and terrorists possess the capacity to attack vessels anywhere, be it in port, in restricted waterways, and even in the open ocean. The open ocean is generally considered to be the most dangerous place to encounter pirates. This is because in the open ocean pirates usually kill the crew because they are unwilling to leave witnesses, and it is easy to dispose of the bodies.[4]

Pirate and Terrorist Activities in the United States and the Caribbean

Since the arrival of Europeans in the Caribbean, piracy has become a legacy. Piracy flourished during the sixteenth to nineteenth centuries before it was brought under control by the might of the British Navy, with assistance from the other European and U.S. navies. In this modern era, piracy is relatively low-key compared to other regions, like Southeast Asia. Piracy still exists in the region; however, the Caribbean states can do little to eradicate it. A point of concern would be the region's inability to properly respond to increased pirate or maritime terrorist activity.

In the United States and the Caribbean regions, terrorist attacks to date have occurred on land or in the air. However, as land and air targets become more difficult to attack, and as the composition of maritime cargoes increase in importance, the likelihood of terrorists targeting ships becomes an increasing prospect. This possibility is high given the unstable political environment of the fragile economies in the region.

The four Caribbean nationals who were arrested in June 2007, for plotting to attack New York's JFK Airport caused consternation in the region and greatly alarmed *Caribbean Community and Common Market Treaty* (CARICOM) leaders. This action of the four also exemplifies that terrorist cells are increasing and spreading to unlikely places. Additionally, their action may be informed by

---

4. Ibid., 12.

increasing anti-American sentiment in areas like the Caribbean, a region where traditionally there have been strong pro-American sentiments and where nations view the United States as an important ally and major trade partner.

Prime Minister Patrick Manning acknowledged this possibility on June 20, 2007, when he addressed the CARICOM Heads of Government and delegates at the Experts Forum of the Conference on the Caribbean. He stated that "in light of the alleged plot to bomb facilities at the JFK International Airport, our region has taken the initiative to establish a regional mechanism to combat terrorism."[5] He also said that collectively, the region must prepare to utilize every facet of available resources to achieve this aim. Threats to the region were recognized back in October 2002, when Ambassador Odeen Ishmael of Guyana addressed a meeting of the Committee on Hemispheric Security in Washington, DC. Back then, he warned that the trade in illegal drugs had a direct linkage with the increase in small arms in the region. This is because arms and drugs are usually transported on the same vessels. The increased presence of illegal weapons in these small states fuels crime escalation and adversely impacts their peace and security.[6] The incidence of crime, sadly, has not improved over the ensuing years. In a number of regional countries, including Trinidad and Tobago, crime rates are increasing annually even as governments are making every effort to prevent a complete breakdown of law and order. This is reason for concern because destabilized governments in turn could lead to instability in the region, and this will pose a threat to regional security by paving the way for a well-funded terrorist organization to infiltrate and set up shop in the region. Historically, terrorism flourishes in unstable environments.

In the next decade, regional shipping is likely to increase dramatically. This is because Panama proposes to construct a third set of locks by 2015. These new locks will cater to vessels that are currently too large to pass through the canal. Additionally, on October 3, 2006, Nicaragua announced plans to construct its own

---

5. Embassy of the Republic of Trinidad and Tobago. Address by Honourable Patrick Manning, Prime Minister of Trinidad and Tobago at the Experts Forums, "Security and competitiveness in a Global Environment." The Preston Auditorium, World Bank Headquarters, Washington, DC, June 2007. Retrieved November 14, 2007, from http://www.ttembassy.org/062007.html.
6. Ishmael, O. Approaches on Security in the Caribbean Region. Statement by Ambassador Odeen Ishmael of Guyana at the Meeting of the Committee on Hemispheric Security of the OAS. Washington, DC, October 29, 2002. Retrieved November 17, 2007, from *http://www.guyana.org/Speeches/ ishmael_102902.html.*

canal by 2016, at an estimated cost of $20 billion (U.S. dollars). If Nicaragua completes the canal, it will accommodate 250,000-ton vessels. Panama's proposed expansion project will only allow vessels to a maximum of 120,000 tons.[7] The proposed increased maritime capacity for both countries would attract an increased shipping volume, which potentially could act as a magnet for maritime terrorists.

Piracy worldwide is declining, but it is not likely to be totally eradicated. There is piracy occurring in the Caribbean region, but so far attacks have been restricted to small craft like fishing boats and yachts. The danger, however, is that the region seems unable to prevent these acts of piracy because of the inadequacy of the CARICOM states to effectively patrol their territorial areas of responsibility. It can be assumed, therefore, that should the situation degenerate and terrorists enter the equation, the Caribbean nations' forces will still be ineffective to act.

Table 6.1 contains a compilation of pirate attacks in the South American and Caribbean region, for the period 2000 to 2006. During this period, there were 230 recorded attacks, while at the same period the Malacca Straits recorded 342 attacks, and the South China Sea region recorded 830 attacks out of a worldwide total of 2,512 recorded attacks.[8] Approximately one-half of the attacks from this region occurred within the Caribbean Sea, an area that is the domain of the CARICOM states. Additionally, these attacks occurred in territorial waters or in port areas. In 2006, the physical violence against crews decreased compared to previous years' figures; most likely because of overall increased maritime security awareness. However, of the fifteen deaths worldwide that year, one person was killed in Trinidad and Tobago.[9]

A possible reason for the reduced pirate attacks is that ship crews are more vigilant, especially when sailing in known danger areas. Alternatively, it could be that ships are under-reporting attacks because of consequences like increased insurance charges.

Regional Response to Security Concerns

Regionally, the CARICOM nations established the CARICOM Single Market and Economy (CSME) in 2006. This agreement expected

---

7. Ibid., 5.
8. Bruynell.
9. Ocean Policy Research Foundation, *OPRF MARINT Monthly Report.* January 2007. Retrieved August 29, 2007, from *http://www.sof.or.jp/ocean/report_e/pdf/200701.pdf.*

TABLE 6.1 Regional Analysis of Reports on Acts of Piracy and Armed Robbery Against Ships, South America, and The Caribbean 2000–2006

Acts Reported to Have Been Allegedly Committed/Attempted	2000	2001	2002	2003	2004	2005	2006
Location of incident							
In international waters	3	1	3	9	3	-	-
In territorial waters	26	11	12	3	2	2	6
In port areas	12	11	52	35	23	12	4
Status of ship when attacked							
Steaming	9	11	14	15	4	1	1
At anchor or at berth	30	12	16	42	24	13	8
Not stated	2	-	1	-	-	-	1
Number of persons involved in the attack							
1–4 persons	13	6	25	26	14	9	3
5–10 persons	9	8	20	11	6	3	4
More than 10 persons	4	-	3	-	7	-	-
Not stated	15	9	19	20	1	2	3
Consequences to the crew							
Actual violence used against crew	14	8	10	8	9	4	5
Threat of violence (including crew being tied up but not physically attacked)	8	13	26	9	4	5	1
Ship missing	-	-	-	-	-	-	-
Ship hijacked	-	-	-	2	13	-	-
None/Not stated	19	2	31	38	2	5	4
Weapons used by attackers							
Guns	13	10	14	3	7	1	4
Knives	4	5	14	14	8	9	2
Other	2	1	1	1	-	1	-
None/Not stated	22	7	38	39	13	3	4
Parts of the ship raided							
Master and crew accommodation	10	8	12	6	1	-	-
Cargo area	8	6	9	18	20	9	2
Store rooms	8	1	28	20	4	3	4
Engine room	5	-	-	1	-	-	1
Not stated	5	2	4	3	-	-	-
Total number of incidents reported per year	41	23	67	47	28	14	10
Total number of incidents reported	230						

Source: This information was compiled by the author from the International Maritime Organization (IMO) Annual Reports on reported acts of piracy and armed robbery against ships, 2000–2006.

to fulfill the region's unification aspiration dreamt about since the Federation attempt of the 1950s. An important aspect of this cooperation among member states is the Framework for the Management of Crime and Security in the region, which began in 2005. The importance of this is recognized in international forum as exemplified in the Joint Report by the United Nations Office on Drugs and Crime and the Latin American and Caribbean Region of the World Bank, which stated that the Caribbean has been "caught in the cross fire of international drug trafficking."[10] CARICOM states now recognize the need to develop a more comprehensive and coordinated approach to safeguarding regional security in the face of new and emerging challenges to regional, hemispherical, and global security. As a result, the heads of government have declared that security is now the fourth pillar on which they will jointly pursue the development and progress of the region. The other three pillars are foreign policy, trade and economic development, and functional cooperation. CARICOM heads of government are taking steps to incorporate recognition of this fourth pillar in the revised Treaty of Chaguaramas. In 2006, the nerve centre for this initiative, called the Implementation Agency for Crime and Security, began operations. Its mandate is to foster coordination and collaboration on matters of security among the law enforcement and security agencies throughout the CARICOM region. In 2007, the system was tested when the CARICOM nations hosted the Cricket World Cup Tournament, the world's third largest sport event after the Olympic Games and Federation Internationale Football Association (FIFA) World Cup Football competition. The security reviews were encouraging as there were no reports of any security breaches during the competition. The recent events' concerning the alleged plot to bomb New York's JFK Airport facilities has caused the region to expand this security mandate to include a regional mechanism to combat terrorism.

In April 2001, President George W. Bush, speaking at the launch of the Third Border initiative said that the United States was committed to deepening cooperation with other hemispheric states to fight the spread of HIV and AIDS, respond to natural disasters, and ensure the benefits of globalization are felt in even the smallest economies. These goals were at the heart of the Third Border initiative, which was a joint venture with the United States and the Caribbean nations. The Bush Administration recognized the Caribbean region as its "third border" and admitted that the region

---

10. Manning, 3.

was often overlooked, but now there was a desire to accept these nations as important trade partners.[11]

During a previous administration, the United States began deporting former Caribbean nationals who were convicted felons and living in the United States. Unfortunately, the Caribbean authorities were not informed about the returning nationals or about their criminal past. Additionally, many of these "deportees" had no family residence in the land of their birth and were literally strangers in their homeland. Many resorted to what they knew best—a life of crime. Some banded together and formed criminal gangs and, using the skills acquired in the United States, engaged in a degree of sophisticated criminal activity that almost overwhelmed many local security forces. Many Caribbean states are still suffering the effects of the crime surge brought on by these deported criminals. This current U.S. administration's effort to cooperate with the Caribbean is different from many past attempts. This time, there is an effort at bilateral engagement rather than the U.S. unilateral approach that some previous administrations practiced.

CARICOM has the means through these protocols to seek bilateral agreements with the United States in order to strengthen maritime security within the Caribbean Sea region. The member states all maintain a friendly relationship with the United States and are dependant on this country for trade and general support. This connectedness is an opportunity rather than a threat to the entire region. The threat of terrorism could be the bond that draws CARICOM and the United States even closer. It is in the best interest of the United States to ensure that the Caribbean region does not become vulnerable to terrorist infiltration; therefore, all parties should be willing to negotiate security related matters because of their mutual needs. Both the United States and CARICOM should make efforts to keep the Third Border Initiative active and workable, as this will redound to their mutual benefit.[12]

CARICOM leaders must accept that their region is vulnerable and therefore must be willing to adopt measures to improve security within the region. The greatest vulnerability is in the maritime domain. Trinidad and Tobago now accepts this and is pursuing measures to reduce this situation. The islands should also look extra-regionally and seek advice from countries like Singapore,

---

11. Ereli, A. Joint Statement by the USA, the Caribbean Community and the Dominican Republic on the Third Border Initiative. 2004/28136.htm. January 13, 2004. Retrieved November 17, 2007, from *http://www.state.gov/r/pa/prs/ps/*
12. Ibid.

since that country has developed methods to reduce its vulnerability to pirate and maritime terrorism.[13]

The United States is a major trading partner of all the English-speaking islands of the Caribbean. The islands are a popular tourist destination for many American and European visitors and many Caribbean nationals in turn view the United States as the land of opportunity; whether it is for education purposes or as the "Promised Land" to resettle and establish new lives. The United States sought to improve its border security post September 11, 2001, and some of the measures adopted have had some adverse effects on the Caribbean islands' economies. The requirement for U.S. citizens to possess passports for travel to the Caribbean has resulted in a reduction in the number of American tourists visiting the islands, and this put a financial strain on the islands that depend on tourism for a substantial part of their economy.[14] The full positive effects of the Third Border Initiative are yet to rebound to the good of the region because the U.S. focus is currently in the Middle East. Meanwhile, the islands are still trying to cope with the negative effects of globalization. The loss of preferential markets and competition from larger producers has adversely affected their economies, and faced with escalating costs for food and fuel among others, regional governments have a very difficult task to provide quality living standard for their citizens.

At the same time, Venezuela's President, Hugo Chavez, who maintains strong links with Cuba and Iran, has been making overtures to Caribbean leaders to form an alliance with Latin America. In June 2005, Presidents Castro and Chavez met with fourteen top officials from the Caribbean and they agreed to a Venezuelan plan that included the sale of oil at preferential rates. As part of the plan, named Petro Caribe, Venezuela indicated that it would be willing to accept CARICOM goods like sugar and bananas as part payment for the oil.[15] These initiatives were viewed as Chavez's alternative to the U.S. proposed Free Trade Area of the Americas (FTAA), which now appears to be no longer relevant, given the U.S. immediate priorities in the Middle East. As an alternative, Chavez has called for the establishment of the Bolivarian Alternative Trade Pact, which envisages a

---

13. *Khaleej Times online.* Singapore Navy to escort passing Merchant Ships to stop terrorism. February 28, 2005. Retrieved August 31, 2007, from *http://www.khaleejtimes.com.*

14. Mintz, J. "U.S. Will Tighten Passport Rules," *Washington Post, April 6, 2005.* Retrieved September 20, 2007, from *http://www.washingtonpost.com/ac2/wp-dyn/A28188-2005Apr5.*

15. Trinidad and Tobago News Bulletin Board. Posted 30 June 2005. Retrieved August 29, 2007, from *http://www.trinidadandtobagonews.com.*

South American and Caribbean trade zone that excludes the United States. To date, all the islands except Barbados and Trinidad and Tobago have signed the agreement; however, Barbados has indicated that if oil prices continue to increase it will have no option but to accept Venezuela's offer. If this movement gains popularity in the region and the Caribbean reorients itself toward South America, the United States may lose some of the mass appeal it currently enjoys from the region's population. This situation in turn has the potential for exploitation by any terrorist group that is looking for an opportunity to establish a base for either attracting recruits and or a launch pad for operations against the United States. Caribbean people could be less focused on the United States and may not be particularly alarmed if a stranger voices anti-American sentiments, especially if that person were to offer financial inducements to people who feel abandoned by the United States.

Vulnerability of Ships

Pirates generally employ ambush tactics, and they use armed speedboats to spring surprise attacks on their targeted vessels. Gray, Monday, and Stubblefield described the ambush process as having seven steps: stalk; site; stop; shock; smother; secure, search and snatch; and scram.[16] The first two steps—stalk and site—are the pre-ambush phase of the process. During the stalking step, the ambusher selects the potential target, gathers intelligence on the intended victim, and develops plans on how, when, and where to spring the attack on the vessel. In the sighting step, the attackers arm and position themselves to perform the actual attack. Locations like the Malacca Straits, with their natural choke points and numerous islands that provide concealment, are ideally suited for sighting maritime ambushes. The Caribbean, with its chain of tiny islands, also has some locations that can provide excellent ambush sites. From these locations, pirates and terrorists using speedboats can quickly launch attacks against their slower moving quarry. Another method involves the use of mother ships, in which large vessels that contain small speedboats to be used for the assault are pre-positioned in the likely path of target vessels. When the target is within range, the smaller boats are launched to quickly overpower and seize the target.

The actual ambushes involve the steps of stop, shock, and smother. The targeted vessel must be halted and prevented from

---

16. Ibid., 26–29.

escaping. A number of options are employed to cause a target to be stopped. These include the use of distress signals, impersonation of maritime security forces, and the employment of the swarm tactic, which is a simultaneous attack by several small craft approaching from different directions. Once the vessel is stopped, the attackers employ shock and smother to quickly overwhelm any resistance by the crew that may prevent the successful takeover by the attackers. These steps of the actual ambush usually occur almost simultaneously and, for a successful ambush, must be completed quickly before the targeted crew can muster an effective counterattack or alert maritime security forces that may be within range to initiate a rescue mission.

Secure, search, and snatch are the next steps of the ambush process. The attackers need to quickly complete their mission, whether it is to seize the entire vessel or the crew and/or cargo, ensure none of the crew escape, among other things. The last step is the scram, which is for the attackers to quickly depart the ambush area, leaving as little evidence of their activity as possible.

Again, it is important to note the different aims of pirates and terrorists. Terrorists generally are little concerned with profit, unless it is to provide funding for their cause. Therefore, in a situation of an attack in the open ocean, terrorists will more likely destroy the vessel in order to make a political statement. Modern terrorists have demonstrated their ability to devise ingenious ways to achieve their goals, much to the horror of an unsuspecting population. It is likely, therefore, for terrorists to attack a tanker in the open ocean on the pretext of executing a pirate attack. During the attack, divers may plant explosives on the tanker's hull before allowing it to continue on its journey. The explosives could then be remotely detonated at any opportune moment. Alternately, the terrorists may decide to pattern the September 11, 2001, attacks and endeavor to use the tanker as a weapon. They may take physical control of the vessel before it gets into port, plant explosives within its confines, set a course directly toward the port, and propel the tanker at full speed before detonating the explosives. The effects of such an attack could be greatly increased if the terrorists acquire radiological, chemical, or even nuclear materiel, along with the expertise to create a crude, yet workable weapon to affix to a tanker in order to create a super weapon of mass destruction (WMD).

In the case of Trinidad and Tobago, a pro-U.S. country, its proximity to Venezuela could become a cause for concern, because Venezuela is anti-United States and an associate of Iran, a country that sponsors international terrorism and also possesses a nuclear capability. Trinidad and Tobago does not support Venezuela's Petro

Caribe plan because it poses a direct challenge to the country's national economy. Trinidad and Tobago is, therefore, an economic rival to Venezuela and a trade partner of the United States. Geopolitical differences between Iran and the United States are widening. In October 2007, the United States froze Iran's U.S. assets in a move to force that country to disband its nuclear program, but Iran responded by insisting that its program was too far advanced to stop. There is the likelihood for these two nations' differences to increase with potentially frightening results. Since Iran is assumed to be a sponsor of international terrorism, the Caribbean can become a potential soft target area for organizing terrorist activities against the United States.

Trinidad and Tobago exports most of its LNG to the United States, and this dangerous cargo must be transported there by ship tankers. It is, therefore, in the United States' interest that terrorists do not attempt to use the Caribbean as a potential base of operations and attempt to use the islands as a recruiting ground and a platform from which to launch terrorist activities against the U.S. mainland. Specifically, it is in the United States' interest that potential terrorists do not seek to use one of the LNG tankers as a WMD in one of its ports.

A supertanker traveling from Trinidad and Tobago and loaded with LNG may prove to be the ideal high-value target sought by terrorists. Their cause will be further advanced if the tanker's destination is a U.S. port and the tanker can be hijacked or otherwise infiltrated, unbeknownst to U.S. authorities. Alternatively, a ship may be en route through the Caribbean via the Panama Canal and the occupants may devise a pretext to divert to a U.S. port, and once there, detonate the vessel to create a WMD.

Trinidad and Tobago's Maritime Situation

Trinidad and Tobago is acutely aware of many of the threats that are arrayed against its sovereignty and its people. Some of these threats are transnational crimes like drug and gun running, human trafficking, piracy, and terrorism. Trinidad and Tobago's proximity to Venezuela places it in the direct transshipment path for drugs, like cocaine, destined for the lucrative U.S. market. The drugs are transported in small boats outfitted with powerful engines that can cover the seven-mile distance in a few minutes. These boats also transport weapons and human cargo. There is the possibility that terrorists can also infiltrate the country by this means.

In order to counter the threats to Trinidad and Tobago's sovereignty, the country installed a radar system that enables the security forces to monitor and track all classes and size of vessels that traverse its territorial waters on a twenty-four-hour basis. The radar provides the course, speed, and position of any vessels operating within its operational range. This is a key weapon in the country's arsenal to combat illegal activities, especially within the water that separates it from Venezuela. Additionally, the country proposes to extend this coverage to as far as the island of St. Lucia and will cover Grenada and St. Vincent and the Grenadines as well. This coverage may also be linked with Barbados since that country proposes to upgrade its radar system and link it with its RSS partners. Trinidad and Tobago has begun the process of acquiring military equipment like naval vessels and armed helicopters that will be used in tandem with the radar to provide security and military protection within its territorial waters and the wider Caribbean region. These acquisitions will enable the TTDF to become more effective by increasing the number of maritime patrols and boosting security for shipping within the southern Caribbean region while acting as a deterrent against pirates and possible maritime terrorists.[17]

The CARICOM nations, as part of an integrated security strategy, initiated the Implementation Agency for Crime and Security plan in 2006. CARICOM created this plan to facilitate cooperation and coordination among the CARICOM states' security and military forces. It was tested in 2007 when CARICOM hosted the Cricket World Cup competition, the third largest sporting event after the Olympics and FIFA Soccer World Cup competition. The plan worked well, and it is now fully integrated within CARICOM's framework. The arrest of the three Guyanese and the one Trinidadian who were implicated in an alleged plot to blow up New York's JFK Airport highlighted to CARICOM that terrorism had arrived in the region. This spurred the region to include counterterrorism in its integrated security mandate. Thus, there is a definite commitment among the nations of CARICOM to fully cooperate on security matters. This cooperation will also include working with the U.S. authorities. Bilateral discussions with the United States on matters of border security, maritime, port and airport security, and counterterrorism are an ongoing process. As Thomas Barnett wrote in his book, *The Pentagon's New Map,* "Whether we realize it or not, we are all-right now-standing present at the creation of a new international security order."[18]

---

17. Manning, 3.

In Trinidad and Tobago, approximately twenty to twenty-two tankers depart monthly for U.S. ports like Everett, Massachusetts; Lake Charles, Louisiana; and Elba Island, Georgia. Atlantic LNG controls the Point Fortin facility, which produces and processes the LNG for export. The facility contains two 700-meter jetties that fully meet the *International Shipping and Port Security* (ISPS) standards. The remainder of the facility is governed by an Integrated Emergency Management Plan (IEMP) that includes, among others, a Maritime Emergency Response Plan. Major (Retired) Sarwan Boodram, corporate security manager at the facility, advised that the Maritime Emergency Response Plan speaks to the safety and accommodation of ships at the jetties, turning basin, and approach channel of the Atlantic LNG port. Atlantic LNG, through its Corporate Security Policy and Crisis Management Plan, adopted the Homeland Security Alert States system, and this is in sync with the *Marine Security* (MARSEC) levels similar to that used by the United States. This ensures that its process and non-process areas are covered for all incidents.[19]

When vessels are approaching the Point Fortin port, they are met and escorted to their berthing point by tugs belonging to ALNG. Major Boodram pointed out that ALNG has no responsibility for the vessels since they belong to the owners; therefore, once the vessels sail from the port they become the responsibility of the owners. The captains and crews become directly responsible for their own security. Each vessel is required to have its own Ship Security Plan (SSP) as per the ISPS Code, and therefore, ship captains are responsible for ensuring that their crews are acquainted with the contents of their plans.[20]

Major Boodram further advised that the ports of countries engaged in the energy business are ranked regarding their risk to terrorist attacks. They may be ranked as high, medium, or low risk. Currently, Trinidad and Tobago's ports are ranked as low. However, Admiral William Crowe (Retired) wrote in his report on the Nairobi and Dar es Salaam U.S. Embassies bombings to then Secretary of State, Madeleine Albright, that "Transnational terrorists often strike without warning at vulnerable targets in areas where expectations of terrorist acts against the United States are low."[21] Since this information about the status of Trinidad and Tobago's ports is available

---

18. Barnett, Thomas. 2005.*The Pentagon New Map,* New York, Berkeley Books, 45.
19. Major Sarwan Boodram. Telephone interview by author, August 27, 2007.
20. Ibid.

to anyone, including potential terrorists, and given that many modern terrorists are brilliant strategists, any number of them can seek to take advantage of Trinidad and Tobago's situation.

During Major Boodram's interview, he reconfirmed the information that Lt. Cdr. Braithwaite provided on the role of the TTDF. The TTDF is the body that has responsibility for staffing and operating the *Port Facility Security/Marine Unit* (PFSMU), and the Designated Authority has full control of the waters as well as all actions regarding security incidents at sea around the territorial waters of the country. The *Trinidad and Tobago Cost Guard* (TTCG) and the PFSMU maintain a working relationship with the U.S. Coast Guard (USCG). The USCG provides training opportunities and advice as it relates to port and harbor security and adherence to the ISPS Code. The USCG also provides advice and periodically assesses the effectiveness of security and anti-terrorism measures that are in place in Trinidad and Tobago ports. At present, the TTCG is restricted by a lack of vessels to adequately patrol the country's territorial water; however, this is expected to be resolved with the acquisition of the vessels referred to previously. The TTCG will then be able to perform long-range patrols around Trinidad and Tobago's territorial water and also patrols over a wide swathe of the Caribbean Sea. This action should help to reduce illegal maritime activities and hopefully reduce pirates and deter potential terrorists. Additionally, these vessels could be used to forge a working partnership with the USCG in order to provide extended protection for tankers throughout their journey in the Caribbean because that is when they may be most vulnerable to pirate and/or terrorist attacks.[22]

Roles of the Trinidad and Tobago Defense Force

The Trinidad and Tobago government mandated the TTDF with responsibility for the security of ports and the surveillance and monitoring of all shipping in the country. This relates specifically to security matters. The TTDF sought and got approval from the government to establish a special unit called the PFSMU and gave it the mandate to ensure that the nation's ports were all ISPS compliant. When the new radar was established, the unit was assigned the task

---

21. Crowe.
22. Lieutenant Commander Michael Braithwaite. Telephone interview by author, September 22, 2007.

of ensuring that it was manned around the clock. The TTDF conducts maritime patrols within the country's territorial waters; however, when the new assets become available, this capacity will be significantly enhanced and patrols will be extended over a much wider area to include neighboring island's territory. This will be in keeping with the Implementation Agency for Crime and Security plan and may even be linked with the United States in a strategic partnership.

The TTDF and the USCG have long maintained a good working relationship. Within recent times, this bond was strengthened with the USCG providing training and advice to the TTDF on port and harbor security matters and matters on adherence to the ISPS Code. The USCG also assists the TTDF by providing assessment of the effectiveness of the security and antiterrorist measures that have been adopted and put into practice at the various ports in the country. There is still room for improvement as there is the opportunity for the United States to share information on potential and actual terrorists that operate within the region. It must be noted that three of the alleged plotters of the proposed JFK Airport bombing were arrested in Trinidad and Tobago, and this was made possible through information sharing between the law enforcement organizations of both countries. This is an excellent example of what can be achieved through joint cooperation between nations. It may be possible that the Third Border Initiative could be the catalyst to strengthen bilateral arrangements between the United States and CARICOM, including sharing security information that could impact the region.

Security Measures Used by International Agencies

Most international ports have adopted the ISPS Code, and this has helped to increase their security awareness. Some nations that are very dependant on shipping have adopted additional security measures that exceed the requirements of the ISPS. Singapore is one nation that has gone this route because at any point in time, as many as 1,000 ships may be alongside its ports. It is estimated that more than 12,000 oil tankers and 3,000 chemical tankers use its ports annually. The Singapore government was the first in Southeast Asia to adopt the ISPS Code and the U.S. Container Security Initiative. This nation also introduced a number of additional initiatives designed to protect its maritime reputation. Singapore introduced the Harbor Craft Transponder System (HARTS), used to identify all ships in harbor. In special instances, some ships are assigned Accompanying Sea Security Teams (ASSeT) that remain with the vessels until their cargo is offloaded or until the ships depart Singapore waters. For vessels below 500 tons, Singapore requires that the vessel fill out a self-security assessment checklist before entry into port. The authorities also restrict access to water around oil terminals and other installations. Additionally, there are many sea checkpoints around entry areas to the harbors, and these are constantly patrolled to provide added protection. Ship captains are required to provide their crew lists, and all crew members must be positively identified before being allowed access to their vessels.[23]

The maritime area around Singapore is very dangerous; therefore, the country installed a vessel traffic information system that provides navigation information to ships traveling through its territorial domain. Dr. Sam Bateman, a maritime security analyst who is a fellow of the Institute of Defense and Strategic Studies, Nanyang Technological University, Singapore, wrote that Singapore introduced the "Harbor Craft Transponder System (HARTS) that requires each watercraft using its ports to be fitted with a transponder that identifies the craft to monitors onshore."[24] Small vessels that do not require compilation to the ISPS Code are required by Singapore's laws to fill out a "Ship Self Security Assessment Checklist" before entry into the port's waterways. This system can track up to 5,000 vessels in real time and has the capability to provide electronic navigational charts and other voice and data information to vessels.[25]

Singapore also uses special security teams to protect selected ships while they are in Singapore's waters. These teams called ASSeT comprise of members of the Singapore Military who travel on the vessels while they are on their way to port and remain until their cargoes are securely offloaded. If the ships are traversing Singapore's territorial waters to another destination, the teams remain on board until they have cleared territorial waters.[26] For ships heading to or from Singapore and traveling through the Singapore and Malacca Straits, Singapore's laws mandate that they use a Differential Global Positional System and STRAITREP so that

23. *Khaleej Times on line.* Singapore Navy to Escort Merchant Ships to Stop Terrorism. 28, February, 2005, *http://www.tkhaleejtimes.com/index00.asp* (accessed 31, August, 2007).
24. Bateman, 82.
25. Ibid.
26. *Khaleej Times on line.* Singapore Navy to Escort Merchant Ships to Stop Terrorism. 28, February, 2005, *http://www.tkhaleejtimes.com/index00.asp* (accessed 31, August, 2007).

these vessels will maintain contact with Singapore's Maritime Authorities. In this way there can be some assurance that pirates have not attacked and taken over the vessel.[27]

The research also examined U.S. security methods. Following the events of September 11, 2001, the USCG trained a cadre of specialists to provide escort duty on selected ships while they were in U.S. ports. This cadre is similar to Singapore's ASSeT body, as they both perform similar tasks. In 2005, following an initiative from President George Bush, the Departments of Defense and Homeland Security published the *National Strategy for Maritime Security* (NSMS) designed to synchronize the U.S. maritime security program to defeat maritime terrorism. The four strategic objectives of the NSMS are: prevent terrorist attacks and criminal or hostile acts; protect maritime related population centers and infrastructure; minimize damage and expedite recovery; and safeguard the ocean and its resources. From these objectives the NSMS outlines these five strategic actions:

First is the objective of enhancing international cooperation. This action is designed to involve all nations that have an interest in maritime security as well as the ability and willingness to take steps to defeat terrorism and maritime crime. The United States will take steps to ensure that all nations fulfill their responsibilities to prevent and respond to terrorist or criminal actions with timely and effective enforcement. This includes developing and expanding means for rapid exchanges among governments of relevant intelligence and law enforcement information concerning suspect terrorist and/or criminal activity in the maritime domain.

Second is to maximize domain awareness. This involves the effective understanding of all activities, events, and trends within the maritime domain capable of threatening the safety, security, economy, or environment of the United States and its citizens. It is important, therefore, to gain knowledge of the enemy's capabilities, intentions, methods, objectives, goals, ideologies, strengths, vulnerabilities, and centers of gravity. This knowledge will assist to develop appropriate responses and countermeasures. Success in this will be heavily dependant on information sharing and requires increased cooperation among the various U.S. and international sectors.

A third action is to embed security into commercial practices. Potential adversaries are opportunistic and will attempt to exploit existing vulnerabilities. They will seek to choose the time and place

---

27. International Maritime Organization. *Maritime Safety Committee Circular* 622/Rev 1, June 16, 1999, 4.

to act according to the weakness that they identified and/or observed. Private owners can improve defenses against terrorists by embedding security measures that reduce vulnerabilities. This is achievable by developing a close partnership between government and the private sector in order to identify and correct the vulnerabilities.

Fourth is the deployment of layered security. The public and private sectors can prevent terrorism and/or criminal activity by using diverse and complementary measures. This can be achieved by applying security measures to vulnerable points. These points are transportation, staff, passengers, conveyances, access control, cargo and baggage, ports, and security en route. The security measures work best by continually evolving through calculated improvements that are geared to introduce uncertainty into the adversary's deliberate planning process and efforts to conduct surveillance or reconnaissance.

Finally, the assurance of the continuity of the marine transport system is essential and paramount. The United States will be prepared to maintain vital commerce and defense readiness in the aftermath of any terrorist attack or other disruptive incidents. This requires properly defined and documented roles for responders. There must be contingency plans, including response plans, and these should be exercised to ensure that players know their roles and functions. Selected personnel must also be trained, equipped, and periodically tested in their roles.[28]

The United States recognizes that securing the maritime domain successfully will not come from acting alone, but through a powerful coalition of nations maintaining a strong, united, international front. In the Caribbean region, this is the opportunity for CARICOM to seek to forge strong regional ties with the United States in order to jointly safeguard the southern maritime approaches to continental United States.

Many threats and concerns face mariners in some sea lanes and chokepoints of the ocean. As a result, the International Maritime Organization produced MSC/Circ 623 for ship captains and crews and MSC/Circ 622 for governments. These documents contain recommendations for countermeasures to protect vessels against pirates and maritime terrorists. The measures are geared toward security forces and rescue coordination centers.

The maritime nations also banded together and created new conventions that closed the gaps in maritime law regarding piracy and maritime terrorism. The new protocols are contained in the

---

28. Ibid., 13–24.

Convention for the Suppression of Unlawful Acts against the Safety of Maritime Navigation (SUA Convention). This allows coastal states to extend jurisdiction beyond their territorial limits and, in special circumstances, extend into adjacent states' territorial waters. Additionally, other protocols provide for prosecuting individuals who use ships as weapons, as a means of conducting terrorist attacks, or for transporting terrorists or cargo to be used in connection with a WMD program.[29]

Some ships have adopted their own onboard security measures, and there is at least one documented successful defense against an attack. On November 5, 2005, the 10,000-ton passenger liner, *Seabourn Spirit,* with 151 passengers on board was attacked by pirates 115 kilometers off the coast of Somalia. The pirates were in two speedboats, and they were armed with machine guns and rocket propelled grenades. The ship's crew repelled the attack using a pressure hose to keep the boats at bay and a long-range acoustic device. The long-range acoustic device operates by emitting a powerful sound wave that affects the hearing and can potentially cause permanent deafness. The pirates were defeated and forced to give up their attack, and the vessel was able to complete its journey. Two members of the crew were honored by the Queen of England for their bravery on May 16, 2007.[30]

29. International Maritime Organization. Maritime Safety Committee Circular, 622/Rev 1, June 16, 1999, 4.
30. Braid, M., and Calder, S. "Pirates Fire at Luxury Seabourn Spirit," *The Independent (UK), ece5nov2005.* Retrieved September 5, 2007, from *http://news.independent.co.uk/worldlafrica/articles325171.*

6.2
Russia, Pirates, and Maritime Terrorism

SERGUEI CHELOUKHINE
CHARLES A. LIEBERMAN

"hostis humani generis"[1]

Introduction

Water covers approximately 70 percent of the earth, and more than 80 percent of the world's goods are transported via waterways. The global maritime transport system is comprised of more than 46,000 large vessels and some 4,000 major ports; thus, successful maritime attacks have the potential to have a devastating impact on the international economy, as maritime economic activity accounts for trillions of dollars each year.

Acts of piracy have been increasing worldwide in recent decades, as have the audacity of the attacks and demands for ransom. In recent years, individuals conducting maritime attacks, or pirates, have taken control of an oil supertanker and a cargo ship carrying tens of millions of dollars in military equipment. The threats posed by these maritime attacks, or piracy, require a comprehensive response from both sovereign nation states and the international community. The United Nations (UN), in reaction to the upward trend in these attacks, passed two resolutions to address this growing menace. In this chapter, the authors conduct an analysis of the threat of maritime attacks, specifically with regard to Russia, examining the regions of greatest activity and providing a foundation for understanding the variation among regions.

---

1. *"hostis humani generis,"* Latin for enemy of mankind, is a term used to describe pirates. McDaniel, 2000.

Russia is the world's largest country with five main areas of maritime activity: the Pacific Ocean, the Baltic and North Seas, the Barents Sea, the Caspian Sea, and the Black Sea. From a geopolitical and economic perspective, only the Black Sea region is considered to be a dangerous region. Some experts are skeptical about the level of threat and propose that the security risk in the Black Sea is exaggerated. Nevertheless, during the Black Sea hostage crisis, which took place on the Black Sea during the First Chechen War, the Panamanian-registered ferry, *Avrazya,* was hijacked on January 16, 1996, in the Russian port of Sochi. The hostage crisis ended without bloodshed with the safe release of the over 200 captives.[2] Despite the number of active ports and vessels docking and embarking from ports since then, there have been very few reports of piracy or maritime terrorism in recent decades within the territorial waters of Russia.

Russia, as an active, international trading nation, has more than 3,800 ships in its registry (out of which more than 1,400 are cargo-carrying ships) and more than 50 commercial ports. Russia's waterways and ports span a wide range of geo-political climates, including Europe, Asia, the Far East, and the Arctic Circle, whose rigorous climate creates very specific safety considerations. Furthermore, the weather conditions of the Arctic Circle would also render many Russian ports inaccessible in winter were it not for the fleet of massive nuclear icebreakers, a vessel developed and perfected in Russia.[3]

The terrorist attacks of September 11, 2001 (9/11) made clear, in the most explicit and frightening manner, the susceptibility of international transportation both as a potential target for terrorist action and, possibly even more ominously, as a potential weapon of mass destruction. Consequently, other incidents, such as the attack on the French oil tanker MV *Limburg* off the coast of Yemen in October 2002 and the March 2004 train bombings in Madrid, confirmed that the world transportation systems, whether on land, sea, or air, are vulnerable to domestic and international terrorist attacks.[4]

Illustrating the vulnerability of military and commercial vessels, on October 12, 2000, two al Qaeda operatives on a small, motorized fishing boat carrying an explosive device conducted a suicide attack, ramming into the USS *Cole,* a U.S. military vessel anchored at a port in Aden, Yemen. The explosive device, which was estimated to be about 300 kilograms, ripped a 72-square-meter hole in

---

2. Harrigan, 1996.
3. Mitropoulos, 2005.
4. Smith, 2002; BBC News, 2004.

the side of the ship, injuring more than forty and leading to seventeen fatalities.[5] On October 23, 2000, eleven days after the attack on the USS *Cole*, the Liberation Tigers of Tamil Eelam (LTTE) conducted a simultaneous suicide attack running two boats carrying explosive devices into the passenger ferries "Sri Lanka" one of which sunk, while the second was severely damaged, leading to more than 400 fatalities.[6] Another maritime attack included the targeting of an Israeli ship by Hamas terrorists; however, this attack did not damage the target due to the explosive device's premature detonation.[7]

The civilized world was horrified by those tragic events; however, they also had a galvanizing effect, creating a new and strong determination to address terrorism by tackling the matter of security in the broadest sense. The International Maritime Organization (IMO) raised a fast and thorough response to the likelihood of terrorists conducting attacks against ships, seeking to use ships themselves as weapons, or using the proceeds of shipping activities to subsidize their unlawful operations.[8] As part of this response, in 2002, the IMO adopted a comprehensive new regulatory rule that sets out in detail what governments, ship operators, ships' crews, port facility operators, and others involved in the business of shipping should do in order to prevent and minimize this very real threat. In July 2002, the IMO and World Customs Organization signed a Memorandum of Understanding for cooperation on container examinations and integrity in multimodal transport and matters relating to the ship and port interface. Following a request by the International Conference on Maritime Security, a new seafarers' identity document was developed establishing a more rigorous identity regime for seafarers.[9]

Recently, terrorist organizations have created their own maritime fleets and committed acts of terrorism not only on land and in the air, but also on the sea. Maritime piracy is an international crime utilizing methods and tactics that are very similar to the tactics employed in terrorist attacks. There is an important difference in regards to the goal of the executors: the goal of piracy is predominantly enrichment and profit, while the goal of terrorism is principally ideological, including social, economic, religious, or political objectives.

---

5. Fenton, 2001.
6. Chaliand and Blin, 2007, p. 353.
7. Roschchupkin, 2009.
8. International Maritime Organization. *http://www.imo.org/.*
9. Mitropoulos, 2000.

In 1981, in response to increased maritime crime, the International Maritime Bureau (IMB), a quasi-governmental organization of the International Chamber of Commerce (ICC), was created. The IMB was designed to combat all types of maritime and trade crime, including documentary credit fraud, charter party fraud, cargo theft, and piracy. According to the IMB: "Piracy is the act of boarding any vessel with intent to commit theft" or any other crime, and with an intent or capacity to use force in furtherance of that act.[10] In order to distinguish piracy from hijacking, a piracy crime requires that two vessels be involved in the incident. The second requirement is that the crime has been undertaken for private, not political, purposes.[11] The IMB's definition covers actual or attempted attacks whether the ship is berthed, at anchor, or at sea.

Piracy of the sixteenth and seventeenth centuries fell into decline due to four primary reasons:

1. *Technology:* The increased size and speed of merchant vessels severely disadvantaged pursuing pirates;
2. *Naval Presence:* The nineteenth and twentieth centuries saw an increasing level of international naval patrols along most ocean highways and particularly in support of colonial networks;
3. *Government Administration:* During the nineteenth and twentieth centuries, most islands and coastal areas were regularly administered by sovereign nations that utilized military vessels to protect their merchant fleets.
4. *Laws and Regulations:* There was a general recognition of piracy as a serious international offense that would not be tolerated by countries determined to protect their national fleets and able to do so. Punishments for acts of piracy were severe and often fatal.[12]

Despite the consensus that piracy was nearly eradicated before the First World War, it continues to be a threat today. The four factors discussed have now begun to encourage and enhance piracy:

1. *Technology:* Technological advances have reduced the need for large crews, which increases the vulnerability of modern vessels. In addition, these advances have

---

10. ICC International Maritime Bureau, 2003.
11. McDaniel, 2000.
12. ICC-International Maritime Bureau, 2003.

improved the weapons of speed, shock, surprise, and fire-power utilized in maritime attacks.

2. *Naval Presence:* Due to the increased range of communication and speed of vessels, in conjunction with the use of aircraft, sovereign nations tend to have less need for numerous military vessels. Dramatically decreased international ocean patrols have left merchant vessels virtually unprotected on the high seas.

3. *Governmental Administration:* Many former colonies that became independent subsequent to foreign rule did not maintain military ties, which led to the financial inability of some governments to afford effective naval assets. The lack of an effective navy provides a greater opportunity for maritime attacks.

4. *Laws and Regulations:* The view that piracy is a serious international crime, or even a crime of which anyone should take notice, has eroded. For example, the hijacking of an airline would likely create media frenzy, while the hijackings of merchant vessels, until recently, received minimal media coverage, despite the economic and environmental impact of these attacks.

With most of the world's gross tonnage fleet under flags of convenience, such as Panama, Honduras, and Liberia, there is little political will to address high seas piracy. Vessels traveling under flags of convenience are frequently targeted in maritime attacks. The nations that provide flags of convenience have neither the interest nor the ability to mount an effective deterrent, as neither Honduras nor Panama has naval military power that extends beyond their territorial waters. IMB officials describe the present involvement by world governments against piracy "in shambles." Piracy is on the rise because there is an abundance of valuable commodities (suitable target), and no one to stop it (an absence of capable guardians).[13] This relates to Routine Activity Theory, an

---

13. The International Transport Workers Federation (ITF) defines Flags of Convenience as:
"Where the beneficial ownership and control of a vessel is found to lie elsewhere than in the country of the flag the vessel is flying, the vessel is considered as sailing under a flag of convenience. In cases, however, where the identification of the beneficial owner is not clear, any vessel where there is no genuine link between the flag state and the person(s), or corporate entity, with effective control over the operation of the vessel shall be considered as sailing under an FOC"; Authors are grateful to Dr. Jon Shane for some ideas and thoughts he shared with us.

environmental criminological theory that proposes that crime will be more likely to occur when three things happen at the same time and place: a suitable target is available, there is a lack of capable guardian to prevent the crime from happening, and a likely or motivated offender is present.[14]

Risk Intelligence, a Danish organization that analyzes threats from piracy, organized crime, terrorism, insurgency, and military conflicts, proposes that the number of pirate groups, armed with automatic weapons, RPGs, satellite phones, radar, and Global Positioning System (GPS), concentrated in Kismayu and Haradere regions of Eastern Somalia has increased to five.[15] Pirates are known to operate from larger vessels, usually a modified fishing or other commercial boat, hundreds of miles from the coast, from which they identify suitable targets and employ speedboats to board the vessels, a process that takes approximately ten to twenty minutes.

Historically, the method most often employed in the fight against pirates was to intercept and sink the pirate vessel. Due to international maritime agreements, most nation states no longer employ such methods. As a result, the response by nation states to maritime attacks is limited and military vessels have been known to release attackers.[16] This undermines the deterrence of intervening in a maritime attack, as the criminological theory of deterrence requires celerity (swiftness), severity (proportionate), and certainty of punishment.[17]

The majority of sources analyzing algorithms of modern piracy provide the following classification of twenty-first century pirates: the first category is made by typical criminals who make primitive crimes, for example, stealing goods; the second category are members of the organized criminal communities who perform tricky operations and dispose of stolen goods (such pirates are especially various in Southeast Asia, and some of them are part of Chinese "triads"); and the third category consists of representatives of the semi-military organizations, who sometimes even have official sta-

---

14. Cohn and Felson, 1979.

15. *http://www.riskintelligence.eu/default.asp?komp=visnyhed&id=4&lang=en;* Somalia: Pirates and Islamists Clash in Central Region. *http://allafrica.com/ stories/200805250014.html* Accessed March 29, 2009; Global Positioning System. http://www.gps.gov/

16. Western European countries are reluctant to detain or arrest pirates due to uncertainty of how to address the detainees. Double Dutch: Commandos capture Somali pirates and free 20 hostages . . . but release the bandits because they are not from the Netherlands.

17. Deterrence theory. Bentham, 1789; Beccaria, 1764.

tus within a weak state. In some cases, armed groups, supervised by field commanders, require regular income for maintenance of power and control over a territory, which tends to be the case with pirates in Somalia and Indonesia.[18]

The authors propose four typologies among the methods of operation employed in maritime attacks. The first typology involves pirates that board the targeted ship and steal from the ship's coffers and personnel, which usually results in tens of thousands of dollars ($US) in proceeds. The second typology involves the targeting of the ship's cargo, in addition to the ship's coffers and personnel. Pirates unload the goods from the targeted vessel, which may require anchoring in a harbor. The commandeered vessel may also be transported to a port where pirates have friendly relations and the cargo can be sold to local buyers. The profit of such operations can reach millions of dollars and is much greater than the proceeds from cargo sold as contraband.[19]

In the third typology, pirates detain the ship and take the staff, passengers, and cargo hostage and demand ransom. The magnitude of the ransom varies. Though usually not disclosed, the amount typically reaches several, if not tens, of millions of dollars. For example, Somalia pirates, after holding a ship laden with Russian tanks, released the vessel after being paid up to $3.5 million, the biggest ransom on record.[20]

The fourth typology, which was prevalent in the 1990s, involved hijacking the ship, killing the crew, forging paperwork and certificates, and registering the vessel anew. However, in the twenty-first century this method has waned as a result of evolving international regulations that disallow these criminals from obtaining new registrations for the stolen vessels.[21] For example, through the end of the 1990s, temporary licenses and registrations allowed a vessel to use the flags of Panama and Honduras, which were easily obtainable in any consulate of those countries. Subsequent to the new registration, the vessel either was sold or assigned to carry cargo that was heavily insured, and then that cargo would conveniently disappear on the way to its final destination, allowing the new owners to collect the insurance money.

Moreover, pirates are actively involved in human trafficking, the transportation of illegal narcotics and weapons, and cooperation with organized crime groups. There is a high probability that in the

---

18. McDaniel, 2000.
19. Ibid.
20. Crilly, 2009.
21. Alderton and Winchester, 2002.

near future pirates and other criminal groups will have access to, or even possess, both surface and underwater vessels, which will provide them with greater mobility and opportunity to avoid intervention by governmental and international authorities.

Features of the Maritime Terrorists Actions

In the past decade, the number of terrorist groups utilizing maritime arracks has increased. According to the International Maritime Bureau (2009b), there were a worldwide total of 293 incidents of piracy against ships in 2008, an increase of more than 11 percent from 2007 when there were 263 incidents reported. In 2008, forty-nine vessels were hijacked, 889 crew taken hostage, and another forty-six vessels reported being fired upon. Among the crew, there were thirty-two injured, eleven killed, and twenty-one were reported missing and presumed dead. The use of firearms increased from 72 in 2007 to 139 in 2008, indicating a greater threat of violence and fatalities as a result of these attacks.[22] Tactically, the method employed in an attack will depend on the location and status of the vessel, which may be in a port, on roadstead, or in territorial or international waters. Recent attacks have also employed technology to increase the effectiveness of the attack, including magnetic mines, which can be attached to a vessel undetected, and autonomous underwater vehicles (AUV) or unmanned underwater vehicles (UUV), which are basically underwater robots, high-speed boats, sea scooters, mini submarines, and the torpedoes operated by suicide attackers, also known as kamikaze operated torpedoes.[23]

During the past five years, there were three attempts of illegal (underground) building and the use of such submarines in Bogotá and Cartagena, Colombia, Africa, and in Southern India. However, terrorists can buy such submarines, even in countries in Western Europe, Russia, and Iran. During the past decade, terrorists began to utilize the tactics and methods that Japanese kamikazes employed to attack U.S. naval ships in World War II, such as the *Kaiten*—a converted torpedo. These vessels were, in essence, human torpedoes whose successful operation involved the death of its crew.[24]

---

22. ICC Commercial Crime Service. *http://www.icc-ccs.org/*
23. von Alt, 2003.
24. Navarro, 1997; Forero, 2008; Sakhuja, 2005; Meyer, 2008; "Kaiten" type Human Torpedoes. World War II Period Photographs & Drawings *http://www.history.navy.mil/photos/sh-fornv/japan/japtp-ss/kaiten.htm*

Among the strategies employed in maritime attacks are attacks on anchored vessels. A moored vessel is typically attacked by divers equipped with light underwater equipment who attach mines or explosive devices to vulnerable sections of the ship, such as the hull. Attackers can be transported to a designated port by land, air, or sea, possibly the use of an underwater vehicle or submarine. The use of small, low-profile boats at night greatly increases the probability of maintaining surprise, which can increase the effectiveness and probability of success in an attack due to the difficulty in being detected by the radar of the targeted ship and the lower levels of staffing. This tactic of conducting a maritime terrorist operation at night using multiple boats attacking from different directions, or wolf pack, was copied from the German World War II tactic, *Rudeltaktik,* which involved numerous submarines conducting simultaneous attacks at night.[25] This tactic has proven effective during attacks targeting cargo vessels, large cruise liners, and even military vessels. These low-profile boats are often equipped with demountable riggings that disguise them as fishing schooners or coast guard vessels. In such cases, attackers wear clothes that masquerade them as fishermen or government vessels, such as customs, border patrol, or navy.[26]

These methods of disguise and misdirection have been employed by the Islamic fundamentalist terrorists, the Revolutionary Armed Forces of Colombia (*Fuerzas Armadas Revolucionarios de Colombia,* FARC), the Liberation Tigers of Tamil Eelam (LTTE), the Basque Fatherland and Liberty (*Euskadi ta Askatasuna,* ETA), and the Philippine Sea Saboteurs.[27] These terrorist organizations not only create their own specialized combat forces, but also buy high-tech equipment such as gliders, planes, and helicopters.

Recently, in seized al Qaeda files from Afghanistan, authorities obtained information about planned attacks on the east coast of the United States by cargo ships belonging to Al Qaeda. The plan involved attacks using Soviet-made Scud missile launchers installed in the holds of multiple ships, which would approach the U.S. coast within range of the missiles (about 300 miles) and launch

25. A Multi-Agent System for Tracking the Intent of Surface Contacts in Ports and Waterways. Defense Science and Technology Agency. Singapore Government. *http://www.pbs.org/wnet/warship/wordlog_subs_print.html http://www.dsta.gov.sg/index.php/573-A-Multi-Agent-System-for-Tracking-the-Intent-of-Surface-Contacts-in-Ports-and-Waterways/*
26. Jasparro, 2009; Burnett, 2002.
27. Maritime Terrorism. *Ursa Major. http://ursamajor2002.narod.ru/NEXT.HTM*

missiles targeting large cities. The authors suggest that this is an example of the potential threat posed by terrorists that may shift the focus of their maritime activities from regions such as the Middle East to the Western Atlantic in order to target vessels of Western nations.[28]

The Organization and Acquisition

Many terrorists, including Islamic fundamentalist terrorists and al Qaeda, are likely to adopt the methods of operation employed by the LTTE in maritime attacks. The LTTE has the world's largest military fleet, effectively operating as a part of two independent structures. The first component is the "Sea Tigers," which represents an amphibian group numbering about 4,000 fighters. Organizationally they share sections: "Tigresses" (approximately 1,000 women), "Black Tigers" (kamikazes), and fighting divers.[29] The "Sea Tigers" group consists of eleven sections:

1. fighting naval divisions;
2. underwater bombers;
3. striking forces "Sea Tigers";
4. engineering and ship-building commandos;
5. radar and telecommunications;
6. an arsenal of sea arms;
7. maritime school;
8. a political propaganda and financing;
9. rear maintenance of an exclusive economic zone;
10. supervision and investigations; and
11. cultural and registration (provide educational, ideological, and basic training for newly recruited).[30]

The "Sea Tigers" are equipped with machine guns, rocket propelled grenade launchers (RPG), and mortars; Japanese manufactured radio and navigation systems; and German optics. Their workshops make floating and ship-bottom mines and underwater bombs. According to the Indian Security Services, "Sea Tigers" have destroyed almost one-third of the navy fleet of Sri Lanka by applying "the wolf packs" and the kamikaze tactics. In addition, the "Sea Tigers" have conducted attacks on Indian and western fishing

---

28. Farah, 2005.
29. Bghattacharji, 2009.
30. Graeme and Gunaratna, 2004, p. 200.

vessels entering the Ceylon's maritime waters. LTTE is believed to have a fleet comprised of about twenty ships disguised as commercial vessels that are used for the transportation of weapons, drugs, insurgents, mercenaries, and human trafficking. Officially, most of these vessels belong to dummy companies registered in Panama, Honduras, Liberia, and other countries. Transportation of commercial cargo serves as a cover for diversionary purposes.[31]

The U.S. Intelligence Services have reported the facts of financing Hamas and the Palestinian Islamic Jihad (PIJ) from Qatar and Bahrain. The CIA's special attention was directed toward a presence of divisions of well-prepared combat-ready navy divers who received rather complex and time-consuming training.[32] These divers are believed to utilize Soviet-manufactured self-contained underwater breathing apparatus (SCUBA) equipment, specifically respiratory devices of closed cycle CLVE-57, combat aqualungs ABM-1, and diver propulsion vehicle (DPV) Protey-3.[33] The technique of the Palestinian divers' actions is indistinguishable from those applied by the Russian Intelligence-Diversionary divisions of the Main Intelligence Directorate GRU "Dolphin" unit.[34]

During Soviet rule in Russia, the headquarters were located in Cossack Bay, near Sevastopol in Crimea. These "Dolphin" units were disbanded in the early 1990s, and now these well-trained underwater *spetsnaz* are not involved with maritime operations on behalf of Russia. Included among the individuals formerly assigned to "Dolphin" units were natives of the North Caucasus, Bashkiria, and Tatarstan, which are predominantly Muslim regions of the Russian Federation. Some of these experts, who are currently not engaged in any government-sponsored activities by Russia, could find employment with non-state actors, including security operations or, conversely, organized criminal operations where their knowledge and expertise would be both appreciated and well compensated.[35]

The regions with high levels of maritime attacks include the South China Sea, the Caribbean, and coastal regions of Africa, Asia, and South America. Many of these waterways include regions where terrorists and insurgents have strong support and/or a base of

---

31. Ramachandran, 2006.
32. Tracking the Terrorist Money Trail, 2008.
33. Samko, 1999.
34. Otryad Delfin [Detachment Dolphin]. *http://ursamajor2002.narod.ru/delfin.htm*
35. Spetsnaz: Russian martial art hand to hand combat. *http://www.spetsnaz-gru.com/*

operation. In 2008, there were 35 official[36] reports of pirate attacks near the coastline of Indonesia and Philippines. In addition to the regions mentioned, the number of pirate attacks in the Mediterranean and Black Seas, primarily in the waters near Lebanon, Syria, Turkey, and Georgia, have increased considerably over the course of the past five years.[37]

The region with the greatest reported pirate activity is in the waters off the eastern coast of Somalia and the Gulf of Aden, which account for over 100 incidents. On September 24, 2008, the first successful hijacking of a vessel loaded with military ammunition and tanks in the modern era was reported. In recent decades, Somalia pirates have attacked all types of ships, collecting millions of dollars in ransoms. The second most active region for pirate attacks is the waters off the western coast of Nigeria, with over forty incidents reported and approximately 100 attacks not reported to officials.[38] Other active regions include the coastal waters of Bangladesh and Tanzania; however, in that region pirate attacks focus primarily on vessels in ports. Furthermore, pirate activity in this region decreased in 2008 with twenty-eight incidents, compared with 121 in 2003, near Indonesia and two against seven incidents in the Strait of Malacca in 2007; however, these statistics only consider attacks in which the ship owners file an official report of the maritime attack.[39]

There are many similarities and differences among the four regions with the highest activity of maritime attacks. The most significant issues among these regions are the presence of a weak local government in close proximity, which creates conditions that make adequate governmental response problematic; certain geographic conditions that provide greater opportunity for attackers; and high levels of maritime traffic. Even in the regions with the highest level of activity, only about one percent of the vessels are targeted by attackers.

Contemporary maritime piracy is a modern phenomenon and not easy to understand. Although Murphy (2007) posits that there is no evidence of linkage between piracy and terrorism, other researchers suggest that some of the money extorted by Somalia pirates is provided to Islamic fundamentalist groups associated with terrorism.[40] Despite conjecture, there is little empirical evidence to connect organized maritime crime or piracy, which is primarily

---

36. IMB, 2009b.
37. Mitropoulos, 2000.
38. Megalommatis, 2009.
39. Vijayan, 2009.
40. Murphy, 2007; Clayton, 2008.

driven by profit, with terrorism, which is primarily driven by some political, social, or religious ideology. While there have been efforts to increase maritime security worldwide, a vast majority of ports and harbors have minimal security, making them attractive targets to both organized crime and terrorists. In addition, addressing maritime piracy and terrorism is difficult due to territorial waters and a wide range of local resources (human, military, economic, etc.) creating obstacles for law enforcement agencies. Pirates and terrorists exploit maritime limits and borders in order to escape arrest and prosecution. However, a recent response by regional leaders in Somalia's northern Puntland region are alleged to have put together a militia of fishermen to catch pirates.[41]

The October 1985 hijacking in the Mediterranean of the *Achille Lauro,* an Italian cruise liner, provides an example of the application of pirate tactics in a terrorist attack. During the attack, the Palestine Liberation Front (PLP) conducted the infamous execution of one U.S. citizen, Leon Klinghoffer, who was thrown overboard with his wheelchair after being executed.[42] The Philippine organization Abu Sayyaf (its founder Abubakar Dzhanialani, as well as Osama bin Laden, fought against the Soviet army in Afghanistan), in a bomb attack on a passenger ferry in Manila Bay in February 2004, killed 100 people.[43] Abu Sayyaf has utilized maritime attacks as a primary source of funding.[44]

In recent decades, armed assaults on commercial vessels has tripled. Over the course of one year, from 1999 to 2000, armed assaults on commercial vessels have increased approximately 40 percent; two-thirds of those attacks occured in Asian-Pacific region.[45] The Gulf of Aden is one of the major sea routes connecting Europe and Asia, with approximately 20,000 ships pass through annually carrying one-third of the world's oil.

The International Maritime Bureau provides annual statistics for maritime attacks, including piracy and armed robbery, from 2003 through 2008, in addition to the first quarter of 2009. Prior to 2009, there was a downward trend in the number of attacks, in which the

---

41. BBC News, 2009: Somali vigilantes capture pirates.
42. Reynolds, 2004.
43. CFR: *Abu Sayyaf Group (Philippines, Islamist separatists),* 2008. *http://www.cfr.org/publication/9235/;* BBC News: *Bomb caused Philippine ferry fire,* 2004. *http://news.bbc.co.uk/2/hi/asia-pacific/3732356.stm*
44. BBC News: *Guide to the Philippines conflict,* 2007. *http://news.bbc.co.uk/2/hi/asia-pacific/1695576.stm*
45. Pirate Attacks Increased in 2007, Maritime Group Says. *The New York Times.* January 10, 2008. *http://www.nytimes.com/2008/01/10/world/africa/10pirates.html?fta*

number of attacks decreased from 445 in 2003 to 293 in 2008. However, the numbers for the first quarter of 2009, including 102 attacks from January 1 through March 31, provide evidence of an upward trend in maritime attacks.[46]

By December 2008, pirates held hostages on eleven ships with 200 sailors.[47] Among them, the Ukrainian vessel, *MV Faina,* en route to Kenya, was hijacked in September, with cargo that contained thirty-three Soviet-made T-72 tanks, 150 anti-tank grenade launchers (RPG), antiaircraft mount, and other military purpose ammunition. For the release of the *Fania,* pirates demanded a record ransom, in excess of $30 million, eventually receiving $3.5 million, the highest pirate ransom reported to date. During the first four months of 2009, Somalia pirates have hijacked twenty-five vessels and have held more than 260 crew hostage, which indicates a continued increase in maritime attacks in the region.[48]

Political Instability

Piracy predominantly occurs in the territorial waters of countries with political instability, where poverty and corruption are often endemic. Personal possessions and cargo are usually the target, which indicates that these are crimes of opportunity. Among weak or failed states, local authorities only pay lip service to victims of maritime attacks. For ship owners and shipping companies, the time and effort involved in the assisting local authorities is perceived as an economic burden, as the time required to question crew or passengers could cost millions in delays. The reluctance to report an incident or even cooperate with the local authority's investigation subsequent to a maritime attack tends to mask the true extent and nature of piracy.[49]

Fueled by unrest and rising poverty in some failing or failed states, piracy has soared, posing a significant threat to the economic development of countries around the world, not just regions with high rates of piracy, such as Somalia and Indonesia. As conditions persist, those living in nations beset with political strife or civil unrest begin to experience great social strain. Since the government structure is

---

46. International Maritime Bureau, 2009 January; International Maritime Bureau, 2009 April.
47. Azikiwe, 2008.
48. Myasnikov, 2008; Gittaa, 2009; Crilly, 2009; International Maritime Bureau.
49. McDaniel, 2000.

too weak to provide for its citizens (economically and politically, health and human services, security, employment, economic stability, and leadership), individuals begin to innovate. In an environment where there is a tremendous disparity between goals and means, where, in many cases, fundamental necessities (such as food, clothing, and shelter) are scarce, great pressure mounts, making some people feel compelled to engage in crime, such as piracy. Anomic conditions cultivate two types of pirates: the low-level, opportunistic criminal and the higher-level, organized criminal.

While piracy in the territorial waters of Somalia and the Gulf of Aden is rooted in the past, the problem did not draw much attention until recent events. Through the beginning of 2008, there was little media attention or information reported regarding maritime attacks. April 2008 marked one of the first highly publicized maritime attacks, with the hijacking of *Le Ponat,* a 290-foot luxury sailboat. Hours after the ransom was paid and the ship freed, French commandos commenced an operation that led to the capture of six pirates and their portion of the ransom.[50] Following this event, reports of maritime attacks began appearing more often and likely affected the UN adoption of resolutions that allow foreign ships to pursue pirates in Somalia's territorial waters.[51] This resolution only created the illusion of a framework for response, as maritime attacks in the region have increased during the first quarter of 2009. In addition, the scale and dynamics of Somalia's piracy threat may be greater than that which is reported.

The UN recently called for international efforts to enhance security in Somalia, proposing that increased security on land will lead to increased security in territorial waters. "Piracy is not a waterborne disease. It is a symptom of anarchy and insecurity on the ground."[52] Somalia has a history of political instability and civil war. The last time this desert country possessed anything resembling a functional government, with tax collection, social services, and law enforcement, was under Siad Barre, who was perceived by many to be a dictator. After Barre was driven out by a national rebellion early in 1991, political power throughout most of Somalia fell into the hands of feuding warlords, who, like grand dukes from the European Middle Ages, deployed their private armies to battle for power, even as hundreds of thousands of their nation's people were

---

50. Axe, 2009.
51. Trevelyan, 2008.
52. UN Department of Public Information (2009, April 23): Priorities for International Efforts to Enhance Security in Somalia. *http://www.un.org/News/Press/docs/2009/sgsm12203.doc.htm*

dying of hunger. Outside intervention, despite good intentions, has done little to help and has often made things worse.[53]

A problem that continues to foster piracy in Somalia is the positive impact on the economic fortunes of many of its residents, leading to business in which hundreds, if not thousands of people are profiting. The small number of individuals involved in the initial attack, usually ranging from seven to ten, go out in powerful speedboats armed with heavy weapons. Once they seize the ship, a larger number of individuals, up to fifty, stay on board the vessel, while another fifty wait on shore in case anything goes wrong.

While under control of the pirates, the vessel is moved, frequently to port Eyl on the east coast of Somalia, which already has became a capital of the "pirates' republic." Hundreds, if not thousands, of people are involved in this process, which includes specifics in division of labor, distribution, and infrastructure.[54] Given all the other people involved in the industry of piracy, including those who feed the hostages, it has become a mainstay of the Puntland's economy. Eyl has become a town tailor-made for pirates and their hostages. Special restaurants have even been set up to prepare food for the crews of the hijacked ships.[55]

Thanks to large ransoms paid for hijacked vessels, the Puntland's economy, based on piracy, is developing very fast. In 2007, the pirates' income from ransom was about 30 million dollars.[56] Although this amount may not seem very high when compared with the billions of dollars in cargo shipped each year, semi-independent Puntland's budget, where the port of Eyl is located, has a budget of only 20 million dollars, 10 million less than the income from piracy in the region. Pirates have the resources to buy modern firearms as well as communication and navigation equipment. Pirates increase their local power, while local authorities are ill equipped to address this growing problem. The town is a safe haven for pirates, leading to the suggestion that some local officials in the Puntland administration have links with pirates. Many of the pirates are allegedly from the Majarteen clan, which is the same clan as the former president of Somalia, Abdullahi Yusuf, who resigned in December 2008.[57]

53. James, 1995.
54. Blair, 2008.
55. Harper, 2008.
56. Ibid.
57. Harper, 2008; Gettelmen, 2008.

Even if the international community will conduct an anti-pirates operation in Eyl, its consequences are difficult to predict. The Somali authorities have allowed pursuing pirates in Somalia's territorial waters; however, land operation would be regarded as a violation of its sovereignty.

Legal and Economic Matters

In regards to the international regulatory framework to combat terrorism, the 1985 incident in which terrorists hijacked the Italian cruise ship *Achille Lauro* in the eastern Mediterranean and killed a passenger before agreeing to terms to end their siege provided the catalyst to develop a series of technical measures to prevent unlawful acts against passengers and crews on board ships. Later, in March 1988, the International Maritime Organization (IMO) adopted in Rome the Convention for the Suppression of Unlawful Acts against the safety (SUA) of maritime navigation and its protocol relating to offshore platforms.[58] The principal purpose of the SUA Convention was to ensure that anyone committing unlawful acts against the safety of navigation will not be given shelter in any country; instead they will either be prosecuted or extradited to a state where they will stand trial. The unlawful acts covered by the SUA Convention include the following: the seizure of ships by force; acts of violence against persons on board ships; and the placing of devices on board a ship that are likely to destroy or damage it.

In the wake of 9/11, it became clear that the previous work of IMO was insufficient. The international maritime community needed a new, more rigorous, and more comprehensive set of measures to address the question of maritime security. To this end, in November 2001, the IMO Assembly called for a thorough review of all existing measures to combat acts of violence and crime at sea.[59] The boundaries between acts of terrorism and crime are often indistinct within the overall perspective of the UN's fight against terrorism and organized crime. The UN Convention against Transnational Organized Crime was adopted by the General Assembly in November 2000.[60]

The June 2008 vote on Resolution 1816 by the UN Security Council was the first sign of international action against piracy. After

---

58. Mitropoulos, 2000.
59. Ibid.
60. United Nations Convention against Transnational Organized Crime, 2000.

a difficult struggle (because of the reluctance of countries such as Indonesia, which suspected a precedent), France and the United States obtained a derogation from the UN Law of the Sea Convention, adopted in 1982 in Montego Bay, Jamaica. This treaty recognized the sovereignty of a coastal state in its territorial waters and in its "area of economic exclusivity," about 250 miles (400 km), and only authorized repression of acts of piracy on the high seas.[61]

After four months, in October 2008, the UN Security Council has accepted the new resolution, 1846 (2008). Acting under the Charter's Chapter VII, the Council decided that during the next twelves months, states and regional organizations cooperating with Somalia's Transitional Federal Government (TFG) may enter Somalia's territorial waters and use "all necessary means"—such as deploying naval vessels and military aircraft, as well as seizing and disposing of boats, vessels, arms, and related equipment used for piracy—to fight piracy and armed robbery at sea off the Somalia coast, in accordance with relevant international law.[62]

States and regional organizations cooperating with Somalian authorities were also requested to provide the Council and the Secretary General with a progress report on their actions within nine months. While warships may enter Somalia's territorial waters with the agreement of the transitional government in Mogadishu (the only internationally recognized form of government) "to repress acts of piracy and armed robbery at sea," this "right to pursue" does not include a mechanism to supervise the bases and ports used by the pirates. France and Spain have called for the creation of an international maritime police force (like an Interpol for the world's waterways) and are seeking an endorsement from the UN and the European Union (EU). Russia, which dispatched a patrol from the Indian Ocean after *Faina* was hijacked, would also like to take action against pirates as the United States and Europe have done, within the framework of Resolution 1816.[63]

In November 2008, the EU Minister of Foreign Affairs made the decision to begin EU NAVFOR Somalia, also known as Operation Atalanta, which is aimed at fighting piracy in the waters off the coast of Somalia; the first naval operation in the history of the European Union, Atalanta attained initial operational capability on December 13, 2008.[64]

---

61. UN Security Council. Resolution 1816, 2008.
62. UN Security Council. Resolution 1846, 2008.
63. Leymarie, 2008.
64. Vogel, 2009; European Security and Defense Policy (ESDP). *http://ue.eu.int/showPage.aspx?id=1518&lang=en*

*Deeply concerned by the outbreak of acts of piracy and armed rob-
bery off the Somalia coast, the European Union launched military
operation EU NAVFOR Somalia (operation "Atalanta"), which is
conducted in support of UN Security Council Resolutions 1814
(2008), 1816 (2008), 1838 (2008), and 1846 (2008) in order to contribute to:*

- *the protection of vessels of the WFP (World Food
  Programme) delivering food aid to displaced persons in
  Somalia;*
- *the protection of vulnerable vessels cruising off the Somalia
  coast, and the deterrence, prevention, and repression of
  acts of piracy and armed robbery off the Somalia coast.*[65]

According to the German Minister of Defense, Mr. Franz Josef
Jung, the overall objective of Atalanta is to combat piracy, provide
security on the sea, and protect international trade. The German
frigate *Karlsruhe* is tasked with helping protect commercial and
civilian sea traffic from pirates.[66] The question remains: Can a single German warship, supported by just five other frigates and reconnaissance aircraft drawn from Great Britain, Greece, France,
Belgium, the Netherlands, Sweden, and Spain, really manage to
accomplish much of anything in the region? Operation Atalanta is
tasked with deterring piracy in an area encompassing 3 million
square kilometers (1.16 million square miles), stretching from the
Gulf of Aden, which connects the Indian Ocean to the Mediterranean
through the Red Sea, to the Somalia coast and out to the southern
part of the Arabian Peninsula, an area equivalent to all of Western
Europe. Rear Admiral Philip Jones of the Royal Navy, who has been
put in charge of the joint EU operation, expressed concerns that the
area is so vast that hundreds of ships could not maintain effective
surveillance.[67]

Moreover, in addition to Great Britain, France, Germany,
Greece, the Netherlands, Spain, Portugal, and Sweden, the Norway,
which is not a member of the European Union, will take part to fight
pirates. Currently, in the Gulf of Aden there are two French frigates
and Spain's intelligence plane. In addition, since 2002, there are
NATO ships conducting antiterrorist Operation Enduring Freedom,

---

65. European Security and Defense Policy (ESDP). *http://ue.eu.int/
showPage.aspx?id=1518&lang=en*
66. Mayr, 2008.
67. Ibid.

including the Italian destroyer and two frigates from Greece and Great Britain.

However, Operation Atalanta is interfaced with some complexities. Prior to the beginning of the operation, countries participating should have settled all legislative formalities concerning participation of the naval forces in combat against pirates and developed a mandate by which the all European naval seamen will be allocated to the region. The basic dispute is whether navy sailors can arrest pirates and hand them over to justice, or for this purpose, the representatives of law enforcement should be present on the ship. The question is not as simple as it may seem due to legal issues of the participating states. Article 87a of the German Constitution specifies the following:

1. *The Federation shall establish Armed Forces for purposes of defense. Their numerical strength and general organizational structure must be shown in the budget.*
2. *Apart from defense, the Armed Forces may be employed only to the extent expressly permitted by this Basic Law.*
3. *During a state of defense or a state of tension, the Armed Forces shall have the power to protect civilian property and to perform traffic control functions to the extent necessary to accomplish their defense mission. Moreover, during a state of defense or a state of tension, the Armed Forces may also be authorized to support police measures for the protection of civilian property; in this event, the Armed Forces shall cooperate with the competent authorities.*
4. *In order to avert an imminent danger to the existence or free democratic basic order of the Federation or of a Land, the Federal Government, if the conditions referred to in paragraph (2) of Article 91 obtain and the police forces and the Federal Border Police prove inadequate, may employ the Armed Forces to support the police and the Federal Border Police in protecting civilian property and in combating organized armed insurgents. Any such employment of the Armed Forces shall be discontinued if the Bundestag or the Bundesrat so demands.*[68]

Therefore, according to the German Constitution, army and police function are strictly divided, and authorities are concerned that if those functions were united again, it would set a dangerous

---

68. Basic Law for the Federal Republic of Germany (Grundgesetz, GG). Article 87a [Establishment and powers of the Armed Forces].

precedent allocating the *Bundeswehr* with police functions, which could allow them be used to suppress protests, as is the case in Russia and other former Soviet states.

A problem associated with the EU naval forces deployed in the Gulf of Aden and the coast of Somalia is the conflict of mandates between the EU, NATO, and the individual participating states. Another issue to be determined is the extent to which the EU is willing to extend itself in regards to a worldwide problem. The resources allocated by the participating states may cause a financial strain on these countries, primarily due to worldwide economic conditions. At some point, the EU and other nations involved in the deployment of resources in this region will question who is benefiting from their protection, such as the multi-billion dollar shipping companies and ship owners. A possible solution to ease the financial burden on participating states is to charge a tax on vessels transporting goods in these hostile waterways; as insurance companies already profit from the maritime trade, providing compensation for the necessary protection for these vessels. In addition, transport fees could be used to provide funding to help rebuild the infrastructure of Somalia so that local authorities could assist in eliminating the ports that are safe havens for the pirates in the region.

Russia

The authors posit that, despite its high level of maritime traffic, Russia does not have a high level of maritime attacks within their territorial waters for several reasons. The first reason is that Russia has a strong central government, which allows it to act definitively against perceived enemies, such as in the case of the maritime incident with Georgian forces (a discussion of that case follows). In addition, Russia has one of the largest and best-equipped navies in the world, providing a deterrent to any individuals or groups that would engage in behavior that could be perceived as hostile.

The second reason Russia does not have a high level of maritime attacks is the presence of strong governments among neighboring states. Most of the states that share waterways with Russia are stable and have a strong central government, which does not allow for the presence of nearby ports that would harbor pirates or other organized criminals attempting to unload stolen cargo without the fear of retribution, from either Russia or the neighboring states' military or police forces.

The third reason Russia does not have a high level of maritime attacks is due to their historical response concerning piracy and pirates. During the fourteenth century, Russia employed military forces and local militias to combat pirates on the Don and Volga Rivers as well as the Black and Azov Seas. An example of the pirates that engaged in robbery and murder in medieval Russia were the *ushkuiniks,* who originated in the 1320s in Novgorod. Their name originated from the word *ushkui,* a type of flat-bottom medieval Russian boat, easily transported over portages between the Don and Volga Rivers. In Novgorod, Russian nobles, or boyars, used the *ushkuiniks,* who numbered in the thousands, to demonstrate military power and influence, as well as to advance their trade interests throughout the Volga region.

During the famous campaign of 1360, the *ushkuiniks* sailed from Novgorod by the portages to the Volga River. Under command of Anfal Nikitin, the *ushkuiniks* captured the famous trade emporium, Zhukotin, in Volga Bulgaria.[69] A khan of the Golden Horde, a provincial governor of Zhukotin, was furious and ordered Grand Prince Dmitry to capture the *ushkuiniks* and bring them to justice. Without any knowledge on the part of their superiors in Novgorod, the *ushkuiniks* approached Novgorod and punished Grand Prince Dmitry for his hostile action by slaughtering the Armenian and Tatar merchants. This led to a diplomatic furor and Grand Prince Dmitry demanded apologies from the Novgorod Republic for the pirate's actions.

In 1371, the *ushkuiniks* captured Yaroslavl and Kostroma along with a number of other upper Volga cities. About three years later the *ushkuiniks* sailed with about ninety ships on a famous series of raids to pillage and loot the Vyatka region. In 1375, the *ushkuiniks* defeated the Kostroma militia and, after looting, burnt the city. A short time after that, the uskuiniks looted Novgorod and then sailed down the Volga city of Astrakhan where they were annihilated by a Tatar general.

In 1391, the *ushkuiniks* had recovered from their defeat and once again felt strong enough to resume pirate activities. In the same year, they captured both Zhukotin and Kazan cities. Muscovy's power was on the ascendant, however, and the Novgorod Republic moved into action. In the beginning of the fif-

---

69. *Zhukotin* in Russian chronicles was a medieval Bolgar city during the tenth to fifteenth centuries. The city was situated on the right bank of Kama, near the modern city of Chistopol. In the tenth to thirteenth centuries it was one of the most important furniture trade centers of Volga Bulgaria. In 1236, Chistopol was ruined by Batu Khan's troops during the Mongol invasion of Volga Bulgaria. Following the Russian pirate raids in the fourteenth and fifteenth centuries, the city's power declined.

teenth century, the Novgorod Republic began putting the *ushkuiniks'* filibustering activities down. This was the end of the *uskuinik* piracy on the Volga River. There were, from time to time, small *ushkuinik* flotillas that appeared on the river, but they were quickly dispersed and destroyed by the military ships and various militias.[70]

From the social and economic point of view, the only "pirate republic" ever originated in Europe was the sixteenth century *Zaporizhian Sich (Sich)* in the Ukraine. Situated in the remote steppe, the *Sich* was populated with Russian, Ukrainian, and Polish peasants, in addition to runaways, from either feudal masters or Ottoman galleys, outlaws, and destitute gentry. The remoteness of the steppe, as well as the rapids on the Dnepr River effectively protected this place from invasion. The main target of the inhabitants of *Sich*, who called themselves *kozaki* (Cossacks) were rich settlements at the Black Sea shores of the Ottoman Empire. In the Ukraine, the *kozaki* were using the Dnepr River as a highway to riches and conquest against the Ottoman Turks. These *kozaki ushkuiniki* (Cossack pirates) attacked, both on the water and by land, caravans and trade vessels up and down the Dnepr. The *kozaki ushkuiniki* made a number of forays up the rivers into the regions that are now known as Romania and Bulgaria. In the mid-sixteenth century, the *kozaki ushkuiniks* began to subside from acts of piracy and revert back to being a predominantly horseback culture.

The sixteenth century Muscovite's *Sobornoe Ulozhenie,* a law that included severe punishments for acts of piracy, required all navy, military, and militia to break on the wheel or sever both hands of all captured in the commission of an act of piracy without a trial.[71] These punishments were also applied to individuals that were harboring pirates or pirate ships. As a result of the changes in laws and punishments, acts of piracy diminished and did not reappear in Russian waterways to any significant degree through modern times.

In the twenty-first century, the international community has begun working together, through the UN, in order to address the increasing threat posed by acts of piracy throughout the world, especially in regards to pirates in the Gulf of Aden. As a result of the daily attempts to hijack ships, many countries, including the United States, EU, South Korea, India, and Russia, have sent military ships into the region. However, the presence of foreign military vessels

---

70. Brockhaus and Efron Encyclopedic Dictionary. Moscow 1890, Russian Language *http://encycl.opentopia.com/term/Ushkuiniks*
71. Sobornoe Ulozhenie, 1649.

has not diminished piracy in the region; to the contrary, recent pirate activities have increased, as indicated in the IMB report for the first quarter of 2009.

In October 2008, Russia tasked *Neustrashimy* (Fearless), a military vessel carrying *Spetsnaz* (marines) and *Spetsgruppa Vympel* (special forces commandos), to patrol the waters and protect vessels in the Gulf of Aden. The *Neustrashimy* had been given permission from the current president of Somalia's Transitional Federal Government (TFG) to conduct military operations against those that engage in maritime attacks; however, the TFG parliament had not approved of Russian intervention. The permission extended to both Somalia territorial waters and land, provided the operations would be coordinated with the TFG. While Russian military operations appeared to be a viable option, no orders were issued to attack the pirates on the *Faina*.

That ship's armament includes SS-N-25 Switchblade anti-ship missiles, SA-N-9 Gauntlet SAM, a 100-mm gun, torpedoes, depth charges, and a Ka-27 ASW helicopter.[72] The increase of a foreign military presence does not contribute to a peaceful solution if the hijackers are prepared to die, as is evident from the numerous attacks in Iraq and Afghanistan. While the arrival of the Russian warship might assist in making the waterways around the Horn of Africa safer in the future, there must also be some proactive measures designed to address the underlying causes of piracy in the region. Merely waiting for the Russian destroyer would only give reason for further delay in the proactive search for a peaceful resolution concerning the case at hand.

Somalia's ambassador to the Russian Federation Mohammed Handule has said: "The Russian navy ships have obtained permission of the Somalia president to fight pirates in Somalia's water and on the land."[73] However, there is little central control over the coastal areas, such as Puntland, which is locally controlled, has claimed independence from the Somalia government, and does not allow negotiations with Somalia's ministers. Other local Somalia tribes have also declared independence and have proclaimed their states.[74]

In addition to the Russian vessel *Neustrashimy*, South Korea and India have expressed intent to deploy destroyers to the region.

---

72. Russian warship en route for anti-piracy mission off Somalia. *Global Research*, October 22, 2008. *http://www.globalresearch.ca/index.php?context=va&aid=10645*
73. Demianov, 2008.
74. Myasnikov, 2008.

Russia is planning to send more warships to the Somalia coast, along with some commandos and a particularly Russian style of counter-piracy operations. The Russians plan to use the aggressive tactics against any suspected pirates encountered, including methods that were successful in ending the activities of the *ushkuiniks*. For example, on April 28, 2009, a Russian warship seized a pirate vessel with twenty-nine people on board off the Somalia coast, recovering numerous weapons and navigation equipment. These captured pirates had launched two unsuccessful attacks against a tanker with a Russian crew.[75]

This could cause diplomatic problems with the other nations providing warships for counter-piracy operations off the Somalia coast, since the ships currently present in the area have followed a policy of not attempting rescue operations (lest hostages get hurt) and not firing on pirates unless fired on first; however, this approach may only serve to encourage the pirates, as they do not fear engagement by military vessels.

Russia brought commandos from *Spetsgruppa Vympel,* hostage rescue experts formed two decades ago as a spin-off from the original Russian army *Spetsnaz* commandos, in order to provide similarly trained units to serve other functions. The 1970s and 1980s marked the first appearance of *Spetsgruppa* (Special Group). Established in 1974, *Spetsgruppa Alfa* (Special Group A), was tasked with anti-terrorist assignments, or special raids, similar to U.S. Delta Force or British Special Air Service (SAS).[76] *Spetsgruppa Alfa* is now part of the Federal Security Bureau (*Federalnya Sluzhba Bezopasnosti,* FSB), which replaced the *Komitet Gosudarstvennoi Bezopasnosti* (KGB). During the establishment of *Spetsgruppa Alfa,* another section of the KGB organized *Spetsgruppa Vympel,* which is primarily deployed in hostage situations.[77]

Russia has received an abundance of negative media publicity for its brutal, but effective, counter-terror operations in Chechnya. Similarly, the authors suggest that the August 2008 invasion of Georgia was a punitive action intended to intimidate the Georgian government, which resulted in negative media publicity and criticism from Western nations. While these actions may have been

---

75. BBC News: *Russia captures Somalia pirates.*
76. Spetsgruppa A: *http://www.specialoperations.com/Foreign/Russia/KGB.htm; Delta Force: http://www.army.com/enlist/delta-force.html; Special Air Service: http://www.sasregiment.org.uk/*
77. A Russian Solution to the Somalia Pirates. *http://www.strategypage.com/htmw/htseamo/articles/20081125.aspx?comments=Y*

effective on the surface, they may also be Pyrrhic victories if the international community does not approve of the methods employed. The authors posit that if the Russians were to use similar brutal tactics against the Somalia pirates, many nations would express reservations, and then subsequently enjoy the benefits of a piracy free Somalia coast and Gulf of Aden. However, there needs to be a balance between the effectiveness of the methods and tactics utilized to address the threat posed by piracy and terrorism and the legitimacy of force employed in order to maintain diplomatic relations with other nations.

In regards to the hijacking of the *Faina,* while most crew members were Ukrainians, two of the captured crew as well as the ship's captain, who died of a cerebral hemorrhage during his captivity, were Russians, which obligated Russia to be involved in the response. The otherwise ineffective Transitional Federal Government (TFG) of Somalia has ongoing diplomatic relations with the Kremlin and, for whatever recognition from such a regime is worth, is one of the few to follow Russia in recognizing the independence of the breakaway Georgian regions of South Ossetia and Abkhazia. The TFG's envoy in Moscow, Mohamed Mohamud Handule, has reportedly signed an oil exploration agreement with Russia's *Zarubezh Geologia* and is courting similar deals with Gazprom and Lukoil. Even without any concessions in Somalia, Russia's increasing engagement in Africa makes it imperative for them to have safe maritime access to the continent. Finally, while it has been reported of late in *blizhnee zarubezhie* ("near abroad"), Russia's ambitions to be a major global actor also require it to play the part when other leading world powers are acting in concert against a common challenge to the international security and safety of maritime operations.

Conclusion

While maritime attacks pose a significant threat to the world, specifically via their threat to the world economy, there are differences in activity that can provide a foundation for future responses. A chain is only as strong as its weakest link, and in relation to international efforts to thwart maritime attacks, the international community must work in conjunction with states that have a weak central government, or weak links, in order to deter the recent upward trend in maritime attacks. While the Russian response to maritime attacks may be effective, the authors propose that any response must be consistent with international agreements in order to provide legitimate responses to this threat and maintain cooperation among sovereign nations. Without cooperation between states, it is unlikely that any response to maritime attacks will be effective for an extended timeframe.

Through the end of the twentieth and beginning of the twenty-first centuries, an overwhelming majority of piracy and maritime terrorist attacks took place in the waterways of developing countries, whose authorities were limited in their ability to independently fight against pirates and terrorists. However, in the past five years maritime terrorists, using modern boats and weapons, have begun to conduct operations in the waterways of more developed nations. Pirates and terrorists will likely continue to target modern vessels, such as cruise liners and cargo ships, unless the international community can come to some useful and effective agreements in regards to the prosecution and punishment of those engaging in these activities.

The authors propose that one effective way to counteract piracy and maritime terrorism in the short term is the continued deployment, via international cooperation and engagement with the UN, of military vessels to regions with high levels of activity, so that these vessels can respond to distress calls and prevent successful attacks, which could serve as an effective deterrent. However, in the long term, the key to diminishing the threat of piracy and maritime terrorism is to assist governments that are prone to high levels of activity so that they can respond appropriately and effectively and be partners in the international efforts to enhance the safety and security of the waterways worldwide. As long as there is easy access to friendly ports, maritime attacks conducted by pirates and terrorists will continue to present an ongoing economic, environmental, and military threat.

References

Alderton, T., and N. Winchester. 2002. Regulation, Representation and the flag market. *Journal for Maritime Research.* September, ISSN: 1469–1957. Retrieved March 23, 2009, from *http://www.jmr.nmm.ac.uk/server/show/conJmrArticle.53*

Associated Press. 2008. Pirate Attacks Increased in 2007, Maritime Group Says. *New York Times,* January 10, 2008. Retrieved March 24, 2009, from *http://www.nytimes.com/2008/01/10/world/africa/10pirates.html?_r=1&fta*

Axe, D. 2009. Five pirated crews who didn't fare as well as the Americans. *Esquire,* April 9, 2009. Retrieved April 20, 2009, from *http://www. esquire.com/the-side/feature/somali-pirate-attack-rescues-040909*

Azikiwe, A. 2009. Will the New Somalia Government Bring Peace and Stability to the Country? *Pan-African News Wire,* February 9, 2009. Retrieved April 20, 2009, from *http://panafricannews.blogspot.com/ 2009/02/will-new-somalia-government-bring-peace.html*

Basic Law for the Federal Republic of Germany (Grundgesetz, GG). Article 87a [Establishment and powers of the Armed Forces]. Retrieved April 16, 2009, from *http://www.iuscomp.org/gla/statutes/GG.htm#87a*

BBC News. 2009. Russia captures Somalia pirates. April 28, 2009. Retrieved April 29, 2009, from *http://news.bbc.co.uk/2/hi/africa/8023951.stm*

BBC News. 2009. Somali vigilantes capture pirates. April 28, 2009. Retrieved April 29, 2009, from *http://news.bbc.co.uk/2/hi/africa/8022820.stm*

BBC News. 2009. Guide to the Philippines conflict. March 31, 2009. Retrieved April 18, 2009, from *http://news.bbc.co.uk/2/hi/asia-pacific/7887521.stm*

BBC News. 2004. Bomb caused Philippine ferry fire. October 11, 2004. Retrieved April 18, 2009, from *http://news.bbc.co.uk/2/hi/asia-pacific/3732356.stm*

BBC News. 2004. Timeline: Madrid investigation. April 28, 2004. Retrieved April 18, 2009, from *http://news.bbc.co.uk/2/hi/europe/3597885.stm*

BBC News. 1985. Gunmen hijack Italian cruise liner. October 7, 1985. Retrieved April 18, 2009, from *http://news.bbc.co.uk/onthisday/hi/dates/ stories/october/7/newsid_2518000/2518697.stm*

Beccaria, C. 1963. *Of crimes and punishments.* Indianapolis, IN: Bobbs-Merrill (Original work published in 1764).

Bentham, J. 1948. *An introduction to the principles of morals and legislation.* New York: Kegan Paul (Original work published 1789).

Blair, D. 2008. Somali pirate port becomes boom town. *Telegraph,* November 19, 2008. Retrieved April 20, 2009, from *http://www.telegraph.co.uk/news/worldnews/africaandindianocean/ somalia/3479001/Somali-pirate-port-becomes-boom-town.html*

Brockhaus and Efron Encyclopedic Dictionary. 1890. Moscow, Russian Language.

Burnett, J. 2002. *Dangerous Waters: Modern Piracy and Terror on the High Seas.* New York: Dutton Adult, Penguin Group.

Chaliand, G., and A. Blin. 2007. *The History of Terrorism: From Antiquity to al Qaeda*. Berkley, CA: University of California Press.

Clayton, J. 2008. Somalia pirates plunder is used to fund terrorism, experts fear. *Times Online*, September 17, 2008. Retrieved April 19, 2009, from *http://www.timesonline.co.uk/tol/news/world/africa/article4769682.ece*

Crilly, R. 2009. Somali pirates are paid record $3.5 million ransom for MV Faina. *Timesonline*, February 5, 2009. Retrieved April 19, 2009, from *http://www.timesonline.co.uk/tol/news/world/africa/article5663504.ece*

Demianov, A. 2008. Adenskoe srazhenie [Aden's Battle] ZAO *"Lenta.ru,"* November 18, 2008. Retrieved April 20, 2009, from *http://lenta.ru/articles/2008/11/14/pirates/*

Farah, D. 1997. Russian Mob, Drug Cartels Joining Forces. *Washington Post Foreign Service*, September 29, 1997. Retrieved April 25, 2009, from *http://www.washingtonpost.com/wp-srv/inatl/longterm/russiagov/stories/mafia092997.htm*

Farah, J. 2005. Al-Qaeda's U.S. nuclear targets: Captured documents, terrorists reveal bin Laden's preferred dates, places for 'American Hiroshima'. *WorldNet DailyExclusive*, July 18, 2005. Retrieved April 25, 2009, from *http://www.worldnetdaily.com/news/article.asp?ARTICLE_ID=45313*

Fenton, B. 2001. Seventeen Americans die in bomb attack on warship. *Telegraph*, June 19, 2001. Retrieved April 20, 2009, from *http://www.telegraph.co.uk/news/worldnews/middleeast/yemen/1370204/17-Americans-die-in-bomb-attack-on-warship.html*

Forero, J. 2008. Colombia Traffickers Moving Drugs Via Submersibles. NPR, February 11, 2008. Retrieved April 20, 2009, from *http://www.npr.org/templates/story/story.php?storyId=18707501*

Frank, J. 2008. Somali pirates strike deeper on the high seas. *Lloyd's List*, August 28, 2008. Retrieved April 20, 2009, from *http://www.lloydslist.com/ll/news/somali-pirates-strike-deeper-on-the-high-seas/1219839806623.htm*

Gettelmen, J. 2008. Somalia's Fate Still Unclear After Leader Quits. *The New York Times*, December 29, 2008. Retrieved April 19, 2009, from *http://www.nytimes.com/2008/12/30/world/africa/30somalia.html?ref=world*

Gittaa, M. 2009. Piracy off the East African Coast. *The African*, February 23, 2009. Retrieved March 29, 2009, from *http://www.africanmag.com/FORUM-724-design004*

Graeme C. and R. Gunaratna. 2004. *Counterterrorism: A reference handbook*. Santa Barbara, CA: ABC-CLIO.

Harper, M. 2008. Life in Somalia's pirate town. *BBC News,* September 18, 2008. Retrieved March 19, 2009, from *http://news.bbc.co.uk/2/hi/ africa/7623329.stm*

Harrigan, S. 1996. Hijacked ferry due in Istanbul. *CNN World News,* January 18, 1996. Retrieved March 29, 2009, from *http://www.cnn.com/WORLD/ 9601/chechen_rebels/01-18/10_am/index.html*

ICC International Maritime Bureau. 2009a. *Piracy and Armed Robbery against Ships: Report for the Period 1 January–31 March 2009.* London, UK: ICC International Maritime Bureau.

ICC International Maritime Bureau. 2009b. *Piracy and Armed Robbery against Ships: Annual Report 1 January–31 December 2008.* London, UK: ICC International Maritime Bureau.

ICC International Maritime Bureau. 2003. ICC commercial crime service: A division of the international chamber of commerce. Retrieved April 21, 2009, from *http://www.iccwbo.org/*

James, G. 1995, January 3. Somalia's Overthrown Dictator, Mohammed Siad Barre, Is Dead. *New York Times,* January 3, 1995. Retrieved April 21, 2009, from *http://www.nytimes.com/1995/01/03/obituaries/somalia-s-overthrown-dictator-mohammed-siad-barre-is-dead.html*

Jasparro, C. 2009. Somalia's Piracy Offers Lessons in Global Governance: Protecting the global commons requires more than a military response. *Yale Global Online,* April 6, 2009. Retrieved April 21, 2009, from *http://yaleglobal.yale.edu/article.print?id=12210*

Leymarie, L. 2008. The Pirates of Puntland. *Middle East Online,* December 11, 2008. Retrieved March 29, 2009, from *http://www.middle-east-online.com/ENGLISH/?id=29161*

Luft, G. and A. Korin. 2004. Terrorism Goes to Sea. *Council on Foreign Relations,* December 2004. Retrieved March 29, 2009, from *http://www.cfr.org/publication/7545/terrorism_goes_to_sea.html*

Mayr, W. 2008. German Navy Mission Encounters More than Pirates. *Spiegel Online International,* December 22, 2008. Retrieved March 24, 2009, from *http://www.spiegel.de/international/world/0,1518,598035,00.html*

McDaniel, M. S. 2000. Modern high seas piracy. *The Cargo Letter.* November 20, 2000. Retrieved March 24, 2009, from *http://cargolaw.com/ presentations_pirates.html*

Megalommatis, S. M. 2009. Ecoterra—Somali Marine & Coastal Monitor–Part VII. MV BOW-ASIR Hijacked and Piracy Revivified. *California Chronicle,* March 27, 2009. Retrieved March 27, 2009, from *http://www.californiachronicle.com/articles/view/96207*

Meyer, C. 2008. Colombia's Cocaine Cartels Learn a New Trick. *Speigel Online International,* June 27, 2008. Retrieved March 29, 2009, from *http://www.spiegel.de/international/world/0,1518,562603,00.html*

Mitropoulos, E. 2000. Address by the Secretary-General of the International Maritime Organization. *Fifth Regional Seapower Symposium for the Mediterranean and Black Sea Navies,* October 13, 2000. Retrieved March 24, 2009, from *http://www.imo.org/About/mainframe.asp? topic_id= 847&doc_id=4364*

Mitropoulos, E. 2005. A new era dawns in IMO's history. *International Maritime Organization.* Moscow, July 2005. Retrieved March 24, 2009, from *http://www.imo.org/About/mainframe.asp?topic_id=1028& doc_id=5071*

Middleton, R. 2008. Piracy in Somalia: Threatening Global Trade, Feeding Local Wars. *Chatham House (the Royal Institute of International Affairs),* October 2008. Retrieved March 24, 2009, from *http://www.chathamhouse.org.uk/files/12203_1008piracysomalia.pdf*

Murphy, M. N. 2007. *Contemporary Piracy and Maritime Terrorism.* New York: Routledge.

Myasnikov, V. 2008. Piratstvo stanovitsya globalnoi problemoi. Kogda v more vyidut terroristy, mir sodrognetsya. [Pirates Became a Global Problem. When Terrorists Hijack the Sea, the World Will Be Shocked]. *Nezavisimoe voennoe obozrenie.* Moscow.

Navarro, M. 1997. Russian Submarine Drifts Into Center of a Brazen Drug Plot. *New York Times,* March 7, 1997. Retrieved March 24, 2009, from *http://www.nytimes.com/1997/03/07/us/russian-submarine-drifts-into-center-of-a-brazen-drug-plot.html?scp=1&sq=columbia%20drug% 20dealer%20submarine&st=cse*

Pirate Attacks Increased in 2007, Maritime Group Says. *The New York Times.* January 10, 2008. Retrieved April 10, 2009, from *http://www.nytimes.com/2008/01/10/world/africa/10pirates.html?fta*

Potential Hikes in Shipping Rates Involving Gulf of Aden Transits. Bloomberg. September 29, 2008. Retrieved March 24, 2009, from *https://origin-www.glgroup.com/News/Potential-Hikes-in-Shipping-Rates-Involving-Gulf-of-Aden-Transits-28099.html*

Ramachandran, S. 2006. The Sea Tigers of Tamil Eelam. *Asia Times Online,* August 31, 2006. Retrieved April 10, 2009, from *http://www.atimes.com/ atimes/South_Asia/HH31Df01.html*

Reynolds, P. 2004. Abbas: Palestinian throwback. *BBC News Online,* March 10, 2004. Retrieved March 29, 2009, from *http://news.bbc.co.uk/2/hi/ middle_east/2952879.stm*

Roschchupkin, V. 2009. Na superkatere pod flagom s "Veselym Rodgerom" [On the super speedboat under the flag of "Jolly Roger"]. *Nezavisimaya gazeta* January 30, 2009. Retrieved March 29, 2009, from *http://nvo.ng.ru/printed/221752*

Sakhuja, V. 2005. Mini submarine: a vessel of choice with drug cartels and terrorists. *South-Asia Analysis Group,* March 30, 2005. Retrieved March 29, 2009, from *http://www.southasiaanalysis.org/%5Cpapers14% 5Cpaper1312.html*

Samko, Y. 1999. Podvodnye Apparaty VMF USSR Russia [Underwater Vehicles of the USSR and Russia Navies]. *Center for Arms Control, Energy and Environmental Studies.* March 15, 1999. Retrieved March 27, 2009, from *http://www.armscontrol.ru/subs/rescue/t0399.htm*

Shane, J. 2003. Vessel Security and Modern Piracy. Unpublished paper. Rutgers University.

Smith, C. S. 2002. Fire on French Tanker Off Yemen Raises Terrorism Fears. *New York Times,* October 7, 2002. Retrieved April 19, 2009, from *http://www.nytimes.com/2002/10/07/world/fire-on-french-tanker-off-yemen-raises-terrorism-fears.html*

Sobornoe Ulozhenie [Law Code of the Assemble of the Land]. 1649. Chapter 8, "Redemption of Military Captives"; Chapter 10, "The Judicial Process." Moscow 1649. Retrieved March 29, 2009, from *www.uoregon.edu/~kimball/1649-Ulj.htm*

Tracking the Terrorist Money Trail. 2008. *Radio Free Europe Radio Liberty,* November 16, 2008. Retrieved March 29, 2009, from *http://www.rferl.org/content/Interview_Tracking_The_Terrorist_Money_Trail/ 1349657.html*

Trevelyan, L. 2008. US gets tough on Somali pirates. *BBC News,* December 11, 2008. Retrieved April 29, 2009, from *http://news.bbc.co.uk/ 2/hi/africa/7776664.stm*

Vesti News. 2008. "Svitser Korsakov" Otkupilsya ot Somaliyskikh Piratov ["Svitser Korsakov" Paid Ransom to Somalia Pirates]. ZAO "Lenta.ru," March 18, 2008. Retrieved March 20, 2009, from *http://lenta.ru/ news/2008/03/18/korsakov/*

UN Security Council. 2008. Resolution 1846: Regional organizations may use all necessary means. *UN Department of Public Information, News and Media Division.* Retrieved March 29, 2009, from *http://un.org/ News/Press/docs/2008/sc9514.doc.htm*

UN Security Council 2008. Resolution 1816: Adopted Unanimously with
Somalia's Consent; Measures Do Not Affect Rights, Obligations under
Law of Sea Convention. *UN Department of Public Information, News and
Media Division.* Retrieved March 29, 2009, from *http://www.un.org/
News/Press/docs/2008/sc9344.doc.htm*

United Nations. 2000. United Nations Convention against Transnational
Organized Crime. Retrieved March 29, 2009, from *http://www.uncjin.org/
Documents/Conventions/dcatoc/final_documents_2/convention_eng.pdf*

Vijayan, K. C. 2009. Pirate attacks continue. *The Straits Times,* April 21, 2009.
Retrieved April 22, 2009, from *http://www.straitstimes.com/
Breaking%2BNews/Singapore/Story/STIStory_366690.html*

Vogel, T. 2009. Military missions up for review. *European Voice.* March 5,
2009. Retrieved March 29, 2009, from *http://www.europeanvoice.com/
article/imported/military-missions-up-for-review/64174.aspx*

von Alt, C. 2003. Autonomous Underwater Vehicles. *Autonomous Underwater
Lagrangian Platforms and Sensors Workshop.* March 24, 2003. Retrieved
March 29, 2009, from *http://www.geo-prose.com/ALPS/white_papers/alt.pdf*

6.3
Maritime Attacks at the Horn of Africa

Terrorists in Yemen and Pirates in Somalia

MICHAEL C. WALKER

Introduction

Over the past several years, the piracy problem has shifted from the Straits of Malacca and Indonesia to the Gulf of Aden and the northern Indian Ocean. According to the International Maritime Bureau (IMB), the area around the Straits of Malacca/Indonesia area accounted for 33.5 percent of all reported piracy attacks in 2003, while the Gulf of Aden/Somalia accounted for only 4.7 percent (ICC International Maritime Bureau, 2009a). By 2008, however, the positions of each of these areas were reversed, with the Gulf of Aden/Somalia accounting for 37.9 percent of all known piracy attacks and the Straits of Malacca/Indonesia area accounting for only 10.2 percent (ICC International Maritime Bureau, 2009a). This shift has been attributed to several factors, mainly that the three countries surrounding the Strait of Malacca (Indonesia, Malaysia, and Singapore) have committed resources and manpower to eliminate piracy in the area. Piracy flourishes around the Horn of Africa, on the other hand, because the two countries closest to the problem, Somalia and Yemen, can be considered failed states.

The Horn of Africa is one of the most important shipping areas in the world today. Most ships from the oil fields of the Middle East travel through this area in order to get their cargo to its destination in the west. Ships have two options when leaving the Arabian Sea: one is to travel west through the Gulf of Aden through the strait called the Bab el-Mandeb, a twenty-mile-wide chokepoint, into the Red Sea and then through the Suez Canal into the Mediterranean

Sea; the alternative would be to travel south from the Arabian Sea into the Indian Ocean and to the Cape of Good Hope at the southern end of Africa, a route thousands of miles longer and one that takes many more days to complete (the operating costs for large vessels can be $20,000 to $30,000 per day) (Knickmeyer, 2008). Until recently, many ships that were slow and had low freeboards were sent around southern Africa rather than risk the journey through the Gulf of Aden. Currently, due to the increased use of mother ships by the pirates (which allow them to venture hundreds of miles out at sea prior to deploying their fast boats) the alternative route can expose the ships to piratical attack (as was the case with the *Sirius Star* and the *Alabama*).

Compounding the problem in this part of the world is the territory to be patrolled to prevent piracy and/or to apprehend the pirates. Commodore Keith Winstanley, deputy commander of coalition naval forces in the Middle East, stated, "We are covering 2.5 million square miles of water. Policing all of it would take more ships than we could ever get" (Jopson and Wright, 2008).

Terrorist Attacks in Yemen

USS *The Sullivans*

Abd al Rahim al Nashiri and Khalid Shiek Mohammed were both operational coordinators for al Qaeda and, according to The 9/11 Commission Report, "were involved during 1998 and 1999 in preparing to attack a ship off the coast of Yemen with a boatload of explosives" (National Commission on Terrorist Attacks upon the United States, 2002). They had originally planned to target a commercial vessel, specifically an oil tanker, but the plan changed when they were instructed by Osama bin Laden to target an American warship instead. Military ships, especially United States naval ships, have "iconic status as symbols of state power" (Murphy, 2008).

In January 2000, an attempt was made to launch a Vehicle-borne Improvised Explosive Device (VBIED) attack against the U.S. warship, the USS *The Sullivans,* near the port of Aden, Yemen. The attackers loaded their small fiberglass workboat with explosives and made for the ship but, due to the weight of the explosives on board, their boat took on water and sank far from its target (Langewiesche, 2004).

USS *Cole*

Khallad and Nashiri were not to be deterred by their initial failure to attack a warship using a vessel as a device to carry out the attack. Nine months after the failed attack on the USS *The Sullivans,* the destroyer USS *Cole* (DDG-67) made a refueling stop at the port of Aden and the members of the terrorist cell saw their opportunity. On October 12, 2000, al Qaeda operatives launched a small boat, laden with explosives, from the shores of Aden. "They piloted the explosives-laden boat along the USS *Cole,* made friendly gestures to crew members, and detonated the bomb" (National Commission on Terrorist Attacks upon the United States, 2002, p. 191). The blast tore a hole in the side of the destroyer, killing seventeen members of its crew. Another thirty-nine sailors were injured in the attack.

An FBI investigation into the *Cole* attack disclosed that a Yemeni follower of al Qaeda, Jamal al-Badawi, worked with Khallad and Nashiri and was the local mastermind of the attack and had recruited the bombers. In 2004, al-Badawi was sentenced to death by a Yemeni court but, prior to his execution, was able to escape from prison with twenty-two other prisoners—a prison break that most believe was an inside job. In October 2007, al-Badawi turned himself in to authorities and pledged his allegiance to Yemen's president, Ali Abdullah Saleh. By late October the same year, al-Badawi was set free (Isikoff, 2007). Although al-Badawi is still under indictment in New York for the *Cole* bombing, he has not been recaptured.

MV *Limburg*

On Sunday morning, October 6, 2002, a threat from al Qaeda leader Osama bin Laden to "target key sectors of your [western] economy until you stop injustices and aggression" was broadcast by Arabic satellite television (Murphy, 2009, p. 202). On that date, almost two years after the USS *Cole* was attacked by suicide bombers in a small boat as it lay at anchor, a small fiberglass dinghy laden with explosives approached one of the largest ships in the world, which was within miles of the place where the *Cole* was struck.

The target that Sunday morning was the French-owned Very Large Crude Carrier (VLCC), the MV *Limburg* (now named the *Maritime Jewel*). The *Limburg* was almost stationary and waiting to pick up a pilot outside the Yemeni port of Mina al-Dabah, near the town of Mukallah, on Yemen's Arabian Sea coast. The 300,000 dwt *Limburg* was a new, double-hulled vessel in good condition. It was to add 1.5 million barrels of heavy crude oil to the cargo it was already carrying upon arrival in Yemen: 400,000 barrels of heavy crude from the Iranian port of Kharj. After taking on its additional crude, the *Limburg* was bound for Malaysia (Lehr, 2009).

There were few security precautions in place aboard the Limburg. The ship is enormous and those on board felt that they were protected by the ship's massive size. It was common at that time for smaller boats to approach a large vessel when it enters a port; nobody paid much attention and nobody, in spite of the lesson of the *USS Cole,* suspected that they might carry explosives (Burnett, 2002).

Lehr (2009) describes the attack on the *Limburg* as follows:

> On that Sunday . . . the ship's master, Hubert Ardillon and another officer, noticed a small vessel approaching fast. The vessel impacted on the port side, a violent explosion occurred, and the *Limburg* burst into flames. The force of the explosion was strong enough to penetrate the double hull of the ship and create a hole 6–8 m [18 to 24 feet] wide. Several crew members were injured by the blast, and 90,000 barrels of oil spilled into the Arabian Sea. The master ordered the ship to be evacuated. In the hasty process of evacuation from the burning tanker, one crew member drowned. The fire would be extinguished within hours, and thanks to the double hull, the *Limburg* did not sink—as it was probably expected by the terrorists. (p. 60)

According to Burnett (2002), "The attack, identical to the one against the *Cole* two years earlier, could have been prevented had lessons been learned. . . . [S]hip captains who felt that they were above it all, invulnerable to attack because their ships were too big or too important, received a rude awakening" (p. 298).

A statement allegedly issued by Osama bin Laden following the *Limburg* attack was quoted by Lehr (2009): "By exploding the oil tanker in Yemen, the holy warriors hit the umbilical cord and lifeline of the crusader community, reminding the enemy of the heavy cost of blood and the gravity of losses they will pay as a price for their continued aggression on our community and looting of our wealth" (p. 60).

The attack on the *Limburg* did have an economic effect but not the one that bin Laden was counting on. The effect of the attack fell squarely on the shoulders of Yemen.

> Insurance rates for ships calling at Yemeni ports increased immediately and substantially. As a direct consequence, shippers of all

types of goods shunned Yemeni ports; throughput of containers fell from 43,000 TEUs [twenty-foot equivilent units] in September 2002 to 3,000 TEUs in November and then almost ceased; three thousand port workers were laid off. (Murphy, 2009, pp. 202–203)

Although the attack also had an effect on the price of oil, it was limited. Oil prices increased 1.3 percent after the attack but receded quickly (Murphy, 2009).

Factors Contributing to the Terrorist Attacks in Yemen

An article in the Economist read, "Last March [2008], al-Qaeda websites posted a message advising members to head to Yemen. . . . With its rough terrain, weak central state and gun-slinging tribal culture, Yemen may prove a fairly secure redoubt for al Qaeda" (*Economist*, 2009). Yemen is one of the most failed states on earth and, with its strategic location on the north side of the Gulf of Aden and its border on the Arabian Sea, is the perfect location from which al Qaeda operatives can prey on maritime interests. Internally, Yemen is plagued by many ills including systemic corruption, depletion of its fresh water supplies, tribal warfare, and power struggles both from separatist groups and among its ruling elite (*Economist*, 2009).

A number of factors seem to influence the success of a maritime terrorist strike according to Murphy (2008): ". . . a permissive legal regime, inadequate security, access to base areas and maritime expertise, state support, and leaders who are persuaded of the seas' importance." The root cause of the attacks in Yemen, as it will also be demonstrated in Somalia, is the weak state of the national government. The attack on the USS *The Sullivans,* the USS *Cole,* and the *Limburg* was completed by an al Qaeda cell which had good leadership and tactics, had access to maritime expertise, and, according to Murphy (2008), "was able to take advantage of the weak legal and security environment prevailing in Yemen."

Combating Piracy in Yemen

Although Yemen organized a coast guard following the 2002 terrorist attack on the tanker *Limburg,* until recently it was under-equipped, under-funded, and its personnel rather untrained in handling acts of terrorism or piracy. This is somewhat unusual given that, of all the piratical attacks that occur in the Gulf of Aden, which forms the southern border of Yemen, most occur in the north of the Gulf, closer to Yemen, than on the Somali side of the Gulf (ICC International Maritime Bureau, 2009a).

As recently as September 2008, a regional commander of the Yemeni Coast Guard, Loft al-Baraty, when interviewed on the piracy threat, responded that he was worried because of the weapons and fast ships that the pirates amassed with the millions they received in ransoms. He concluded, "The French know how to deal with them, killing one of them. This is very nice" (Knickmeyer, 2008).

The Yemeni Coast Guard had, at the time of Knickmeyer's article (2008), only 1,200 personnel and no vessel longer than seventy-five feet. In another interview, the twenty-year-old commander of a Yemeni coast guard vessel, Ahmed al-Gunaid, reported that he had heard a call for assistance from a pirate attack only once and that, by the time he was able to reach the Japanese oil tanker, the pirates had been gone for two hours. He stated that was probably best since, "I know if I'm in combat with them . . . three or four RPGs, and I'm done." (Knickmeyer, 2008)

In September 2008, the Yemeni government announced the formation of an anti-piracy unit of the Somali Coast Guard to battle piracy in the Gulf of Aden, the Arabian Sea, the Red Sea, and the Bab el-Mandab Strait. The unit's mission is "to enhance the protection of ships and stop Somali pirates" in these areas, according to a coast guard official. Each of the sixteen patrol boats, which were acquired from Australia, will contain "60 marines trained to combat piracy [and] the vessels will contain artillery, radar and advanced communications" equipment (*World Tribune,* 2008).

The last weekend in April 2009 was a very busy one for the Yemeni anti-piracy patrols. On Sunday, April 26, Yemeni forces freed three vessels from Somali pirates (Al-Shawthabi, 2009). Later that day, the oil tanker *Gana,* a small vessel capable of carrying 3,000 tons of product but empty at the time, was attacked by Somali pirates off the coast of Shafrah, Yemen. At dawn Monday anti-piracy commandos using helicopters stormed the *Gana* in an attempt to regain control of the ship and its twenty-three crew members. According to sources interviewed by the Saba (the Yemeni News Service), the operation "resulted in three Somali pirates killed, two injured and other five arrested . . . [but the source stated] that two Yemeni coast guards were also wounded in the exchange of fire" (Al-Shawthabi, 2009). The Somali pirates, however, apparently placed a bomb on the *Gana* that exploded during the raid, causing the ship to take on water and possibly sink (*Yemen Post,* 2009).

Piratical Attacks in Somalia

Background

Prior to its unification in 1960, Somalia was two separate entities—British Somaliland and Italian Somaliland. A coup took place in 1969, led by Mohamed Siad Barre, which led to the establishment of an authoritarian socialist regime. In May 1991, northern clans broke away and formed an independent Republic of Somaliland that, although not officially recognized by any government, was designed as a constitutional democracy. The regions comprising the Horn of Africa formed a self-declared, semi-autonomous state of Puntland at the same time. The third section of Somalia is the southern region around the capital, Mogadishu. In 1995, a Transitional Federal Government (TFG) was established to run the country but this failed and was replaced by the Union of Islamic Courts (UIC). An invasion by Ethiopia occurred in December 2006, leading to the collapse of the UIC government. Ethiopian troops withdrew from the country at the end of 2008 and a new government was set-up. In April 2009, Somalia's Parliament "voted unanimously . . . to institute Islamic law (Sharia), a measure lawmakers say they hope will strengthen popular support for the government and siphon it away from the Islamist militias fighting an insurgency here" (Ibrahim, 2009). Ibrahim (2009) goes on to say that, "Most Somalis generally welcome the introduction of Sharia, suggesting that it was the only solution that Somalis could agree on."

A Failed State

Gettleman (2009a, p. 62) describes Somalia as one of the most dangerous places in the world where, "When you land at Mogadishu's international airport, the first form you fill out asks for name, address, and caliber of weapon" and "where you can get kidnapped or shot in the head faster than you can wipe the sweat off your brow." The violence prevalent on land has migrated into the waters off of the Somalian coastline, all 1879 miles of it (CIA World Factbook–Somalia). The pirates have threatened to block shipping in the Gulf of Aden, through which over 20,000 ships pass annually (Gettleman, 2009, p. 62), and now attack ships in the Indian Ocean, along which Somalia has a coastline of over 1250 miles (longer than the distance from Miami to New York).

According to Davis (2008):

> Incidents of piracy off the coast of Somalia are directly propor-
> tional to the political environment. During the summer of 2006, the
> Union of Islamic Courts (UIC) came to power in Somalia.
> Immediately afterward, the UIC announced that they would punish
> those engaged in piracy according to Sharia law. (p. 119)

The attacks ceased for a while but then the pirates attacked the
MV *Veesham I,* a cargo ship from the United Arab Emirates. A boatload of six pirates boarded the ship and demanded a $1 million ran-
som. The UIC, according to Davis, launched an attack on the pirates
and recaptured the ship, ending the hijacking. One month later,
Ethiopia gained political control of Somalia and, "with the UIC gone,
the organized gangs of pirates no longer feared governmental retribution for their offshore attacks" (Davis, 2008, p. 120).

Piracy in Somalia vs. the Straits of Malacca

As one can see by reviewing Figure 6.1, piratical attacks in the Gulf
of Aden/Somalia region have been on a steady rise, with the exception of the year 2006 when the UIC ran the Somali government,
while attacks in Indonesia/Malacca Straits have plummeted. The
sharp decline in Southeast Asian piracy has been attributed to a
coalition of forces in the area.

From 2007 to 2008, piracy in the Gulf of Aden/Somalia region
rose 152.3 percent (from 44 attacks or attempts in 2007 to 111 in

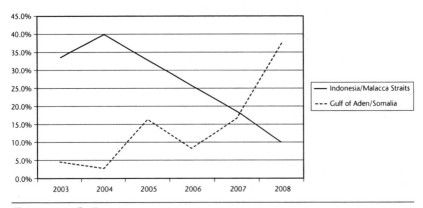

FIGURE 6.1
Piracy in Selected Areas as a Percent of Piracy Worldwide
Source: ICC International Maritime Bureau, 2009a

2008) while piracy in Indonesia/Malacca Straits declined by 40 percent (from 50 to 30 incidents).

Pirates still operating in the Indonesian/Malacca Straits area were more likely to attack a ship at dock or at anchor (53.6%) than one underway (46.4%). One hundred percent of the attacks in the Gulf of Aden/Somalia region occurred on ships underway. The reasons for this are based upon the objective of the pirates and their methods of operation. Many pirate attacks in Southeast Asia are basically robberies where the pirates board a vessel and take anything of value that they can find (Murphy, 2009). Piracy in the Gulf of Aden/Somalia region is committed with the intent of holding the crew and cargo hostage until they are ransomed. Pirates in Southeast Asia are more likely to use small boats and attack their targets under the cover of darkness, while pirates in the Gulf of Aden/Somalia region use mother ships to enable them to travel far from shore, high levels of technology to navigate and to communicate with their handlers on the mainland, and heavy firepower to intimidate the ship's captain and crew into surrendering.

While only sixteen crew members were taken hostage in 2008 in the Indonesia/Malacca Straits area, 815 crew members became hostages in the Gulf of Aden/Somalia theater. Guns and rocket-propelled grenades were used in 102 of the 111 attacks in the Gulf of Aden/Somalia region (in seven cases weapons were not reported or not observed), while knives were the weapons of choice in Indonesia/Malacca Straits (ICC IMB, 009a).

Piratical Tactics and Use of Technology

Mohamed Mohamed, an analyst for BBC Somalia, states that pirate gangs are usually composed of three different types of pirate:

> Ex-fishermen . . . considered the brains of the operation because they know the sea
>
> Ex-militiamen . . . considered the muscle, having fought for various Somali clan warlords
>
> The technical experts . . . computer geeks [who] know how to operate the hi-tech equipment . . . satellite phones, GPS and military hardware. (Hunter, 2008)

Davis (2008) describes the typical Somali pirate attack as follows:

> [They attack in] small, high-powered boats capable of out maneuvering larger cargo ships . . . Somali pirates often board vessels wearing fatigues carrying military-style weapons, specialized GPS,

and communications systems. Once onboard, they quickly seize control of the vessel and begin stealing cargo, shipboard electronics equipment, and personal items and money from the crew. In several instances, ships attempted to out run the pirates . . . with the Somali's faster boats, the attempt is often pointless. Aiming a Rocket Propelled Grenade (RPG) at the vessel, they order the ship to stop. (pp. 120–121)

Another improvement in maritime engineering has greatly benefited the pirates. Due to the increased use of technology and automation to run a large ship, smaller crews are needed. Most large ships operate with only twenty to thirty unarmed crew, so it is relatively easy for a half-dozen armed pirates to take control of the ship. As Davis (2008) writes:

> Even though the cargo ship is much larger than the pirate boat, just a few sailors operate them. If attacked by an RPG, the ship becomes vulnerable to fire and that's one thing no sailor wants. If a ship burns, there's nowhere to go. When combating a fire, the ship must stop or else the prevailing wind caused by the forward motion of the vessel feeds the fire, making matters worse. The captain generally has two choices: risk catastrophic damage to the vessel, risk crew safety and stop, or, protect the ship and stop. . . . The ship will always stop and the pirates know that." (p. 121)

Review of Attack Data for 2008 and First Quarter 2009

In 2008, pirates based in Somalia attacked maritime shipping in the Gulf of Aden, the Arabian Sea, and in the Indian Sea off the east coast of Somalia. Since the International Maritime Bureau, in both their quarterly and annual reports on worldwide piracy, only differentiates between acts of piracy in the Gulf of Aden and in Africa (Somalia), I will base my data analysis on the areas they identify. It is entirely possible that, due to the increased mobility of Somalian pirates, some attacks listed as being off the coast of Kenya can also be attributed to this menace to navigation and commerce, as can be attacks on shipping in the Red Sea. Of the 111 attacks during 2008, nintey-two (82.9%) took place in the Gulf of Aden (ICC International Maritime Bureau, 2009a).

In 2008, the International Maritime Bureau reported that ninety-two attacks occurred in the Gulf of Aden and that, of the total, thirty-two (34.8%) were successful in that the targeted vessel was boarded, while another fifty-eight vessels escaped from the pirates by utilizing a variety of means (attacks by pirates on seventeen vessels came to an end upon the intervention of military forces conducting anti-piracy patrols in the Gulf, and thirty-one vessels managed to escape the pirates by employing evasive maneuvers and/or anti-piracy measures). The attacks took place almost entirely during times of daylight with the median time of attack being 11:03 A.M. local time. Following their capture, five vessels were abandoned by the pirates as a direct result of military intervention, which followed the report of the attack. In the case of the seizure of the fishing vessel *Lina 2,* the pirates left the vessel after shooting its master and stealing three Zodiac boats (ICC International Maritime Bureau, 2009a, pp. 56–57). Of the vessels held for ransom, sixteen were taken to Eyl and one to Bosasso. Seventeen of the hijacked vessels were ransomed from the pirates by the end of 2008 and the remainder are thought to be still under the control of the pirates. The types of vessels attacked in this location ran the gamut with twenty-five classified as bulk cargo carriers; seventeen general cargo; seventeen chemical tankers; fifteen tankers; six container vessels; three fishing vessels; two tugs and two passenger vessels; and one each in the category of heavy load carrier, LPG (liquefied petroleum gas) tanker, vehicle carrier, dhow, and yacht (ICC International Maritime Bureau, 2009a).

Although there were significantly fewer attacks reported off the coast of Somalia, the pirates experienced much more success there. In 2008, nineteen vessels were attacked in this vast area and ten (52.6%) were successfully hijacked by the pirates. The other nine escaped from the pirates by employing evasive maneuvers and/or anti-piracy tactics. As opposed to the attacks in the Gulf of Aden, the military did not account for any cases where their intervention forced the pirates to withdraw from an attack. There was, however, one successful case of a military intervention after a vessel was seized, which resulted in the pirates abandoning the ship. As was the case in attacks in the Gulf of Aden, almost all took place during daylight with the median time of attack being 12:32 P.M. local time. Vessel types attacked off the Somali coast included three each in the categories of fishing vessel, container ship, and general cargo carrier; two bulk carriers and two tankers; and one each classified as barge, chemical tanker, roll-on/roll-off (Ro-Ro) carrier, barge carrier, tug, yacht, and one vessel with classified as unknown (ICC International Maritime Bureau, 2009a).

Piratical attacks surged in the first quarter of 2009 when compared to 2008 as a whole. While there were 111 total attacks in 2008, fifty-seven attacks in the area were reported during the first quarter of 2009. Of these, thirty-seven attacks (64.9%) took place in the Gulf of Aden, while the remaining twenty occurred off the east coast of Somalia (ICC International Maritime Bureau, 2009b).

In the Gulf of Aden during the first quarter of 2009, five of the thirty-seven attacks against maritime interests were successful (13.5%). All five seized ships were taken to the Somali port of Eyl where they were held for ransom. Of these, two were released presumably following payment to the pirates. Thirty-two ships were able to evade boarding and capture by the pirates, twenty (62.5%) employed evasive maneuvers or anti-piracy tactics, while the attacks on the twelve others were thwarted by intervention by the military coalition patrolling the Gulf. In three instances the military not only drove the pirates from the targeted vessel but was able to capture the pirates in the act. As was the case in 2008, only three attacks (8%) took place under the cover of darkness. The median time of attack was 10:35 A.M. local time. Again the vessel types attacked ran the gamut with thirteen being classified as bulk cargo carriers (one, the *S Venus,* was attacked twice on the same day (1/1/09) once at 7:30 A.M. and again at 2:05 P.M.); eight were tankers; six general cargo carriers; two chemical tankers and two product tankers; and one each LPG tanker, roll-on/roll-off vessel, and yacht; and one, the German FGS *Spessart,* was a supply vessel assisting the coalition efforts against piracy in the Gulf (this attack was thwarted by military intervention and the pirates were captured) (ICC International Maritime Bureau, 2009b).

The first quarter of 2009 saw no attacks on shipping off the eastern coast of Somalia during January, February, and the first part of March. This could be attributable to sea and/or weather conditions at that time of year. Attacks on shipping commenced on March 10 and, of the twenty attacks that month, five (25%) were successful. The masters of the fifteen ships eluding capture attributed their success to evasive maneuvers and/or anti-piracy measures. As was the case in 2008, the coalition forces were unavailable to intercede in a piracy attack. Of the twenty attacks, seventeen took place during daylight, with one at night and two with no times reported. The median time reported was 11:17 A.M. local time. Of the vessels attacked, the majority (six) were classified as bulk cargo carriers; three were general cargo vessels (one, the *Ryu Gyong,* was attacked twice—on March 20 and on March 23); two each were listed as chemical tankers, container ships, and fishing vessels; and one attack took place on a catamaran, a dhow, a research vessel, a ro-ro, and a yacht (ICC International Maritime Bureau, 2009b).

MV *Faina*

On September 26, 2008, the MV *Faina* was about 200 miles off the Somalian coast in the Indian Ocean steaming towards its destination of Mombasa, Kenya when it was approached by three speed-boats. The pirates boarded the boat and the ship's communication was cut off—a tactic common with Somali pirates (Gettleman, 2008a). The *Faina* may have appeared to be the type of vessel favored for attack by the pirates: it was large and slow moving and it was an easy target, but the pirates got more than they bargained for both in media attention and in attention by the navies of both Russia and the United States. The *Faina* was carrying what was described to port officials as "project cargo," which usually means heavy machinery, but it actually carried a surprising load of arms: "33 T-72 Soviet-era tanks, 150 grenade launchers, six antiaircraft guns and heaps of ammunition" (Gettleman and Ibrahim, 2009). When news of its cargo spread there was immediate concern that the arms would be taken by the pirates and used to fuel the Somalian insurgency further.

That the *Faina* was carrying arms was unknown to the pirates at the time of the attack. A spokesman for the pirates, Sugule Ali, was quoted by Gettleman (2008b) as stating, "We just saw a big ship . . . so we stopped it." The *Faina's* cargo was valued at approximately $30 million, and many people familiar with the situation speculate that Kenya was to be merely the transshipment point and that the arms would eventually find their way into the southern Sudan (Gettleman, 2008b).

Officially, the Ukrainian arms were bought by the Kenyan government, which is one of America's closest allies in Africa. "'This is a big loss for us,' said Alfred Mutua, a spokesman for the Kenyan government. But, as Mr. Mutua was quick to add, since the ship had not reached Kenya yet, the cargo was still the Ukrainians' responsibility" (Gettleman, 2008a).

Given that each of the T-72 tanks weigh more than 80,000 pounds and that the pirates have no experience offloading or handling that type of machinery—nor do they have access to a port that does—holding the *Faina* and its crew for ransom was their only option (Gettleman, 2008a). There was a concern, however, that the pirates would transfer the more easily handled small arms to supply boats that would carry them to shore. To protect against this possibility, a cordon of both U.S. and Russian naval ships surrounded the *Faina* for the duration of her seizure. The spokesman for the pirates, Mr. Sugule, stated to Gettleman (2008b) that "the pirates were not interested in the weapons and had no plans to sell them to Islamist insurgents battling Somalia's weak transitional government."

Towards the end of January 2009, negotiations between the pirates and the shipping company were being finalized. In the beginning of February, a price of $3.2 million for the release of the *Faina* had been agreed to and the money was parachuted to the vessel. On February 4, 2009, the last pirates left the *Faina*. "'The fact that this case took so long, that's not good,' said one of the pirates, Isse Mohammed, in a telephone interview. 'But we got the cash in hand, and that's good. That's what we're interested in'" (Gettleman and Ibrahim, 2009). The pirate further added that he and his fellows would continue to hunt ships because "that's our business" (Gettleman and Ibrahim, 2009). The *Faina* was released to continue her journey, along with her entire lethal cargo, to Mombasa, Kenya.

MV *Sirius Star*

On November 15, 2008, the Very Large Crude Carrier (VLCC) *Sirius Star* was steaming 450 miles southeast of Kenya when pirates attacked. "Everyone remarked on the exceptionally beautiful day, no wind and the sea like a millpond," said Chief Engineer Peter French (Chapman and Gallagher, 2009).

It was thought that the *Sirius Star* was operating in a safe area, far enough from the Somali coast that it was out of the pirates' reach. The pirates managed to adjust to the new distances involved in attacking their prey through the use of a mother ship. The mother ship in this case was an ocean going tugboat that was hijacked in Nigeria and taken thousands of miles around the Cape of Good Hope. The tug allowed the pirates to prey on shipping hundreds of miles off the east African coast and also helped to make surviving the large swells of the Indian Ocean somewhat tolerable (Frodl, 2009). They had placed high-speed rubber boats on the tug's deck and, according to Frodl (2009), "crept up on the lumbering tanker most likely at night from behind. Tankers used to move at 22 knots, but to save fuel now move only at 15 knots or less" (Frodl, 2009, p. 18).

The pirates, using two speedboats and twenty-five raiders (Roberts, 2009), attacked the vessel from the rear where they were less likely to be spotted by crew members and were unable to be detected by the ship's radar. This is due to a situation referred to as 'sector blanking' where the view to the stern of the ship is blocked from the radar due to the positioning of the radar antenna forward of the ship's stack. The large stack effectively blocks out a pie-shaped section of coverage of between 20 and 25 degrees (Burnett, 2002, p. 147).

According to an account of the hijacking given to Chapman and Gallagher (2009), the Chief Engineer of the *Sirius Star,* Peter French, explained that the ship's captain, Marek Niski, upon seeing that his ship was under attack, first ordered that an attempt be made to repel the pirates by using the ship's fire hoses. That proved to be insufficient as a deterrent and the pirates approached the tanker in a speedboat, placed a ladder on her hull, and scaled the twelve feet to the lower deck. Seeing that the pirates were armed with AK-47s and rocket-propelled grenades, the captain ordered the crew to stand down. One of the pirates entered the ship's bridge after firing a warning shot and ordered the captain to stop the ship. Niski refused the order and stated that a sudden stop would damage the ship's engines. The pirate's two boats and their fuel barge were lifted onto the *Sirius Star* by the ship's crane and Niski was ordered to sail for Somalia. During the days that followed, the pirates took £4,000 in cash from the ship's safe and looted the crew's cabins searching for cash, electronics, and other property (Chapman and Gallagher, 2009).

The *Sirius Star* was the largest vessel ever hijacked. The supertanker is owned by a subsidiary of Saudi Arabian-based Saudi Aramco, Vela International Marine Ltd. It is a ship, at a length of over 1,000 feet, longer than three football fields and, at 300,000 tons, heavier than three U.S. Navy aircraft carriers (Cable News Network, 2009; Frodl, 2009). The *Sirius Star* cost more than $140 million to build and, on the day that she was hijacked, had a load of crude worth more than $110 million (Frodl, 2009). A supertanker like the *Sirius Star* can, on one voyage, carry enough crude that could, when refined, supply enough fuel for all the cars and sport utility vehicles in the United States to burn in one day (Burnett, 2002, p. 12).

Many would think that a small boat approaching a vessel the size of the *Sirius Star* underway would be swamped and sunk either by the vessel's large bow or stern wakes, or by its prop wash but, due to advances in maritime architecture, they would be wrong. Large ships have displacement hulls that use the power of the ship to displace the water in front of it in order for the ship to make way. Smaller boats have planning hulls that, when the boat achieves speed, raise the boat's hull over the water. In years past, large ships had an angled bow that moved water aside but also raised the ship up so that it traveled at a slight pitch with its stern squatting in the water; this produced large bow and stern wakes (larger for increasingly large vessels) as well as a large amount of whitewater prop wash and amounted to a waste of fuel in that the ship was using a lot of energy plowing through the water. Naval architects studied the issue and designed a modification to the ship's bow. The modification normally cannot be noticed unless the ship is without cargo, but it amounts to a bulbous protrusion on the bottom of the bow below the water line. This modification helps the ship ride more evenly and efficiently. It reduces the amount of water displaced by the ship and thus makes it significantly more efficient (Burnett, 2002). According to Burnett (2002):

> The bulbous bow, now found on most vessels, probably has saved shipping companies more money in the long term than any other recent development in naval architecture. But it has also been a boon to predators planning to hijack a ship. Without a midship's wave and stern wake it has become considerably easier for a speedboat to tie up alongside or onto the stern while a vessel is underway. (pp. 251–252)

Many would also think that, even if pirates can get to the sides or stern of a VLCC or other large vessel, it would be almost impossible for them to get up on the deck. They would again be mistaken. While it would still be difficult to board many large vessels amidships, there is an easier way—go to the stern. Not only do you avoid the gaze of crew members, but you can avoid being spotted by the radar. In addition, the deck is closer to the water at the stern. As Burnett (2002) explained:

> The sunken deck, the poop deck, that shorter deck behind the accommodation block, is cut away and drops four meters [12 feet] below the main cargo deck and . . . is much closer to the water than expected. The distance from the water to this deck is only about three and a half meters [10.5 feet]. . . . Anyone standing on the bow of a fishing boat or a large speedboat could be up and over the railing . . . in seconds. (p. 77)

The pirates took the *Sirius Star* to Somalia and anchored the huge ship within three miles of the coast without grounding her, which, according to Frodl, "proved the experts wrong: no ship is too big to hijack and steer safely home" (Frodl, 2009, p. 18). Once the pirates had settled in on their catch, they spent time "constantly chew[ing] the mind-bending drug khat; opened fire on deck with Kalashnikov rifles; used computers to look at internet porn; [and] panicked after mistaking a lighthouse for another ship attacking them; . . . the only one injured was a pirate accidentally shot in the arm by a friend" (Roberts, 2009). When their fellow pirate was shot in the arm the pirates gave him no help; it was left to the crew of the *Sirius Star* to bandage him. When informed that he needed to go ashore for treatment, the other pirates refused (Chapman and Gallagher, 2009).

Negotiations between the pirates and the shipping company continued through the end of 2008. Finally, on January 3, 2009, a deal was agreed to and several days later, after a plane flew over the tanker to count the crew, two pink capsules (containing U.S. currency) were parachuted into the water near the ship. The pirates retrieved the money and, with the help of Captain Niski, it was counted and distributed to the pirates (Chapman and Gallagher, 2009). Although the pirates originally demanded $25 million for the *Sirius Star,* the final ransom paid was $3.5 million (Cable News Network, 2009).

The pirates were jubilant that their hijacking was a success but their happiness did not last long. When the twenty-seven members of the "Central Region Coastguard" sped toward the shore, one boat containing eight pirates sank, killing five of them (Rice and Hassan, 2009). Many theories arose as to what happened in the boat, and the best explanation was given to CNN by one of the pirates involved:

> "Other pirates on the shore wanted a tip from the pirates on the *Sirius Star,* so they started to fire in the air as our people approached the land," Libaan Jaama told CNN. "When our pirates heard the shots, they thought that they would be robbed, so they tried to return to the tanker. In that quick turn the boat capsized. (Cable News Network, 2009)

The mourning for the dead pirates was to be short lived also. Robert Wright of the *Financial Times of London* describes the scene in Hobyo, the southern Somali town where the tanker was moored:

> After the ransom for the *Sirius Star* . . . [was paid,] an impromptu beach party started near Hobyo. . . . The partygoers had come for their share of the $3m ransom. . . . There are carefully worked out formulae determining how much is paid to everyone, from the lowliest guards to gang leaders. (Wright, 2009)

MV *Maersk Alabama*

The 508-foot long United States flagged *Maersk Alabama* was hijacked by four pirates early on Wednesday, April 8, 2009. The 17,000-ton ship was carrying food aid bound for Rwanda, Somalia, and Uganda when it was attacked hundreds of kilometers off the east coast of Somalia (Pitman and Jakes, 2009). The crew of the *Alabama* initially tried using fire hoses to keep the hijackers from boarding but that was unsuccessful. Pirates scrambled on the ship with ropes and hooks from a small boat. "As the pirates shot into the air, Capt. [Richard] Phillips told his crew to lock themselves in a cabin and surrendered himself to safeguard his men, crew members said" (Pitman and Jakes, 2009). Most importantly, however, the crew was able to disable the ship at the time the pirates were coming on board. The pirates initially seized the crew of twenty, but the crew was able to regain control of the ship. At one point, the crew ambushed and held captive one of the pirates, releasing him twelve hours later in what they believed to be an exchange for the *Alabama's* captain, who was being held by the pirates (Mazzetti and Otterman, 2009). Ken Quinn, the second mate on the ship, stated: "We returned him but they didn't return the captain" (Mazzetti and Otterman, 2009).

The pirates then took Phillips and fled the ship in one of the *Alabama's* lifeboats "a twenty-two-foot long covered vessel that has a motor and is large enough for at least twenty people and is equipped with food and water for at least a few days" (Mazzetti and Otterman, 2009).

The four pirates were split between two clans, one from southern Somalia and one from Puntland. It appears that pirates had been attacking another vessel when the *Alabama* came into view. The four attackers were then dispatched to the *Alabama* in a small boat to commandeer it. This "may explain why there were only four pirates aboard the *Alabama*. In previous hijackings, pirates had swarmed merchant ships with four to five boats" (*The New York Times,* 2009).

The crew had radioed for help from military vessels in the area but, at the time of the attack, the closest patrol vessel was about 300 nautical miles away, according to a navy spokesman (Mazzetti and Otterman, 2009).

By Thursday (4/9/09), a United States Navy destroyer, the USS *Bainbridge,* was on scene and a spokesman for Maersk was quoted as stating that the "Navy has command of the situation" and is in contact with the lifeboat, which has been 'disabled' and is now adrift" (Mazzetti and Otterman, 2009). The pirates were demanding $2 million for the release of Captain Phillips (*The New York Times,* 2009).

The *Bainbridge* transferred an eighteen-man security team onto the *Alabama* and released it to travel to Mombasa, Kenya with its cargo and crew while the *Bainbridge* and the frigate *Halyburton* stood by the lifeboat containing Phillips and his four captors (Mazzetti and Otterman, 2009; Barnes and Sanders, 2009). It is interesting to note that the *Bainbridge* was named after the captain of the frigate *Philadelphia* which, in 1803, was captured by Barbary pirates and who, along with his crew of 300, was detained for ransom. United States president Thomas Jefferson refused to pay and the United States led a multinational force to fight the pirates (Beckman and Koh, 2009).

On Thursday, the captain of the *Bainbridge* began talking with the pirates "under instructions from FBI hostage negotiators on board the . . . destroyer." The pirates told the captain of the *Bainbridge* that they would kill Captain Phillips if attacked (Pitman and Jakes, 2009).

It seems that the pirates, now surrounded by three American warships and with helicopters and drones circling them, decided to radio for assistance of their own. According to one report:

> [A] group of pirates on a hijacked German ship attempted to aid their comrades . . . but they were forced to return to the Somali coast when they failed to locate the drifting lifeboat. 'We almost got lost because we could not find the bearing of the lifeboat,' [a pirate] told Reuters. (Kovaleski and Goodnough, 2009)

Obviously, the United States Navy would do all in its power to prevent other vessels from entering the area around the lifeboat and providing any assistance to the pirates since the "U.S. negotiating position will grow stronger . . . as the pirates run low on supplies" (Barnes and Sanders, 2009).

On Friday, Captain Phillips decided to take matters into his own hands. He jumped overboard and tried to swim from the lifeboat to the nearby naval vessels. The pirates fired their AK-47s at him as he tried to swim away and then "beat him after dragging him back aboard the boat" (Barnes and Miller, 2009). Although Phillips' escape attempt may have been an opportunity for the U.S. Navy to take command of the situation, they had no knowledge that Phillips was going to attempt an escape and no way to assist him when he did. Additionally, although a military special operations team had been mobilized, it had not yet reached the *Bainbridge*. The pirates' response to the escape attempt illustrated how dangerous they actually were (Barnes and Miller, 2009).

Somali elders from Gara'ad attempted to negotiate with the Americans concerning the release of Captain Phillips and proposed a solution in which the pirates would release Phillips without receiving a ransom if the pirates would be allowed to escape. The Americans, however, insisted that the pirates release Phillips and be tried for piracy in the Puntland region of Somalia. The elders refused, according to *The New York Times* (2009), and negotiations with the elders ended. By late Saturday, negotiations with the pirates themselves had broken down. The stumbling block was, Somali officials said, "The Americans' insistence the pirates be arrested and brought to justice" (Pitman and Jakes, 2009).

By the time that negotiations had broken down, the situation on the lifeboat was becoming more desperate for the pirates. Abdi Wali Alitaar, a businessman who runs a maritime security firm in the port city of Bosasso was quoted as stating that the pirates were growing tired and may be ready to give up. "They're probably saying to themselves that they've made a very big mistake by taking this American and now they are wondering how they will survive," he said (Barnes and Sanders, 2009). The pirates had run out of food and water and had agreed to accept a delivery from the *Bainbridge.* A small boat made several trips to the lifeboat to deliver supplies (McFadden and Shane, 2009).

On Saturday, members of the Navy SEALs "were flown to the *Bainbridge* by fixed-wing aircraft. They parachuted into the sea with inflatable boats and were picked up" (McFadden and Shane, 2009). The first contingent was onboard the *Bainbridge* at 5:10 A.M. and the second, larger contingent parachuted in at 6:30 P.M. Once there, the SEALs began to position themselves and readied small, Zodiac-style inflatable boats to maneuver near the lifeboat that held the captain and the pirates. The SEAL commander also deployed snipers to target the pirates and shoot them if they tried to harm Captain Phillips. According to a military official, the SEAL snipers had multiple opportunities to shoot the pirates but they "held off . . . hoping they could persuade the pirates to give themselves up peacefully" (Barnes and Miller, 2009).

At 6:30 A.M. Sunday, when the SEALs approached the lifeboat containing Phillips, a pirate, later identified as Abdi Wali Abdulqadir Muse, asked if he could be taken to the *Bainbridge* (Barnes and Miller, 2009). He was suffering from a stab wound on his hand from the struggle during the *Alabama's* takeover, and the wound had become infected. "The military took the pirate aboard, gave him a clean set of clothes and treated his wound" (Barnes and Miller, 2009). The military officials talked the pirate into speaking to the others by radio in order to say he was safe and was being treated well and to encourage their surrender—he did so but they refused.

As Sunday dragged on the ocean became more turbulent and navy officers offered to throw a line to the lifeboat and tow it behind the *Bainbridge,* telling the pirates they would be towed to calmer waters. The pirates agreed and were initially towed 200 feet behind the destroyer. The ride was still choppy and the line was shortened to seventy-five to eighty feet, with the pirates being told that the closer they were to the destroyer, the calmer the ride would be.

Although now in the calm wake of the ship, the pirates appeared to grow more desperate, perhaps feeling that they had lost control of the situation. Additionally, some believe that they were suffering from withdrawal from khat—as withdrawal from the stimulant can cause depression.

The pirates appeared agitated and, before breaking off their last communication with the *Bainbridge,* reiterated that: "If we don't get what we are demanding, we will kill the captain" (Barnes and Miller, 2009).

Shortly thereafter, the snipers saw their opportunity when two pirates moved away from Phillips and peered from a hatch while the third pointed his weapon at the captain's back. Believing that imminent harm was about to be done to Phillips, the snipers fired (Barnes and Miller, 2009). According to one account of the shooting, "It took only three remarkable shots . . . one by each of the snipers firing at a distance at dusk, using night-vision scopes, the officials said. Within minutes, rescuers slid down ropes from the *Bainbridge,* climbed aboard the lifeboat and found the three pirates dead. They then untied Captain Phillips . . ." (McFadden and Shane, 2009).

Aftermath

On Saturday (4/11/09), the *Alabama* arrived in Mombasa, but the crew was not permitted to leave the ship because "the F.B.I.—whose New York office has been charged with investigating the seizure—considered the vessel a crime scene" (*The New York Times,* 2009). The crew was permitted off the ship after it had been processed.

Captain Phillips stayed onboard the *Bainbridge* to be taken to Mombasa and reunited with his crew, but that was not to be the case. The *Bainbridge* was diverted in order to assist another ship that was being hijacked in the Indian Ocean off of Somalia. This delayed his arrival in Kenya, and he missed meeting his crew. Eventually, Captain Phillips was flown back to the United States to be with his family in Vermont. After his release, Captain Phillips said of the SEALs who rescued him: "They're superheroes. They're impossible men doing an impossible job, and they did the impossible with me" (Zezima and Blumenthal, 2009). "I'm not a hero, the military is" Captain Phillips stated. "I'm just a bit part in this story. I'm a small part. I'm a seaman doing the best he can, like all the other seamen out there" (Zezima and Blumenthal, 2009).

The pirate who had surrendered to naval personnel in order to be treated for the infected wound on his hand has been identified as Abdi Wali Abdulqadir Muse. He was from Galka'yo, which is approximately 450 miles north of Mogadishu. He was brought to New York to face trial mainly "because the FBI office there has a history of handling cases in Africa involving major crimes against Americans, such as the al Qaeda bombings of two U.S. embassies in East Africa in 1998" (Associated Press, 2009).

Hot Pursuit into Somali Territorial Waters

One major problem with piracy in Somalia was the pirates' ability to take the seized vessel into Somali territorial waters and thus be free of pursuing vessels. This is due to a quirk in the Law of the Seas that prevents warships from entering the sovereign territory of another nation without being invited to do so. In Somalia's case, with no real government in power, permission to pursue into territorial Somali waters was impossible to obtain. This gave the pirates a refuge for their hijacked ships until a ransom could be paid.

On December 2, 2008, the United Nations unanimously passed Resolution 1846 (2008), which stated that

> during the next 12 months States and regional organizations coop-
> erating with the Somali Transitional Federal Government (TFG)
> may enter Somalia's territorial waters and use 'all necessary
> means'—such as deploying naval vessels and military aircraft, as
> well as seizing and disposing of boats, vessels, arms, and related
> equipment used for piracy—to fight piracy and armed robbery at
> sea off the Somali coast . . ." (Security Council, 2008).

An International Coalition to Battle Piracy

The Gulf of Aden, and now the coast of Somalia, "is patrolled by an anti-piracy flotilla from the European Union and an American-led coalition of ships, plus warships from Iran, Russia, India, China, Japan, and other nations" (Mazzetti and Otterman, 2009). The central operating component of this coalition is Combined Task Force (CTF) 150. CTF 150's mission is, according to Pegg (2009):

> To ensure the security of the strategic sea lanes of communication
> (SLOC) between the Mediterranean and the oil-producing regions
> of the Middle East, principally the Persian Gulf. Essentially, the
> interdiction is to ensure that sea trade and the flow of petroleum in
> the region is secure from any terrorist threats that might exist or
> have the potential to develop. (pp. 34–35)

The CTF usually consists of fourteen to fifteen warships and, since it was formed in 2002, "has boarded numerous vessels, includ-ing dhows, fishing boats, and tankers in its area of responsibility, found and confiscated illicit drugs, and conducted anti-piracy and cordon operations off the coast of Somalia" (Pegg, 2009, p. 35).

Some have expressed the opinion that countries have entered the coalition in order to "flex their muscles" militarily in a region where they may want to exercise control at a later date. China has added warships to the area much to the dismay of its regional competitor India (*Times of London Editorial,* 2008). India has joined the coalition also and:

> Has flexed its maritime muscles by destroying a pirate boat in the Gulf of Aden as part of an international effort to fight the rising tide of hijacks of merchant shipping. . . . Commander Nirad Sinha, a naval spokesman, said the Indian ship had asked the pirate boat— bristling with rocket-propelled grenade launchers—to stop but it responded by threatening to blow up the frigate. (Lamont and Wright, 2008)

Japan, a pacifist nation under its constitution, has deployed two warships into the area, upsetting some who fear a resurgence of Japanese military power. According to Dickie (2009):

> The two destroyers . . . are heading to waters off Somalia as an 'emergency step' of an existing law that allows the [Maritime Self Defense Force] to assist the coast guard in safeguarding Japanese lives and property at sea. The warships . . . will operate under orders essentially limiting them to escorting commercial vessels either owned by Japanese companies, having Japanese nationals on board, or carrying Japanese cargo. (Dickie, 2009)

Who Will Try the Pirates?

Until recently, when pirates were apprehended by coalition forces, they were stripped of their weapons and brought back to Somalia where they were dumped on the beach (Gettleman, 2009b). However, when dealing with the problem of piracy in Somalia, everyone agrees that the pirates must be arrested and tried for their crimes—the problem is where. There are three possible remedies: try the pirates in Somalia; try the pirates in the country whose nation seized them; or find a neutral site for a trial. To try the pirates in Somalia, a failed state and one without a fully functioning government would, at this point, be impossible. Bringing the pirates to the country of the coalition member that detained them would be logistically difficult but it can, and has (in the case of France and the United States), been done. Taking a pirate into another country for trial could be difficult if the pirate were to be found not guilty and then attempt to seek asylum there. A neutral site on which to hold the pirates and have a trial is generally considered to be the best option and Kenya, located to the south of Somalia, has been chosen. The Kenyan government was somewhat eager to deal with the pirates since they were destroying the Kenyan shipping industry through their actions. Additionally, under its agreement with coalition forces, Kenya has agreed to try the pirates in return for assistance in modernizing its antiquated court system (Gettleman, 2009b).

Summary/Conclusions

The jihadist knows no borders and has a global perspective, and al Qaeda will attack wherever they sense a lack of preparedness, weakness, or where they have local allies (Murphy, 2008). All of this holds true when discussing terrorism and piracy at the Horn of Africa. Talk has abounded amongst jihadists about the possibility of sinking ships in order to close narrow shipping areas such as the Bab el-Mandeb (which leads from the Red Sea to the Gulf of Aden and accounts for the transit of 3.3 million barrels of oil daily (Luft and Korin, 2004)) or the Strait of Hormuz (through which 15 million barrels of oil travel daily (Luft and Korin, 2004)). Such a strike would have a huge economic effect on Western interests and on their economies. Many terrorists have stated that Yemen and the Horn of Africa region represent a critical point where they can attack western interests and impact western economies (Murphy, 2008).

Nearly all of the writers on this topic acknowledge that there is only one solution to the piracy problem in the area around the Horn of Africa—government control and normalcy in Somalia. Roger Middleton, a consultant researcher for the Africa Programme at Chatham House, London, put it best when he stated:

> The most powerful weapon against piracy will be peace and opportunity in Somalia. . . . Ignoring Somalia and its problems is not an option that will end well. Piracy is a very real threat to seafarers, the shipping industry, the environment, international trade, and most of all Somalia and Somalis. (Middleton, 2008)

References

Al-Shawthabi, A. R. 2009. Three Pirates Killed Two Injured in Clashes with Yemeni Coast Guard Forces. *Yemen Post Newspaper,* April 28, 2009.

Retrieved April 28, 2009, from: *http://www.yemenpost.net/Detail123456789.aspx?ID=3&SubID=629&MainCat=3*

Associated Press. 2009. Somalian pirate arrives in N.Y. The Philadelphia Inquirer, April 21, 2009. Retrieved April 21, 2009, from: *http://www.philly.com/inquirer/world_us/43327972.html*

Barnes, J. E., and G. Miller. 2009. Moment to shoot Somali pirates had come. *Los Angeles Times,* April 14, 2009. Retrieved April 15, 2009, from: *http://www.latimes.com/news/nationworld/la-fg-pirates14-2009apr14*

Barnes, J. E., and E. Sanders. 2009. U.S. hostage flees Somalia pirates, is caught. *Los Angeles Times,* April 14, 2009. Retrieved April 15, 2009, from: *http://www.latimes.com/news/nationworld/world/la-fg-somali-pirates 11-2009*

Beckman, R., and T. Koh. 2009. Pirates and the Law. *The New York Times,* April 21, 2009. Retrieved April 21, 2009, from: *http://www.nytimes.com/2009/04/22/opinion/22iht-edkoh.html*

Blitz, J., and R. Wright. 2008. Borderless Boarders. *Financial Times,* November 22, 2008. Retrieved April 28, 2009, from: *http://www.lexisnexis.com.ez.lib.jjay.cuny.edu/us/lnacademic/search/newssubmitForm.do*

Burnett, J. S. 2002. *Dangerous Waters: Modern piracy and terror on the high seas.* New York: Plume, The Penguin Group.

Cable News Network. 2009. Exclusive: Pirate tells how comrades drowned. January 12, 2009. Retrieved March 7, 2009, from: *http://www.cnn.com/WORLD/africa/01/12/somalia.pirates/index.html#cnnS TCOther1*

Chapman, A., and I. Gallagher. 2009. Pirates Aboard: Sailor from rescued tanker tells how Somali raiders brought guns, grenades—and goats. The Daily Mail and Mail on Sunday (London), January 25, 2009. Retrieved April 15, 2009, from: *http://www.lexus/nexus.com.ez.lib.jjay.cuny.edu/us/inacademic/returnToKey=20_T6476949732*

CIA World Factbook–Somalia. n.d. Retrieved March 15, 2009, from: *www.cia.gov: https://www.cia.gov/library/publications/the-world-factbook/geos/so.html*

Cummins, C., L. Radnofsky, and J. W. Miller. 2009. French Forces Detain 11 Pirates in Attack on 'Mother Ship'. *The Wall Street Journal,* April 15, 2009. Retrieved April 15, 2009, from: *http://www.online.wsj.com/article/SB123980523765821121.html*

Davis, A. M. 2008. *Terrorism and the Maritime Transportation System: Are we on a collision course?* Livermore, CA: Wing-Span Press.

Dickie, M. 2009. Japan stretches idea of pacificism with anti-piracy mission. *Financial Times (London)*, March 14, 2009, , p. 3.

Economist. 2009. A nice safe haven for jihadists. January 31, 2009, p. 54.

Frodl, M. G. 2009. Choke Point: Hijacked super tanker exposes vulnerability of energy supplies. *National Defense,* March 2009, pp. 18–20.

Gettleman, J. 2008a. Somalia Pirates Capture Tanks and Unwanted Global Notice. *The New York Times,* September 27, 2008. Retrieved April 14, 2009, from: *http:www.nytimes.com/2008/09/27/world/africa/27pirates.html*

Gettleman, J. 2008b. Somali Pirates Tell Their Side: They Only Want Money. *The New York Times,* October 1, 2008. Retrieved April 21, 2009, from: *http://www.nytimes.com/2008/10/01/world/africa/01pirates.html*

Gettleman, J. 2009a. The most dangerous place in the world. *Foreign Policy,* March/April 2009, pp. 62–69.

Gettleman, J. 2009b. The West Turns to Kenya as Piracy Criminal Court. *The New York Times,* April 24, 2009. Retrieved April 25, 2009, from: *http://www.nytimes.com/2009/04/24/world/africa/24kenya.html*

Gettleman, J., and M. Ibrahim. 2009. Somali Pirates Get Ransom and Leave Arms Freighter. *The New York Times,* February 6, 2009. Retrieved April 14, 2009, from: *http://www.nytimes.com/2009/02/06/world/agfrica/06pirates.html*

Hunter, R. 2008. Somali pirates living the high life. BBC News, October 28, 2008. Retrieved March 5, 2009, from: *http://newsvote.bbc.co.uk/mpapps/pagetools/print/news.bbc.co.uk/1/hi/world/africa/765041*

Ibrahim, M. 2009. Somalia Adopts Islamic Law to Deter Insurgency. *The New York Times,* April 19, 2009. Retrieved April 21, 2009, from: *http://www.nytimes.com/2009/04/19/world/africa/19somalia.html*

ICC International Maritime Bureau. 2009a. *Piracy and Armed Robbery Against Ships: Annual Report (1 January–31 December 2008).* London: ICC International Maritime Bureau.

ICC International Maritime Bureau. 2009b. *Piracy and Armed Robbery Against Ships: First Quarter 2009.* London: ICC Maritime Bureau.

Isikoff, M. 2007. A Terrorist Walks Free. *Newsweek,* November 5, 2007, p. 39.

Jopson, B., and R. Wright. 2008. Pirates in shoot-out aboard arms ship. *Financial Times (London),* October 1, 2008, p. 13.

Knickmeyer, E. 2008. On a Vital Route, a Boom in Piracy; Somali Marauders Step Up Attacks in Gulf of Aden, Shipping Costs Soar. *The Washington Post,* September 27, 2008, p. A1.

Kovaleski, S. F., A. Goodnough. 2009. A Placid Man on Land, Caught in a Drama at Sea. *The New York Times,* April 11, 2009. Retrieved April 15, 2009, from: *http://www.nytimes.com/2009/04/11/world/africa/ 11pirates.html*

Lamont, J., and R. Wright. 2008. *Indian navy sinks pirate craft off Aden. Financial Times (London),* Retrieved March 14, 2009, from: *http://www.lexisnexis.com. ez.lib.jjay.cuny.edu/us/lnacademic/results/ docview/docview.do?docLinkInd=true&risb=21_T6477080684&format= GNBFI&sort=BOOLEAN&startDocNo=1&resultsUrlKey=29_T6477080688& cisb=22_T6477080687&treeMax=true&treeWidth=0&csi=293847& docNo=1:*

Langewiesche, W. 2004. *The outlaw sea: A world of freedom, chaos, and crime.* New York: North Point Press.

Lehr, P. 2009. Maritime Terrorism: Locations, Actors, and Capabilities. In R. Herbert-Burns, S. Bateman, and P. Lehr, *Lloyd's MIU Handbook of Maritime Security* (pp. 55–71). Boca Raton, FL: Auerbach Publications.

Luft, G., and A. Korin. 2004. Terrorism Goes to Sea. *Foreign Affairs,* November/December 2004, pp. 61–71.

Mazzetti, M., and S. Otterman. 2009. Standoff With Pirates Shows U.S. Power Has Limits. *The New York Times,* April 10, 2009. Retrieved April 15, 2009, from: *http://www.nytimes.com/2009/04/10/world/africa/ 10pirates.html*

McFadden, R. D., and S. Shane. 2009. In Rescue of Captain, Navy Kills 3 Pirates. *The New York Times,* April 14, 2009. Retrieved April 15, 2009, from: *http://www.nytimes.com/2009/04/13/world/africa/13pirates.html*

Middleton, R. 2008. *Piracy in Somalia: Threatening Global Trade, Feeding Local Wars.* London: Chatham House.

Murphy, M. N. 2009. *Small Boats, Weak States, Dirty Money: The challenge of piracy.* New York: Columbia University Press.

Murphy, M. N. 2008. *The Unwanted Challenge.* U.S. Naval Institute Proceedings, December 2008, 134(12), pp. 48–51. Retrieved March 31, 2009, from: *http://search.ebscohost.com.ez.lib.jjay.cuny.edu/ login.aspx?direct=true&db=aph&AN=35862123&site=ehost-live*

National Commission on Terrorist Attacks upon the United States. 2002. *The 9/11 Commission Report.* New York: W. W. Norton and Company.

Pegg, R. 2009. Maritime forces and security of merchant shipping in the Mediterranean Sea and northern Indian Ocean. In R. Herbert-Burns,

S. Bateman, and P. Lehr, *Lloyd's MIU Handbook of Maritime Security* (pp. 29–37). Boca Raton, FL: Auerbach Publications.

Pitman, T., and L. Jakes. 2009. Navy snipers kill 3 pirates, free U.S. captain held hostage. *The Globe and Mail,* April 13, 2009, p. A9.

Rice, X., and A. Hassan. 2009. Somalia: Death at sea: how pirates' triumph ended in disaster: Five drown after collecting ransom, but rewards are too great to deter hijackers. *The Guardian,* January 17, 2009, p. 25.

Roberts, L. 2009. Pirate Treasure: Exclusive Scots Hostage's Amazing Secret Pictures of His Gun-Toting Captors. *Scottish Daily Record and Sunday Mail,* February 1, 2009. Retrieved April 15, 2009, from EBSCO.

Security Council. 2008. Security Council Decides States, Regional Organizations May Use 'All Necessary Means' to Fight Piracy off Somali Coast for 12-Month Period. United Nations Department of Public Information, December 2, 2008. Retrieved March 5, 2009, from: *http://www.un.org/News/Press/docs//2008/sc9514.doc.htm*

The New York Times. 2009. Negotiations Break Down in Standoff With Pirates. April 12, 2009. Retrieved April 15, 2009, from: *http://www.nytimes.com/2009/04/12/world/africa/12somalia.html*

Times of London Editorial. 2008. China Sets Sail; Piracy has given Beijing a perfect pretext for power projection. *The Times (London),* December 23, 2008, p. 2.

World Tribune. 2008. Yemen coast guard forms unit to police pirates. September 22, 2008. Retrieved April 28, 2009, from: *http://www.worldtribune.com/worldtribune/WTARC/2008/me_yemen0544_09_21.asp*

Wright, R. 2009. Piracy brings rich booty to Somalia. *Financial Times,* March 2, 2009. Retrieved March 7, 2009, from: *http://www.ft.com/cms/s/0c99d484-0751-11de-9294-000077b07658,dwp_uuid=a99ba554-4*

Yemen Post. 2009. Released Yemeni Tanker Could Sink. April 28, 2009. Retrieved April 28, 2009, from: *http://www.yemenpost.net/Detail123456789.aspx?ID=3&SubID=634&MainCat=3*

Zezima, K., and M. L. Blumenthal. 2009. Rescued Captain Returns to Vermont Town. *The New York Times,* April 18, 2009. Retrieved April 21, 2009, from: *http://www.nytimes.com/2009/04/18/us/18captain.html*

CHAPTER 7

FUTURE CONSIDERATIONS AND CONCERNS

7.1
Maritime Terrorism

Risk and Liabiltiy

MICHAEL D. GREENBERG
PETER CHALK
HENRY H. WILLIS
IVAN KHILKO
DAVID S. ORTIZ

The Contemporary Threat of Maritime Terrorism

Intelligence analysts, law enforcement officials, and policymakers have become increasingly concerned in recent years about the possibility of terrorist groups carrying out attacks in the maritime realm. The Council for Security Cooperation in the Asia Pacific (CSCAP) Working Group has offered an expansive definition for the types of events that comprise maritime terrorism:

> . . . the undertaking of terrorist acts and activities (1) within the maritime environment, (2) using or against vessels or fixed platforms at sea or in port, or against any one of their passengers or personnel, (3) against coastal facilities or settlements, including tourist resorts, port areas and port towns or cities. (Quentin, 2003)

Yet despite the breadth of this definition, the world's oceans have not historically been a major locus of terrorist activity. Indeed, according to the RAND Terrorism Database, seaborne strikes have constituted only 2 percent of all international incidents over the last 30 years. What explains the apparent contradiction between current concerns regarding maritime terrorism and existing evidence of terrorist activity?

To answer this question, this chapter evaluates the potential threats of maritime terrorism. We begin by discussing the factors underscoring the current concern with this particular manifestation of militant extremism and the reasons that might motivate terrorists to undertake operations in a marine environment. We then briefly examine the main terrorist organizations that have actually operated at sea, summarizing some of the key strikes that have been linked to these various groups.

Factors Underscoring the Contemporary Perceived Threat of Maritime Terrorism: Vulnerability, Capability, and Intent

It should perhaps not be surprising that until now terrorists have neglected to exploit maritime targets. In the past, maritime terrorism did not correspond well to terrorists' available opportunities, capabilities, or intentions. Many terrorist organizations have neither been located near to coastal regions nor possessed the necessary means to extend their physical reach beyond purely local theaters. Even for those groups that did have a geographic opportunity, there are several problems associated with carrying out waterborne strikes that have, at least historically, worked to offset some of the tactical advantages of the maritime environment.[1]

Operating at sea requires terrorists to have mariner skills, access to appropriate assault and transport vehicles, the ability to mount and sustain operations from a non–land-based environment, and familiarity with certain specialist capabilities (for example, surface and underwater demolition techniques).[2] Limited resources have traditionally precluded such options being available to most groups.

---

1. Again, the advantages to terrorists of maritime settings include the fundamentally anarchic nature of "over the horizon" oceans, together with frequently lax security monitoring over coastal waters, riparian systems, and related facilities and infrastructure.
2. Anonymous Institute of Defense and Strategic Studies representative (2005). See also Wilkinson (1986) and Jenkins et al. (1986).

The inherently conservative nature of terrorists in terms of their chosen attack modalities compounds the constraints imposed by limited opportunities and lack of technical skills. Precisely because groups are constrained by ceilings in operational finance and skill sets, most have deliberately chosen to follow the course of least resistance—adhering to tried and tested methods that are known to work, which offer a reasonably high chance of success, and whose consequences can be relatively easily predicted. Stated more directly, in a world of finite human and material assets, the costs and unpredictability associated with expanding to the maritime realm have typically trumped any potential benefits to terrorists that might have been garnered from initiating such a change in operational direction.

A further consideration has to do with the nature of maritime targets themselves. Since many maritime targets are largely out of sight (something that is particularly true of oceangoing commercial vessels), they are relatively speaking also out of mind. Attacking a ship is, thus, less likely to elicit the same publicity—in either scope or immediacy—as striking land-based venues, which, because they are fixed and typically located near some urban conglomeration, are far more media-accessible (although as is argued below, this may be less true with respect to contingencies involving heavily laden cruise liners and ferries) (Wilkinson, 1986, p. 34; Jenkins et al., 1986, p. 65). This consideration is important, since terrorism, at root, is a tactic that can only be effective if it is able *visibly* to demonstrate its salience and relevance through the so-called propaganda of the deed.[3]

Despite these considerations, the perceived threat of maritime terrorism has risen markedly over the last several years and is now taking on a singular importance in terms of national and international counterterrorism planning.[4] This is particularly true of the United States, which has been at the forefront of attempts to strengthen the global regime of maritime security in the post-September 11 era. The reasons for this heightened level of apprehension are complex and multifaceted, but generally pertain to

---

3. For a discussion on this aspect of the terrorist phenomenon see Chalk (1996, Chapter One). Rather like the philosopher's conundrum regarding the unobserved tree that falls in a forest (i.e., does it make a sound?), one might raise a similar question regarding the effect of an unwitnessed and unpublicized terrorist attack: Does it really accomplish a political purpose?

4. Anonymous former British defense official and Department of Homeland Security Liaison attache (2005). See also Frittelli (2004, pp. 1–3); Wrightson (2005, pp. 1, 7).

concerns that can be grouped in terms of vulnerability, capability, and intent.

Vulnerability of Maritime Targets

The international community appears to have become progressively more cognizant of the general vulnerability of global shipping as a result of the largely unpoliced nature of the high seas, the fact that many littoral governments lack the resources—and in certain cases, the willingness—to enact serious programs of coastal surveillance, and the sheer esoteric character that typifies much of the oceanic environment. As Rupert Herbert-Burns of Lloyd's of London observes:

> The combination of the enormous scope, variety and "room for maneuver" offered by the physical and geographical realities of the [earth's] maritime environment . . . presents a sobering and uncomfortable reality . . . [W]hat compounds this reality further is that the commercial milieu that simultaneously affords . . . the ability to deploy, finance operations, tactical concealment, logistical fluidity and wealth of targets of opportunity—the commercial maritime industry—is itself numerically vast, complex, deliberately opaque and in a perpetual state of flux. (Herbert-Burns, 2005, p. 158)

Exacerbating international concern is the increased dependence of seaborne commercial traffic (which itself has risen markedly over the last five to ten years)[5] on passing through narrow and congested maritime choke points, where, owing to forced restrictions on speed and maneuverability, vessels remain highly vulnerable to offensive interception.[6] Such misgivings have been

---

5. More than 6 million containers enter U.S. ports every year, which accounts for nearly half of the world's present inventory (12–15 million containers are estimated to be moving on the world's oceans at any given point in time). See Sinai (2004, p. 49).

6. Key choke points of concern include the straits of Malacca, Bab el Mandeb, Hormuz, Bosporus, Dardanelles, Dover, and Gibraltar, and the Suez, Panama, and Keele canals. All of these waterways require ships to reduce speed significantly to ensure safe passage (in the Bosporus Strait, for instance, at least six accidents occur every 1 million transit miles); are vital to global commercial, passenger, and military shipping; and constitute viable locations from which to launch maritime attacks using contiguous land-based platforms. Anonymous former British defense official (2005). See also Köknar (2005).

especially palpable in light of moves by a growing number of shipping companies to replace full staffing complements with "skeleton" crews—sometimes numbering no more than half a dozen personnel—as a cost-cutting device. Although this practice has helped to lower overhead operating costs, it has also made gaining control of ships that much easier.

Certain vessels have also been highlighted as remaining particularly vulnerable to deliberate sabotage. As is discussed at greater length in the next chapter, passenger ferries are often singled out in this regard, largely because they tend to be characterized by extremely lax predeparture security screening of passengers, sail according to preset and widely available schedules, and, at least in the case of ships that transport vehicles, necessarily lack stabilizing bulkheads on their lower decks (anonymous UK customs and excise officials, Raytheon and Glenn Defense Marine analysts, and Control Risks Group officials, 2005).

Capability of Terrorist Groups

The inherent openness and opaqueness of the maritime environment has been viewed as particularly worrisome during a time when terrorist capabilities to act on a nonterritorial "footing" may be increasing. Two broad issues have been raised. First, various commentators have argued that the growth of offshore industries combined with the general popularity of maritime sports is serving to expand greatly the potential ease by which groups can gain basic skills and equipment for seaborne attacks.[7] The southern Philippines is often taken as a salient case in point. Here, suspected members of Jemaah Islamiyah (JI) are known to have enrolled in scuba courses run by commercial or resort diving companies, which members of the security forces widely believe have been undertaken for the specific purpose of facilitating underwater attacks against gas and oil pipelines off the coast of Mindanao.[8]

Second, there is a general fear that terrorists could overcome existing shortcomings in seaborne attack capabilities by contracting out to pirate syndicates. Most concern in this regard has focused on

---

7. See, for instance, Jenkins et al. (1986, p. 67).

8. Anonymous defense antiterrorism and intelligence officials and Anti-Terrorism Task Force officials (2005). What appears to have particularly attracted the attention of Philippine and American security personnel is that the alleged JI members actively sought training in deep-sea water diving but exhibited little or no interest in decompression techniques.

the possible employment of maritime crime groups to hijack and deliver major ocean-going vessels (such as oil tankers, container ships, and LNG carriers), which might then either be scuttled to block critical sea-lanes of communication (SLOCs) or detonated to cause a major explosion at a target port of opportunity. While the possible convergence between piracy and terrorism remains highly debatable—not least because these actors are motivated by differing and, in many ways, conflicting objectives[9]—it is a contingency that has been highlighted in several maritime threat assessments over the past five years and is clearly one that security, intelligence, and maritime officials are not prepared to dismiss out of hand (Frittelli, 2004, p. 8; Raymond, 2005, p. 197; Sinai, 2004, p. 51; "ASEAN," 2002; Ijaz, 2003). A case in point was the Lloyd's Joint War Council (JWC) 2005 designation of the Malacca Strait as an "Area of Enhanced [Terrorism] Risk."[10] This determination was based on a disputed threat-vulnerability study carried out by the UK-based Aegis group, which specifically considered anticipated future links between regional Islamist militants and maritime criminals in its analysis.[11]

---

9. The "business" of piracy, for instance, depends directly on a thriving and active global shipping industry while contemporary terrorists associated with the international jihadist network generally seek to disrupt maritime trade as part of their self-defined economic war against the West. The incompatability of these objectives was repeatedly expressed to the authors during interviews with Ministry of Foreign Affairs and Ministry of Home Affairs officials and Control Risks Group analysts (2005).

10. The designation of the Malacca Strait as an area of enhanced risk allows maritime insurance companies to levy a "war surcharge" on ships transiting the waterway up to 0.01 percent of the total value of their cargo; this is over and above the 0.05-percent baseline premium that is routinely imposed on seaborne freight. At the time of writing, no shipping association had actually been required to make the additional payment. Notably, while the Malacca Strait was included on the Lloyd's list of designated regions and countries, Syria, Iran, Sri Lanka, and Yemen were all taken off. The JWC reviews each designation quarterly (anonymous Lloyd's of London analysts, 2005).

11. Anonymous Lloyd's of London analysts (2005). It should be noted that both Singaporean and Western maritime security and intelligence officials dismissed the validity of the Aegis report, noting that the group has no recognized analytical presence in the region and that its assessment was not in line with the empirical risk of attack (terrorist or pirate) in the Malacca Strait (especially when one compares the number of incidents that have occurred with the volume of traffic passing through the strait).

Intent of Terrorist Groups

For several reasons, government and intelligence personnel believe contemporary terrorist groups may be actively seeking to extend operational mandates to the maritime environment. On one level, there is an argument that extremists groups could see utility in instituting sea-based activities as a means for overcoming extant security measures on land, the comprehensiveness of which has dramatically escalated over the last several years. Certainly while heightened internally based immigration and customs arrangements and general target-hardening have emerged as staples of counterterrorism in many countries since September 11, 2001, the overall latitude of action on the world's oceans and coastal waters remains prevalent, offering extremists the opportunity to move, hide, and strike in a manner not possible in a terrestrial theater (Herbert-Burns, 2005, p. 157). In many ways, this process of threat displacement has arguably been further encouraged by international pressure on littoral states to invest in territorially bounded homeland security initiatives. In the case of governments that have consistently struggled to enact effective systems of coastal surveillance (for example, the Philippines, Indonesia, Turkey, Eritrea, and Kenya), such external demands have negatively impacted already limited resources for offshore surveillance (anonymous Raytheon and Glenn Defense Marine analysts and Control Risks Group personnel, 2005). Policy analysts contend that the resultant void would be of particular interest to terrorist groups, given their asymmetric relationship with state adversaries and, therefore, their need to opt for operational environments that are most conducive to their tactical designs (anonymous former defense intelligence official, 2005).

Maritime attacks may also hold an increasing degree of attractiveness in that they have emerged as an alternative means for potentially causing mass economic destabilization. Today roughly 80 percent of global freight moves by sea, much of which takes the form of cargo that is transshipped on the basis of a "just enough, just in time" inventory. Disrupting the mechanics of this highly intensive and efficient trading system has the potential to trigger vast and cascading fiscal effects, particularly if the operations of a major commercial port were severely curtailed.[12] As Michael Richardson explains,

---

12. Anonymous Control Risks Group (UK) personnel (2005). See also Raymond (2005, p. 179).

> The global economy is built on integrated supply chains that feed components and other materials to users just before they are required and just in the right amounts. That way, inventory costs are kept low. If the supply chains are disrupted, it will have repercussions around the world, profoundly affecting business confidence. (Richardson, 2004, p. 7)

Attacking petroleum tankers and offshore energy facilities has been similarly highlighted in terms of generating significant economic externalities.

The suicide attack against the M/V *Limburg* in October 2002 is frequently emphasized as representing a pertinent case in point. Although the incident resulted in only three deaths (two of which were the bombers'), it directly contributed to a short-term collapse of international shipping business in the Gulf of Aden and nearby waters, led to a $0.48/barrel hike in the price of Brent crude oil and, as a result of the tripling of war-risk premiums levied on ships calling at the Aden, caused the Yemeni economy to lose an estimated $3.8 million a month in port revenues.[13]

The disruptive economic dimension of maritime terrorism has been singled out as having specific pertinence to al Qaeda precisely because Osama bin Laden has emphasized that attacking key pillars of the Western commercial and trading system is integral to his self-defined war on the United States and its major allies. Certainly there have been repeated statements attributed to the Saudi renegade and his major cohorts post-September 11, which have explicitly denigrated America as a paper tiger on the verge of financial collapse, with many further urging young Muslims to wage their jihad against Washington by focusing on targets that are liable to have a disruptive economic effect, including shipping (Eedle, 2002; Campbell and Gunaratna, 2003, pp. 73–74; Jehl and Johnston, 2004). This stance was perhaps best exemplified in an al Qaeda communiqué that was issued following the bombing of the M/V *Limburg:*

> By exploding the oil tanker in Yemen, the holy warriors hit the umbilical cord and lifeline of the crusader community, reminding the enemy of the heavy cost of blood and the gravity of losses they will pay as a price for their continued aggression on our community and looting of our wealth.[14]

---

13. See Sheppard (2003, p. 55), Richardson (2004, p. 70), Herbert-Burns (2005, p. 165), and Chalk et al. (2005, p. 22, fn. 20–21).
14. Alleged bin Laden statement cited in Herbert-Burns (2005, p. 165). See also Whitaker (2002).

Besides economic fallout, maritime security experts point to the potential of sea-based terrorism as a further means for inflicting "mass coercive punishment" or triggering a major environmental disaster.

In terms of inflicting coercive punishment, cruise ships and passenger ferries are commonly accepted as representing viable venues for executing large-scale civilian-centric strikes. These types of vessels move and cater to large numbers of people and, at least in the case of luxury liners, they often represent high-prestige, symbolic targets (anonymous former defense intelligence official, 2005). Moreover, thanks to international media and satellite communications, it is now far more probable that these types of attacks will elicit the necessary exposure and publicity that terrorists crave. As one British naval expert put it, "Should a cruise ship be bombed—even in the middle of vast oceans—one can expect that news teams would be on the scene covering the story, if not within minutes, certainly within hours."[15] Even if this were not the case, the advent of modern video technology has provided terrorists with a ready means to record and transmit their messages of death and destruction, as has been so vividly demonstrated with the televised images of beheadings of Westerners in Iraq since 2003.

With regard to creating potential environmental disasters, government officials and environmental groups contend there is good reason to speculate that a decisive terrorist strike could result in extensive ecological damage and, quite possibly, instability. These commentators argue that because heavy crude oil will not disperse or easily emulsify when treated with detergents, a major spill from a stricken petroleum tanker is liable to devastate the marine environment in the immediate vicinity of the release and, if left to drift, could conceivably degrade elongated stretches of fertile coastline (Richardson, 2004, p. 42). For some developing states in Africa and Asia that rely heavily on fish for both indigenous consumption and overseas export earnings, such effects have the potential to feed into wider socioeconomic unrest and could possibly act as a trigger for political instability.[16] Although deliberately causing environmental harm has yet to emerge as a mainstream terrorist tactic, it is certainly one that analysts have postulated as a potential motivator for future acts of extremism, particularly as militants seek to extend the

---

15. Comment made during the Senior Counter-Terrorism Course (SCTC), Asia Pacific Center for Security Studies (APCSS), Honolulu, September 1, 2005.
16. Asia is particularly prone to effects such as these, not least because popular perceptions of governing legitimacy often rest on the ability of the central administration to provide socioeconomic prosperity.

focus of their aggression toward venues that have historically not factored significantly in national or international security planning.[17]

Security analysts note with alarm that these various rationales are already becoming manifest in the sense that not only are international terrorists exhibiting greater tactical sophistication and innovation than in the past—perhaps best exemplified by the September 11 strikes[18]—a growing number also appear to be broadening their militant agendas to include specific experimentation with seaborne modalities. Indeed as Table 7.1 highlights, no fewer than five major maritime terrorist events have taken place since 2000. The main fear is that these incidents may be indicative of a future trend in militant Islamist extremism that increasingly views the maritime realm as both a viable and conducive theater of activity.[19]

Table 7.1 catalogs some of the higher-profile and publicized incidents connected to these groups.

Contemporary Maritime-Capable Terrorist Groups

Several groups have already recognized the inherent advantages of operating at sea and moved conspicuously to integrate waterborne modalities into their overall logistical and attack mandates. The following have been among the better known of these organizations:

- PIRA, which has conspicuously exploited commercial shipping to avail the resupply of weaponry and other war-related materiel[20]

---

17. See, for instance, Penders and Thomas (2002).
18. The sophistication and innovation of September 11 was reflected in several respects: the coordination of multiple aircraft hijackings; long-term planning and surveillance on the part of the perpetrators—much of which was undertaken in hostile, enemy territory; the institution of an effective logistics support infrastructure that literally spanned the globe; and the ability to mount simultaneous, mass casualty attacks using conventional weapons.
19. Anonymous Control Risks Group (UK) personnel and Maritime Intelligence Group analyst (2005). See Sinai (2004, pp. 50–51).
20. Many of these weapons were procured from Libya and transported to Ireland in container vessels fraudulently registered under flags of convenience. In the course of one year during the late 1980s, PIRA took delivery of nearly 120 tonnes of arms and explosives through this conduit, including AK47 assault rifles, Webley pistols, rocket-propelled grenade (RPG) launchers, surface-to-air missiles (SAMs), hand grenades, and a wide assortment of ammunition, detonators, fuses, and SEMTEX-H explosives. See Chalk (1996, p. 42) and "Arming the IRA" (1990).

TABLE 7.1 High-Profile Maritime Terrorism Incidents, 1961–2004.

Incident	Group	Deaths	Remarks
Hijacking of *Santa Maria* (1961)	Portuguese and Spanish rebels	N/A	The *Santa Maria*, a 21,000-ton cruise ship owned by Companhia Colonial of Lisbon, was hijacked by a group of 70 men led by Captain Henriques Galvao (a Portuguese political exile) to bring global attention to the Estado Novo in Portugal and related fascist regime in Spain. The vessel was on a holiday cruise in the southern Caribbean and its more than 600 passengers were held for 11 days before Galvao formally surrendered to the Brazilian navy. The incident constitutes the first modern-day hijack at sea.[a]
Use of a Cypriot-registered coaster, *Claudia*, to transport weapons to Ireland (1973)	Provisional Irish Republican Army (PIRA)	N/A	*Claudia* was intercepted by the Irish Navy while attempting to land a consignment of weapons intended for PIRA. On board were five tons of munitions that included 250 Soviet-made assault rifles, pistols, mines, grenades, and explosives. The vessel was owned by Gunther Leinhauser, a West German arms trafficker, which said that PIRA had given him a "shopping list" of required materiel and that the "order" had been filled by Libya (Wilkinson, 1986, p. 39).
Hijacking of *Achille Lauro* (1985)	Palestine Liberation Front (PLF)	1	Cruise ship hijacked in an attempt to coerce the release of 50 Palestinians being held in Israel. The perpetrators were eventually detained in Sicily. Person Killed was Leon Klinghoffer, a German, wheelchair-bound tourist, who was captured by the world's media as he was pushed overboard.[b]

TABLE 7.1 Continued.

Incident	Group	Deaths	Remarks
Targeting of cruise ships on the Nile River (1992–1994)	Al-Gama's al-Islamiyya	N/A	The group targeted at least four cruise ships during these two years as part of its general effort to undermine the Egyptian tourist sector (a key contributor to the country's economy) (Sinai, 2004, p. 50; Sitilides, 1998).
Hijacking of a Turkish passenger ferry in the Black Sea (1996)	Chechen rebels	N/A	Nine rebel gunmen held 255 passengers hostage for four days during which they threatened to blow up the captured ferry in order to bring international attention to the Chechen cause; the abductors eventually sailed the vessel back to Istanbul where they surrendered.[c]
Suicide bombing of the USS Cole (2000)	Al Qaeda	19	The bombing took place while the Cole was refueling at the Yemeni port of Aden. The assault involved 600 pounds of C4 explosive that was packed in the hull of a suicide attack skiff. Those killed were 17 U.S. sailors, 2 terrorists. In addition to the 17 sailors who were killed, another 39 were injured.[d]
Suicide bombing of the M/V Limburg (2002)[e]	Al Qaeda	3	The attack involved a small, fiberglass boat packed with 100–200 kg of TNT rammed into the tanker as it was preparing to take on a pilot-assisted approach to the Ash Shihr Terminal off the coast of Yemen. The Limburg was lifting 297,000 barrels of crude at the time of the strike, an estimated 50,000 of which spilled into the waters surrounding the stricken vessel. Those killed were 1 crewman and 2 terrorists.

TABLE 7.1 Continued.

Incident	Group	Deaths	Remarks
Use of *Karine A* to transport weapons for anti-Israeli strikes (2002)	Palestinian Authority (PA)	N/A	*Karine A*, a 4,000-ton freighter, was seized in the Red Sea on January 3, 2002. The vessel was carrying a wide assortment of Russian and Iranian arms, including Katyusha rockets (with a 20-kilometer range), antitank missiles (LAW and Sagger), long-range mortar bombs, mines, sniper rifles, ammunition, and more than two tons of high explosives. The US$100 million weapon consignment was linked directly to Yasir Arafat and was allegedly to be used for attacks against Jewish targets in Israel and the Occupied Territories ("IDF Seizes PA Weapons Ship," 2002).
Hijacking of the *M/V Penrider*, a fully laden shipping fuel oil tanker from Singapore to Penang in northern Malaysia (2003)	Gerakan Aceh Merdeka (GAM)	N/A	This is one of the few instances where GAM has directly claimed responsibility for a maritime attack. The group took three hostages (the master, chief engineer, and second engineer), who were eventually released after a $52,000 ransom was paid[f]

TABLE 7.1   Continued.

Incident	Group	Deaths	Remarks
Use of the *Abu Hassan*, an Egyptian-registered fishing trawler, to transport weapons and training manuals to assist militant strikes in Israel	Lebanese Hezbollah	N/A	The Egyptian owner of the trawler was recruited by Hezbollah and trained specifically to carry out maritime support missions. The vessel, which Israeli naval commandos intercepted 35 nautical miles off Rosh Hanikra near Haifa, was being used to ferry a complex weapon and logistics consignment, consisting of fuses for 122mm Qassam rockets, electronic time-delay fuses, a training video for carrying out suicide strikes, and two sets of CD-ROMs containing detailed bomb-making information (Herbert-Burns, 2005, p. 166).
Attacks against the Khawr Al Amaya oil terminal (KAAOT) and Al Basrah oil terminal (ABOT), Iraq (2004)	Jamaat al-Tawhid	3	The attacks were claimed by al Zarqawi as a follow-up to the 2000 *Cole* and 2002 *Limburg* strikes (using the same small-craft, suicide modality) and appeared to be part of an overall strategy of destabilization in Iraq (the terminals were shut down for two days, costing nearly US$40 million in lost revenues) (Warouw, 2005, p. 12; Köknar, 2005).

TABLE 7.1 Continued.

Incident	Group	Deaths	Remarks
Bombing of the Philippine *SuperFerry 14* (2004)	Abu Sayyaf Group (ASG), combined with elements from Jemaah Islamiyah (JI) and the Rajah Soliaman Revolutionary Movement (RSRM)[9]	116	Attack involved 20 sticks of dynamite that were planted in a hollowed-out television set. The bomb set off a fire that quickly spread throughout the ship due to the lack of an effective internal sprinkler system. Of the 116 fatalities, 63 have been identified (at the time of writing) and 53 remain uncounted for. The incident has been listed as the most destructive act of terrorism in maritime history and the fourth most serious international incident since September 11, 2001 (anonymous Anti-Terrorism Task Force officials, 2005).
Suicide attack against the Port of Ashdod, Israel (2004)	Hamas, al-Aqsa Martyr's Brigade	10	The attack took place at Ashdod, one of Israel's busiest seaports, and involved two Palestinian suicide bombers from Hamas and the al-Aqsa Martyr's Brigade. The perpetrators had apparently been smuggled to the terminal inside a commercial container four hours before the operation. Some speculation remains that al Qaeda assisted with logistics of the strike (Köknar, 2005).

[a]Jenkins et al. (1986, p. 69); "Santa Maria Hijacking" (undated). The hijacking was also known as "Operation Dulcinea" by the hijackers.
[b]The PLF's original intention was to seize the *Achille Lauro* and then ram it into the Israeli oil terminal at Ashad. However, the attack team was discovered before this operation could be put into effect, forcing a change in plan (anonymous security and terrorism analyst, 2005).

TABLE 7.1   Continued.

c Sinai (2004, p. 50); Sitilides (1998); Köknar (2005); "Hostage Taking Action by Pro-Chechen Rebels Impairs Turkey's Image" (2001). Allegedly the gunmen had also considered blowing up one of the two suspension bridges that cross the Bosporus to close the Strait to traffic.

d For more on this incident, see Perl and O'Rourke (2001).

e The M/V Limburg has since been renamed and now operates under the designation M/V Maritime Jewel (anonymous International Maritime Bureau personnel and Maritime Intelligence Group analyst, 2005).

f Herbert-Burns (2005, pp. 167–168). See also McGeown (2003) and International Maritime Organization (2003).

g JI is an Indonesia-based jihadist group that has been linked to al Qaeda and allegedly seeks the creation of a pan-regional Islamic caliphate in Southeast Asia. It has been held responsible for several high-profile attacks in the region, including the 2002 Bali bombings (which collectively killed 198 people and remains the single most deadly international terrorist attack since September 11, 2001), suicide strikes on the U.S.-owned Marriott Hotel and Australian Embassy in Jakarta between 2003 and 2004 (with a combined toll of 17 deaths and 248 injuries), and coordinated attacks against tourist hubs, again in Bali, in 2005 (32 killed, over 100 wounded). For two excellent overviews of the group's origins and terrorist activities, see ICG (2002, 2003). The RSRM is a highly fanatical fringe element of Balik Islam, a Philippines-based movement composed of Christian converts to Islam. The group has been linked to both JI and ASG and seeks to replace the existing administration in Manila with a Muslim theocracy to purge what it regards as the artificial influx of Catholic influences first introduced by the Spanish and then consolidated under the Americans (anonymous antiterrorism and intelligence officials, 2005). See also Villaviray (2003) and "Summary of Report" (2004).

- Chechen rebels, who have carried out sporadic attacks agaltist passenger ferries in the vicinity of the Bosporus Strait
- Al-Gama'a al-Islamiyya, which carried out strikes against passenger ships during the early to mid-1990s
- Palestinian organizations, including Hamas, Palestinian Islamic Jihad (PIJ), PA, the Popular Front for the Liberation of Palestine—General Command (PFLP-GC), the Democratic Front for the Liberation of Palestine (DFLP), and PLF. The latter group carried out the infamous hijacking of the *Achille Lauro* in 1985, which remains, arguably, one of the most spectacular seaborne assaults to date.
- Lebanese Hezbollah, which is known to have received training in seaborne techniques from its principal sponsor, Iran, and has made efficient use of the maritime environment for covertly moving weapons, personnel, and materiel[21]
- ASG, which has been responsible for numerous seaborne strikes in the southern Philippines—including the 2004 sinking of *Super-Ferry 14*. Resulting in 116 fatalities, this incident remains the most deadly act of maritime terrorism to have been carried out in the modern era (although it appears as though the extent of the death toll was more "accidental" than deliberate—see Table 6.1).
- GAM, which, prior to its signing of a peace agreement with the Indonesian government in 2005, had been linked to a number of hijackings of tugs, fishing trawlers, and other small craft in the Strait of Malacca[22]

---

21. Anonymous Institute of Defense and Strategic Studies representative (2005). According to a former member of British defense intelligence, Hezbollah has also acquired a Soviet-era patrol boat that it uses for its own coastal "policing" purposes (anonymous former defense intelligence official, 2005).
22. It should be noted that many commentators do not view these strikes as terroristic, as their prime motivation is economic. However, the fact that seized funds have been used specifically to support GAM's insurgency in Aceh suggests that the attacks represent something more than basic criminality and do, in fact, involve a definite political dimension that Herbert-Burns has termed "logistical-support terrorism." See Herbert-Burns and Zucker (2004) and Raymond (2005, p. 197).

- the Liberation Tigers of Tamil Eelam (LTTE), which, in the guise of the group's so-called Sea Tigers, retains the most advanced maritime attack capability of any known sub-state terrorist insurgency
- Jamaat al-Tawhid wa'l-Jihad (or Unity and Jihad Group), a Sunni organization led by Abu Musab al-Zarqawi until his death in June 2006 that has been at the forefront of attacks against U.S.-led coalition forces in Iraq
- al Qaeda, which was behind the bombing of the USS *Cole* in 2000 and the French-registered M/V *Limburg* two years later. Prior to his arrest in 2003, the movement's chief maritime planner, Abdel Rahim al-Nashiri (colloquially known as Ameer al Bahr, or "Prince of the Sea"), was also believed to have been in the latter stages of finalizing plans to attack Western shipping interests in the Strait of Gibraltar.[23] More recently, in August 2005, a Syrian national linked to al Qaeda, Lu'ai Sakra, was linked to a plot to ram explosive-laden speedboats into cruise ships carrying Israeli tourists to Turkey (Ant, 2005; "World Briefing Middle East, 2005).
- Various allegations have additionally surfaced pertaining to the existence of an al Qaeda fleet of ocean-going vessels. According to Lloyd's List and a 2002 Norwegian intelligence report, for instance, prior to September 11, the organization owned at least 23 ships, most of which operated through front companies located in Liberia, Tonga Panama, Belize, and the Isle of Man (all notorious for tolerating registration bureaus that permit irresponsibly lax strictures regarding crewing conditions and documentation requirements) (Köknar, 2005; "What al-Qaida Could Do with 'Terror Navy,'" 2003). A similar U.S. report has put al Qaeda's inventory at 15 merchant carriers, which may or may not include other ships chartered but not specifically

---

23. Percival (2005, p. 9), Richardson (2004, p. 19), Köknar (2005), "Al-Qaeda Has Multi-Faceted Marine Strategy" (2003), Smith (2004). Nashiri had apparently developed a four-point plan for the attacks in the Mediterranean, which included ramming ships with small boats; detonating medium-sized vessels near other craft or at port; crashing aircraft into large carriers such as supertankers; and using suicide divers or underwater parasitic devices (for example, submersible limpet mines) to destroy surface platforms.

owned by the network.[24] There have also been periodic reports that bin Laden has used fishing trawlers procured from family businesses located in Madagascar and parts of Asia to transport weapons, ammunition, and explosives (Sinai, 2004, p. 58). Definitive evidence to back these various claims, however, has never materialized and as such they should necessarily be treated with an air of caution.

Scenarios of Potential Maritime Terrorist Activity in the Future

Looking to predict how terrorists may actually seek to exploit the maritime realm for future operational purposes, intelligence analysts and security experts have highlighted several scenarios in their analytical forecasting. At least seven possibilities are routinely postulated:

- use of a commercial container ship to smuggle chemical, biological, or radiological (CBR) materials for an unconventional attack carried out on land or at a major commercial port such as Rotterdam, Singapore, Hong Kong, Dubai, New York, or Los Angeles
- use of a "trojan horse," such as a fishing trawler, resupply ship, tug, or similar innocuous-looking vessel, to transport weapons and other battle-related materiel
- hijacking of a vessel as a fund-raising exercise to support a campaign of political violence directed toward ethnic, ideological, religious, or separatist designs
- scuttling of a ship in a narrow SLOC in order to block or disrupt maritime traffic
- hijacking of an LNG carrier that is then detonated as a floating bomb or used as a collision weapon
- use of a small, high-speed boat to attack an oil tanker or offshore energy platform to affect international petroleum prices or cause major pollution

---

24. See Sakhuja (2002); Raymond (2005, p. 193); Herbert-Burns (2005, pp. 171–172); Sinai (2004, p. 58); Grier and Bowers (2003); Mintz (2002); and "Al-Qaida Training Manual Shows Seaports Top Target" (2003). According to one former British defense official, al Qaeda owns only one or two ships outright, with most of its assets taking the form of charter vessels (anonymous former defense intelligence official, 2005).

- directly targeting a cruise liner or passenger ferry to cause mass casualties by contaminating the ship's food supply, detonating an on-board or submersible improvised explosive device (IED) or, again, by ramming the vessel with a fast-approach, small, attack craft.[25]

A thorough discussion of all these contingencies is beyond the scope of this analysis. However, to give a flavor of extant vulnerabilities and potential opportunities that might be available to terrorists wishing to operate in the maritime realm in the near to medium term, Chapters Five, Six, and Seven of this book (Greenberg, 2006) are devoted to assessing the risks posed in connection with three specific types of shipping targets: cruise liners, passenger ferries, and container vessels.

These types of shipping targets were selected in part because they receive a great deal of public attention and for two additional reasons. First, attacks against passenger vessels have already occurred and constitute the most frequent occurrence of terrorism in the maritime realm. Second, as years of drug trafficking bear witness, it is relatively easy to compromise the integrity of the oceanic container network for smuggling purposes. Thus, container shipping is vulnerable to terrorists' attempts to smuggle goods.

Consequences of Maritime Terrorism

Passenger and commercial shipping in the maritime domain are both large and highly profitable industries in the United States. Their size and importance alone make it worthwhile to estimate the potential consequences of terrorism to these industries.

Both the U.S. and global economies depend on commercial shipping. U.S. ports handle approximately 20 percent of worldwide maritime trade. The value of national and international products transported through the United States annually is approximately $9.1 trillion, with the international component of that being roughly $2 trillion (almost half of which is container-transported materials). Moreover, the international tonnage of trade transported through the United States is expected to double by 2020, tripling the volume

---

25. Anonymous former defense official and Control Risks Group (UK) personnel (2005). See also Campbell and Gunaratna (2003, pp. 70–89), Herbert-Burns (2005, pp. 163–169), Sinai (2004, pp. 63–64), and Percival (2005, pp. 10–13).

currently transported through the East Coast ports and quadrupling that currently transported through the West Coast ports (Foschi, 2004, pp. 1–46).

Passenger ships, meanwhile, are used in the United States for both commuting and leisure travel. More than 66 million passengers travel by ferry each year in the United States, with the largest ferry systems operating in the Seattle/Tacoma, New York/New Jersey, New Orleans, Boston, and San Francisco Bay areas (American Public Transportation Association, 2006). More than 9 million passengers board cruise ships each year in North America, contributing approximately $14.7 billion to the U.S. economy (Business Research and Economic Advisors, 2005).

Given the foregoing, attacks involving U.S. passenger or container shipping clearly have the potential to affect large numbers of people and important sectors of the U.S. economy. The types of consequences that could be expected after an attack on passenger or container shipping can be broadly defined in terms of who is affected, how they are affected, and by how much they are affected. This chapter provides an ontology to address the first two of these issues. Since the magnitude of attack effects is scenario specific (i.e., dependent on the nature of a particular attack), the last issue is addressed separately through case studies of maritime risks in cruise-, ferry-, and container-related attacks, provided in Chapters Five, Six, and Seven of this book (Greenberg, 2006).

Parties Affected by Maritime Terrorism

The distribution of the consequences of maritime terrorist attacks may be just as relevant to public policy as their magnitude. Terrorist attacks can destroy property that is exclusive to individuals or private firms. Attacks can likewise affect the public sector, by destroying public property and by interfering with revenue sources that provide for public goods and services.

In drawing a similar distinction among the parties affected by terrorism, Jackson and Dixon (2005) distinguish how the scope and motivations of investment decisions differ between individuals, private-sector firms, and public-sector institutions. According to micro-economic theory, individuals act to maximize personal welfare to the extent their resources allow. Similarly, firms maximize the profit generated through the value of present and future revenues. This is in contrast to the assumed responsibility of the public sector to maximize welfare of society as a whole, occasionally through the redistribution of goods, services, and wealth.

Categorizing the consequences of terrorism in terms of its effects on individuals, private-sector firms, and public-sector institutions can help to frame issues of distribution. For example, the distribution of effects across these three sets of parties can influence perceived equity in the aftermath of an attack. The public may view a terrorist attack that predominantly contaminates houses of people living near an industrial facility but who are not employees of the facility very differently than it would a cyberattack that destroys only the infrastructure of a single private firm.

In some important respects, the consequences of a terrorist attack to individuals, private firms, and the public sector are unlikely to be independent. This is true in the obvious sense that the lives lost in a terrorist attack simultaneously involve catastrophic harm to the individuals involved and a loss of human capital to the businesses or agencies that employ them. On a more esoteric level, though, government policies can also have the effect of *redistributing* some of the consequences of an attack in a manner that may shift related burdens among individuals and private-sector firms. For example, under applicable workers' compensation laws, most businesses are required to insure their employees against injury while working. This insurance lessens the burden of accidental injury to victims, by shifting a portion of related costs to private firms, under administrative oversight by government. In a similar manner, civil liability is another mechanism for redistributing the burden of injuries among individuals, private firms, and government agencies.

Although the operation of these kinds of cost-shifting policy mechanisms might itself be construed broadly as a "consequence" in the wake of a terrorist attack, the mechanisms can also be understood independently as a complex set of rules and procedures for limiting, preventing, or remediating some of the effects of hypothetical attacks. In this book, we address the civil liability implications of potential maritime terrorist attacks separately and in detail in Chapter Four (Greenberg, 2006). For current purposes, it suffices to emphasize that the public-sector effects of terrorism may include both immediate harms to public institutions and assets in the wake of an attack, as well as secondary cost-shifting effects through the operation of public institutions like the civil justice system.

Connecting Consequences to Terrorist Events

Whether or not presumed consequences can be observed is affected by the proximity of the causal link between the terrorist event and presumed consequences. *Direct* consequences manifest themselves in the form of loss of human life, physical destruction of property caused by the physical and biological effects of a terrorist event, and response and recovery from the attack.

Many other *indirect* consequences subsequently result from these effects. Businesses may be unable to operate because of policing and infrastructure damage around them. Individuals and businesses depending on those directly affected by an attack may suffer disruptions as a result. Individual and firm decisionmaking may change because of psychological reactions to the consequences of an event. Broader consequences can continue to ripple outward as these disruptions propagate, and individual and firm decisionmaking is influenced by the occurrence of terrorism.

The indirect consequences of terrorism are difficult to estimate. Jackson and Dixon (2005) appropriately noted that the distinction between direct and indirect effects can be quite ambiguous. The magnitude of indirect effects depends on how broadly the scope of a terrorist event is defined. Considering only those entities physically affected and connecting effects in adjacent communities will result in different estimates than would result, for example, from also considering effects on businesses across the nation that suffer logistical disruptions.

As the causal chain of events stretches, it also becomes increasingly difficult to attribute behavior to a particular event.[26] There are two explanations for this. One is that manifestation of indirect consequences depends on choices that individuals and organizations make in response to an event. A company that sits and waits for its supplier to recover may lose significant business, but one that places a replacement order from an unaffected supplier may not suffer at all. How people and organizations do, in fact, respond when faced with particular terrorist events is not well understood, making it difficult to estimate these indirect consequences. A second explanation is that, as the causal proximity grows more distant, effects might fade into the noise of other events shaping economic activity. For example, supplier disruptions that might be expected to limit supply of a commodity and raise prices may be offset by an unrelated oversupply of the same commodity.

---

26. Note that the U.S. civil justice system has long grappled with the problem of bounding the limits of causal relationships in the context of compensating tort claims. Beyond the general observation that indirect causes are often subjective in interpretation and difficult to apprehend fully, the law has frequently taken the position that some categories of injury (e.g., harm to future income in the absence of loss of property or physical or psychological injury) will simply not be compensated in tort, by virtue of the fact that causal relationships involved may be too distant to justify it.

As an alternative to distinguishing between direct and indirect costs, Jackson and Dixon (2005) captured causal relationships between events and consequences by considering attack costs, security and preparedness costs, and costs resulting from behavioral change. Where relevant in the chapters that follow, we describe our estimates of the consequences of terrorist acts in terms of these three types of costs, again as experienced by individuals, private firms, and the public sector.

Types of Consequences of Maritime Terrorism

The consequences of maritime terrorism can manifest in many forms. Table 7.2 presents a summary of the types of consequences of maritime terrorism that might affect individuals, the private sector, and the public sector. Broadly, these consequences fall into one of three groups: *human, economic,* and *intangible* effects.

Human consequences refers to effects on lives caused by fatalities and injuries. *Economic consequences* are those effects easily quantified in financial terms. *Intangible effects* capture those effects that are difficult to measure in human lives or financial metrics either because they are measured in metrics that are not easily translated into lives or financial metrics or because the cause-and-effect linkage is not understood well enough to allow precise estimation and attribution of effects.

Human Consequences of Terrorism

Individuals carry the ultimate burden of the consequences of terrorism. It is people who are injured or killed and who suffer debilitating psychological consequences following terrorist attacks. Moreover, the indirect consequences of fatalities and injuries can flow into both the public and private sectors, particularly in terms of economic costs. Again, the costs associated with fatalities and injuries may be transferred, at least in part, through compensatory mechanisms like insurance and civil tort claims, with some of the burdens associated with human injuries borne by the private sector.

TABLE 7.2	The Scope of Consequences of a Maritime Terrorist Attack		
Affected Party	**Human Consequences**	**Economic Consequences**	**Intagible Consequences**
Individuals	Fatalities Injuries	Loss of salary Loss of property Loss of investments Loss of public services	Psychological consequences leading to changes in saving, earning, and consumption preferences
Private sector		Destruction of property Ships Facilities Transportation infrastructure Products and raw materials Loss of data Life and injury compensation Short-term disruption of business cycle Immediate lag in delivery Loss of customers Loss of revenue business interruption Increased transport costs Internal diseconomies of scale Long-term transportation inefficiency Augmented security measures Increased insurance rates	Loss of human capital in the private sector Changes in consumption and investment preferences Reduced tolerance of risky investments Loss of future revenue streams Decreased foreign confidence Decreased foreign investment Increased cost of foreign trade because of insecurity Shifts in stock market Decrease in tourism and resulting losses in revenue
Public sector		Loss of revenue for government Destruction of public infrastructure Financial costs of response and recover Increased government spending on counterterrorism	Political consequences Loss of human capital in the public sector

In addition, fatalities affect both the public and private sectors in terms of loss of human capital. To the public sector, this most frequently results in a temporary loss of capability (a diseconomy of scale) until organizations can be reorganized. If a large proportion of people with a particular specialty skill (such as nuclear power plant design) or serving a specific function (such as elected government) were affected by a terrorist attack, the results could be severely disruptive and could potentially take years from which to recover. In the private sector, loss of human capital that would not affect the nation's production capabilities can be devastating to individual firms. For example, in the World Trade Center attacks on September 11, 2001, 658 employees of the investment firm of Cantor Fitzgerald died, leading to the collapse of Cantor Fitzgerald's core interdealer business in the United States (Cantor Fitzgerald, undated).

Economic and Intangible Consequences of Property Damage

Terrorist attacks can destroy both physical and intellectual property. Attacks that damage facilities, ships, vehicles, airplanes, infrastructure, or products and raw materials reduce the assets of private firms. In cases in which power is disrupted or computer networks are targeted, loss of data may also reduce firm assets that enable future revenues.

Damage to infrastructure, facilities, and information systems may propagate into both short,- and long-term economic disruptions. Firms may immediately experience delivery delays, loss of revenue from interrupted business, and increased transportation costs. Reduction of demand or supply could eliminate the benefits of economies of scale until facilities and infrastructure can be replaced. As the magnitude and duration of disruptions to infrastructure, facilities, and information systems increase, the consequences can be more permanent. Firms may experience long-term transportation inefficiencies.

In extreme cases, disruptions can lead to long-term or permanent loss of business. Following a large fire in a Philips Electronics manufacturing facility, Ericsson's inability to adapt its supply chain quickly for mobile phone components contributed to the firm's loss of significant market share to competitor Nokia (Sheffi, 2005).

These private-sector effects can spill over into the public sector as well. Business disruptions can lead to significant loss of revenue for local and state governments. The pooled effects of destruction of private infrastructure along with public infrastructure can lead to significant loss of public services, such as freight and public trans-portation. These public-sector effects were most recently demon-strated by the devastation wrought by Hurricane Katrina. Loss of population and business prompted initial projections of a budget shortfall of as much as $1 billion for the state government of Louisiana[27] and freight transportation was disrupted for months by damage to rail, road ($3 billion [Burton and Hicks, 2005]), and port facilities ($1.7 billion [Blanco, 2005] in Louisiana alone).

Economic and Intangible Consequences of Responding to Terrorism

The unfolding of events and reactions following a terrorist attack can result in a cascade of secondary consequences. In addition to the direct costs of emergency response to the attack, subsequent changes in the nation's posture toward terrorism and the economic impact of those changes can also be construed as consequences of terrorism. Experience from the events of September 11, 2001, strongly suggest that terrorist events will be followed by increased public- and private-sector security investments or increases in insurance rates as firms and the public sector react to new per-ceived and realized threats (Zycher, 2003).

Terrorism-induced changes in risk perception may also lead individuals and firms to change their consumption and investment preferences. Some business sectors might experience loss of future revenue. This could be particularly significant for luxury and substi-tutable industries, such as jewelry or travel tourism, respectively.

Large terrorist events might also provoke shifts in foreign policy and have domestic political consequences. By analogy to the costs of the Iraq war, Linda Bilmes and Joseph Stiglitz (2006) have sug-gested that costs from shifting political focus might compound other human and economic consequences of the Iraq war, thereby con-tributing to reduced confidence in the national economy, and ulti-mately leading to the macroeconomic effect of decreased foreign investment. This kind of effect could alter even technological inno-vation, if severe uncertainty about the future were to lead to a reduced tolerance for risk investments. These kinds of effects could lead to shifts and loss of value in domestic securities markets.

Though these consequences are poorly understood and difficult to estimate, it is prudent to consider proactively how they may arise and how alternative responses might amplify or counter them.

---

27. Hochberg (2005). Note that apparent increases in sales tax receipts from increased purchases ultimately eased the projected deficits.

Scenario-based tools, such as day-after gaming, may be particularly useful for assessing risk management for these types of consequences.

Methods of Estimating Consequences of Maritime Terrorism

Past maritime terrorist events provide the most direct means of estimating the consequences of future attacks. However, there are two significant limitations to relying on this type of historical analysis. First, terrorist attacks on maritime targets are fortunately infrequent. As discussed in Chapter Two (Greenberg, 2006), a few events can be used as benchmarks for the potential consequences of terrorist attacks. However, the small number of events is limiting because it does not provide a representative sample of attack modes that terrorism analysts have discussed. Second, historical analysis does not provide a means for extrapolating to events that may occur as terrorists adapt and affect maritime systems in new ways.

Therefore, additional approaches are necessary to augment this direct historical analysis. In the analysis of risks of cruise, passenger, and container ships in the subsequent chapters, we used three additional sources of information.

First, terrorist attacks in nonmaritime arenas can provide a measure of typical fatalities and injuries from different attack modes. While maritime attacks are relatively rare, terrorists have been active with land-based and aviation-based attacks for decades. Reviewing shootings, suicide bombings in crowds, and hijackings in other scenarios can provide a better understanding of what the consequences of these attacks might be in the maritime domain.

Second, modeling and simulation can provide estimates of direct and indirect impacts of terrorism. Physical models have been used to understand the impacts of weapons on structures and humans. These can be used to estimate the casualties from conventional, nuclear, radiological, and biological weapons. Direct economic effects can often be easily estimated through modeling and simulation, though uncertainty in the extent of disruptions must be addressed. Economic models, such as input-output models, represent the interdependencies of sectors in the economy. Day-after games and scenario analysis can be used to elicit expert estimates of consequences and how firms and individuals will respond to terrorist events. All of these tools can be used to estimate the indirect effects of terrorism on regional and national economies.

Finally, non–terrorist-related events that cause disruptions provide additional proxies for infrastructure disruptions that might occur following terrorist attacks.[28] Natural disasters like the Northridge Earthquake, Hurricane Andrew, and Hurricane Katrina provide case studies of large-scale regional disruption. Labor disputes like the 2002 West Coast port lockout provide another source of case studies that can be used as a proxy for disruptions.

---

28. Although natural disasters (for example) can provide useful proxies for the infrastructure disruptions that might follow from terrorist attacks, disasters are not a good proxy for the civil liability consequences of attacks, because attacks are unique in that they involve the independent criminal actions of terrorists. We discuss the tort liability implications of this distinction in Chapter Four of this book (Greenberg, 2006).

7.2
Criminological Theories and the Problems of Modern Piracy

Jon M. Shane
Charles A. Lieberman

Introduction

Piracy and other maritime attacks have occurred nearly as long as there have been vessels on the waterways.[1] Among the many criminological theories, environmental and ecological theories are most appropriate to explain the origins and opportunities for piracy. When society's norms and institutions breakdown because of conflicting expectations, corruption, and political instability, social control becomes ineffectual. Local institutions—schools, churches, government—lose the ability to exert control over people and geographical areas. When social controls wither and conventional traditions disintegrate, society loses the ability to regulate itself, which gives way to a culture that begins to identify with deviant behaviors that become normalized. This reversion to a "state of nature" enables criminal groups to rise and propagate in an environment dominated by a survivalist ideology. Criminal factions supplant conventional institutions and exert an influence over the denizen that fosters tolerance for criminal behavior because the inhabitants have lost the capacity to exercise control. Living in this environment produces social isolation, where there is little or no contact with mainstream society. As a result, crime and violence are seen as a near inevitable consequence of life.

---

[1] May, 2008.

People living in this environment develop a disposition (motivation) to act in a criminal manner as a means to fulfill basic human needs.[2] Piracy is predicated on rather crude operating methods that bring offenders into contact with valuable targets that are easily converted into cash. Because piracy typically takes place in vast ocean waters, the targets are largely unprotected. When someone sufficiently motivated by social circumstances (e.g., inherited traits, hunger, poverty, unemployment and lack of conventional lifestyle) comes into contact with durable goods that are easily converted to cash and often insufficiently protected, piracy becomes a viable economic pursuit. Fortunately, there are ways to disrupt the intersection of motivated offenders, suitable targets, and capable guardians that can reduce the likelihood of a piracy occurring.

Piracy Defined

In 1981, in response to increased maritime crime, the International Maritime Bureau (IMB), a quasi-governmental organization of the International Chamber of Commerce (ICC) was created. The IMB was designed to combat all types of maritime and trade crime, including documentary credit fraud, charter party fraud, cargo theft, and piracy. According to the IMB, "piracy is the act of boarding any vessel with an intent to commit theft or any other crime, and with an intent or capacity to use force in furtherance of that act."[3]

Piracy is distinguished from simple hijacking in two respects: first, an act of piracy requires that two vessels are involved in the incident; second, an act of piracy requires that the crime has been undertaken for private, not political, purposes.[4] The IMB's definition covers actual or attempted attacks, whether the ship is berthed, at anchor, or at sea. Petty thefts are excluded unless the thieves are armed. This definition seems quite practical for today's needs and is broad enough to cover the widening variety of types of attacks being seen today. Commercial crime is growing quickly, as is evidenced the IMB's *Weekly Piracy Report*. The nature of piracy has changed significantly since the sixteenth and seventeenth centuries. Today's pirate is often more barbaric and better prepared, due to the implementation of technological advancements, to fight than ever before.

---

2. Maslow, 1943.
3. ICC IMB, 1998.
4. McDaniel, 2000.

The Nature of Piracy

The days of the swashbuckler swinging on a chandelier, brandishing a trusty cutlass, are long gone. Disguised by a patch over one eye, oversized hoop earrings, and a puffy shirt, the pirates' outfit of yesteryear has given way to the modern pirates' accouterments: high-powered weapons, vanguard communications, and the ominous black balaclava. It is sophistication and celerity (the swiftness of small motorized vessels) that enable the modern terrorist-pirate to ply their trade, making the shipping industry more and more vulnerable to attack. The 2008 IMB Annual Report revealed 1,845 actual or attempted acts of piracy occurred worldwide between 2003 and 2008. In addition, an IMB report for the first quarter of 2009 provides a comparison for first quarter attacks from 2004 through 2009 (See Table 4.1).[5]

During the period 2003–2008, there appeared to be a downward trend in actual and attempted attacks despite a slight increase in the number of attacks in 2007–2008 (Figure 7.1). This trend is primarily due to the high number of attacks (N_{2003} = 445) in 2003, compared with the declining numbers in the subsequent three years (N_{2004} = 329; N_{2005} = 276; N_{2006} = 239).

Based on the numbers for 2007 and 2008 (N_{2007} = 263; N_{2008} = 293), the downward trend indicated by an analysis of the IMB 2008 Annual Report appeared to be reversing. In addition, the IMB report

TABLE 7.3	Actual and Attemped Attacks, 2003–2008		
Year	Total Attacks	Year	Jan-Mar Attacks
2003	445	2004	79
2004	329	2005	56
2005	276	2006	61
2006	239	2007	41
2007	263	2008	49
2008	293	2009	102
2003–2008	1,845	2004–2009	388
ICC IMB 2008 Piracy and Armed Robbery Against Ships Annual Report ICC IMB 2009 Report for the Period 1 January–31, March 2009			

5. ICC IMB, January 2009; ICC IMB, April 2009.

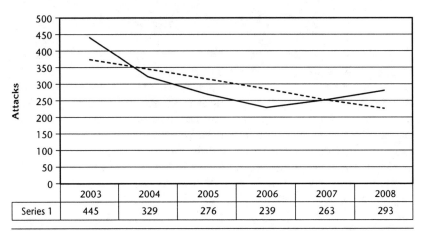

	2003	2004	2005	2006	2007	2008
Series 1	445	329	276	239	263	293

FIGURE 7.1
Actual and Attempted Attacks, 2003–2008. *The solid line represents the number of attacks; the dotted line represents the trends over time for the attacks.*

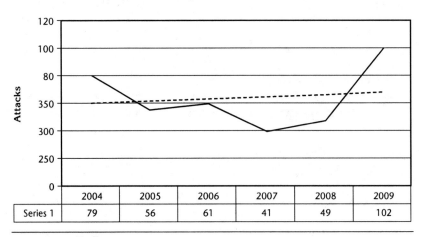

	2004	2005	2006	2007	2008	2009
Series 1	79	56	61	41	49	102

FIGURE 7.2
1st Quarter Actual and Attempted Attacks, 2004–2009. *The solid line represents the number of attacks; the dotted line represents the trends over time for the attacks.*

for the first quarter for 2009 suggests an upward trend, as the number of attacks for the first quarter of 2009 ($N_{1stQ2009} = 102$) is nearly double the average ($N_{1stQavg2005-2008} = 51.75$) of the prior four years (Figure 7.2).

An examination of recent attacks provides a picture of the types of ships most frequently targeted by pirates. Tankers tend to be most often targeted ($N_{Tanker} = 85$), accounting for more than one-third of all attacks in 2008, and the numbers for the first quarter of 2009 project a 46 percent increase.

TABLE 7.4	Attacks by Vessel Type		
Vessel	**2008**	**Jan–Mar 2009**	**Projected 2009**
Container	49	16	64
Bulk Carrier	48	32	128
Chemical Tanker	39	12	48
General Cargo	38	10	40
Tanker	30	11	44
Tug	16	1	4
Product Tanker	16	4	16
Total	**236**	**86**	**344**

The depiction of maritime attacks by vessel type in Figure 7.3, comparing the numbers for 2008 with the projections for 2009 based on the first quarter of 2009, provides some insight into the decision-making process among pirates. For most of the vessel types, the projection of attacks for 2009 remains fairly consistent; however, there is an upward trend for attacks on bulk carriers. This increased targeting of bulk carriers may be due to the size and speed of the vessel, as they tend to be very large, therefore easily identifiable from a distance, and relatively slow, especially in comparison to the speedboats employed by many pirates. Another factor that could have an impact on the increased targeting of bulk

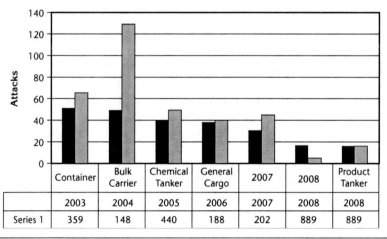

FIGURE 7.3
Attacks by Vessel Type

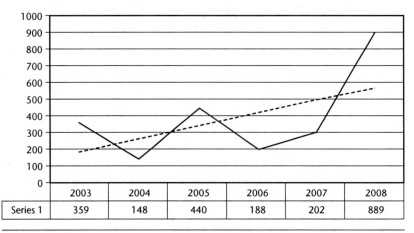

Series 1	2003	2004	2005	2006	2007	2008
	359	148	440	188	202	889

FIGURE 7.4
Hostages Taken, 2003–2008. *The solid line represents the number of hostages taken; the dotted line represents the trend for hostages taken.*

carriers, which account for approximately one-third of all cargo vessels, is their increased usage in maritime trade since their inception in the 1950s.

Attacks like the one in the Gulf of Aden in October 2002, when the French tanker *Limburg* was rammed by a boat packed with explosives, are difficult to prevent. "No shipboard response can protect the ship in these circumstances."[6]

An unsettling trend in maritime attacks is the significant increase in hostage taking. The number of hostages taken in 2008 is triple the average number of hostages between 2003 and 2007 (Figure 7.4). One possible explanation for this upward trend is the realization that hostages provide greater leverage during negations and the potential for higher ransoms. In April 2009, Somalia pirates seized the *Maersk Alabama* and her crew and held them for ransom. Captain Richard Phillips was held for several days before U.S. navy snipers shot and killed three of four pirates; the fourth was brought to the United States for prosecution.[7]

An examination of the IMB Piracy and Armed Robbery against Ships Report—Annual Report 2008, provides evidence that the overwhelming majority of attacks took place against ships either anchored or steaming, with only 6.5 percent of the attacks taking place against berthed ships. Attacks against anchored ships accounted for 35.5 percent, with 104 attacks. Attacks against

---

6. ICC-International Maritime Bureau, 2003a.
7. McFadden and Shane, 2009.

steaming ships accounted for 58 percent, with 169 attacks. However, only approximately half of those attacks against steaming ships were successful, with 87 successful attacks and 82 unsuccessful attempts. The size of a commercial vessel can make it a "soft target," as the crew simply cannot maintain an adequate watch while underway. Vigilant anti-piracy measures still remain the best deterrent to illegal boarding.[8]

Nexus to Criminological Theory

The social conditions associated with piracy typically include poverty, hunger, unemployment, poor housing, and political instability. Those who exploit the vulnerabilities created by social disorganization are doing so in response to the strain and frustration that manifest from a lack of life's basic necessities such as food, shelter, and clothing. In these regions of the world, there is a subculture willing to support individual criminal behavior, operating in an environment too corrupt to stop it.

Political instability, which results from a weak or non-existent central government, produces a social phenomenon known as *anomie*.[9] Anomie is a condition in which social and moral norms are weak, conflicting, or simply absent. Emile Durkheim (1893) proposed that the lack of norms—a state of normlessness—creates deviant behavior and ultimately social upheaval. For example, Somalia, where piracy is prevalent, has been without an effective central government since President Siad Barre was overthrown in 1991.[10] The country suffers from widespread fighting among warring militias, famine, and disease that has eroded the social and moral norms that regulate behavior plunging the country into lawlessness. Somalia and countries like it represent a regression to a "state of nature"—a hypothetical social state similar to anarchy that existed before the rule of law and the state's monopoly on the use of force.[11]

Similar conditions exist in Indonesia, where the sprawling nation of 13,000 islands was thrust into social and political upheaval when former President Suharto resigned amid a mounting economic crisis in 1998. It is widely accepted that when pirates strike in the Straits of Malacca, they will easily evade detection by taking refuge

---

8. ICC International Maritime Bureau, 2003b.
9. Durkheim, 1893.
10. BBC News, 2009.
11. Hobbes, 1651.

among the numerous island hide-outs away from a government too corrupt to care. Piracy has gained a foothold in Indonesia due to the country's economic instability, which poses threats to other developing areas of Asia as well.

As conditions persist and government structures weaken, opportunities for criminal activity arise. Opportunities exist because international commerce relies on ports and waterways that are adjacent to economically and politically unstable countries. Since there is no domestic force (i.e., police or viable military) to stop the pirates in these countries, they can easily set upon unguarded vessels passing through international waters, seize the crew and their cargo, return to land, and liquidate the goods. Opportunities for piracy can be explained from three perspectives that converge into a single explanation known as opportunity theory: first, the routine activities approach;[12] second, the rational choice perspective;[13] and third, crime pattern theory.[14]

Opportunity Theory

This approach to controlling crime consists of three opportunity-reducing principles: first, directing crime control measures at highly specific forms of crime; second, managing, designing, or manipulating the immediate environment in as systematic and permanent way as possible; and third, increasing the perceived risk or effort to commit a crime, or reducing the rewards or removing the excuses for committing a crime.[15]

Routine Activities Approach

The routine activities approach suggests crime is more likely to occur when three conditions are satisfied: 1) the presence of a motivated offender; 2) the presence of a suitable target; and 3) the absence of a capable guardian (Figure 7.5).[16] The presence of a motivated offender is a given; the theory assumes an offender is predisposed to acting on his or her criminal inclinations, for without an overt act there would not be a crime. Motivation for piracy is the oppressive social and moral foreground pirates are subjected to in their homeland, including poverty, unemployment, political and social strife, and economic deprivation.

---

12. Cohen and Felson, 1979.
13. Cornish and Clarke, 1986.
14. Brantingham and Brantingham, 1984.
15. Clarke, 1997: 4; see also Felson and Clarke, 1998.
16. Felson, 1998.

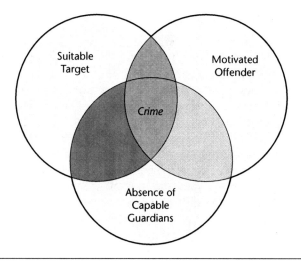

FIGURE 7.5

Suitable targets are those that exhibit these four qualities: 1) value, 2) inertia, 3) visibility, and 4) access.[17] Pirates typically go after targets that are easily converted to cash; however, some targets may be symbolic. Inertia refers to the target's weight and how easily it can be carried away or disposed of. Visibility refers to the target's sightlines. A large seagoing vessel such as a tanker or container ship can be easily spotted from the shore line or from a boat used by pirates to scout the waters. Lastly, pirates must have access to the target. Pirates can pull up alongside a vessel and board it by using a grappling hook or similar climbing device.

The last segment of routine activities is the absence of capable guardians. The motivation to commit an act of piracy follows Travis Hirschi's line of thought that crime occurs in the absence of controls.[18] When temptations are high and controls are low, a motivated pirate can strike more easily. A guardian is not necessarily a formal agent (e.g., police officer, soldier, teacher) but anyone who can serve as a reminder that someone is watching. The lynchpin is "capable." Since most high seas piracy is an armed takeover, pirates can easily force an unarmed crew into submission and render them incapable of defending the ship. In this sense, even though a crew of able-bodied adults is aboard, they are no match for the overwhelming force applied by armed pirates.

---

17. Felson, 1998: 54–55.
18. Hirschi, 1969.

Crime Pattern Theory

Crime pattern theory suggests people are intertwined with their environment and crime is a product of how they move about and converge in time and space.[19] This theory is useful for understanding how opportunities are concentrated at particular times in particle places. Pirates that embark from developing countries may seem to lack the technical wherewithal to hijack a ship. Admittedly, their operations are crude; however, through corruption or basic reconnaissance they gain access to information about what type of cargo may be aboard, what routes the ships sail, the ships' port of call, when the ships will sail, and how often ships pass through certain regions (i.e., time of day, day of week, season). Armed with this knowledge, it is easy to recognize patterns of shipping and to intercept the ships along their primary travel route.

Rational Choice Perspective

The rational choice perspective focuses on offender decision making. The premise is that offenders weigh the costs (i.e., pain and punishment) and benefits (i.e., pleasure and gain) before committing a crime. Except, their decisions are never perfect and they rely on information that constrains their decisions, which results in flawed outcomes (i.e., arrest, injury, death, monetary loss).[20] Because the conditions in the pirates' homeland are so oppressive, the pleasure associated with seizing a ship's cargo and converting it to cash outweighs the pain associated with capture. The profile of the typical pirate operating in the Straits of Malacca is one of an "opportunist, who is perhaps working from a local village, or a local community. He may have had military training and he is doing it basically for his own gain and advantage."[21] Other reported cases involve juveniles who have been kidnapped and forced into piracy.[22] Liquidating stolen goods may involve cooperation from local officials who use the proceeds to further corrupt already destabilized governments.

Together, routine activities, crime pattern theory, and rational choice, form "opportunity theory," which suggests specific situations, environments, and products can be intentionally manipulated

---

19. Brantingham and Brantingham, 1984, 1991.
20. Cornish and Clarke, 1986.
21. Bateman, 2001.
22. Zambito, Boyle and Connor, 2009.

to reduce crime. That is, interventions can be specifically constructed to "design-out" crime.[23] There is a large body of historical and contemporary research[24] supporting this theory through a wide range of criminal behaviors including delinquency[25], deceit[26], burglary[27], and auto theft.[28] The consistent premise of this line of inquiry is that increasing risk or effort and reducing the benefits of crime—dimensions that can be intentionally controlled by industry, government, and individual citizens—has much to do with someone's decision to commit or forego criminal activity.

Despite the problems plaguing certain developing regions and the propensity of pirate youth to use violence to achieve their goals, a ship's master may unwittingly precipitate their own demise through the routine activities of shipping. Vessel security is dependent upon the activities of the crew and the master's itinerary. The route traveled, the season, the port of call, the regulations that govern shipping, the time of departure and arrival, and the nature of the cargo, among the many, all contribute to the routine of shipping. In the interest of time, inasmuch as time is money, ship masters rely on the familiar; that which has saved time and effort in the past is likely to do so in the future, thus keeping deliveries on schedule. Deliveries that are on-time are dependable and cheaper, dependability and low cost ensure higher profit, irrespective of crew safety. The quickest, shortest route known to the master may also be known to the motivated pirate.

Once patterns are established, they become predictable. Predictable patterns breed complacency and complacency breeds vulnerability. The opportunities for pirates to strike generated by routine shipping activities eventually create "hot-spots"—areas that produce a disproportionate amount of crime. Some of the "hot-spots" for piracy today are Southeast Asia, the Horn of Africa, and Indonesia. With an understanding of how opportunity theory works, it is useful to describe the structure of opportunity.

---

23. Felson and Clarke, 1998; Jeffrey, 1971; Newman, 1972, 1996.
24. Visit the Center for Problem Oriented Policing (*www.popcenter.org*) for more than 1,000 examples of problem-oriented projects by police departments, as well as a collection of problem-specific guides and other resources on situational crime prevention.
25. Burt, 1925.
26. Farrington and Knight, 1980; Hartshorne and May, 1928.
27. Brantingham and Brantingham, 1975; Reppetto, 1974; Scar, 1973.
28. Wilkins, 1964.

Reducing Opportunity

Clarke's (1997) description of opportunity structure includes victims, targets, and facilitators (Figure 7.6). The *target* is the commodities aboard the ship (e.g., palm oil, lumber, textiles, and household goods). The *victim* is the ship's crew or the ship itself, and the *facilitators* are the means by which piracy is carried out (i.e., speed boats, heavy weapons, communications). The source of targets and their nature is a product of (i) the *physical environment* including the (e.g., design and size of the ship), and (ii) the *routine activities* of the shipping industry including patterns of trade among nations, season, weather, supply and demand of commodities, number of crew, speed of travel, and ocean currents, which can affect guardianship. The physical environment, routine activities and the broader socio-demographic structure (i.e., poverty, unem-

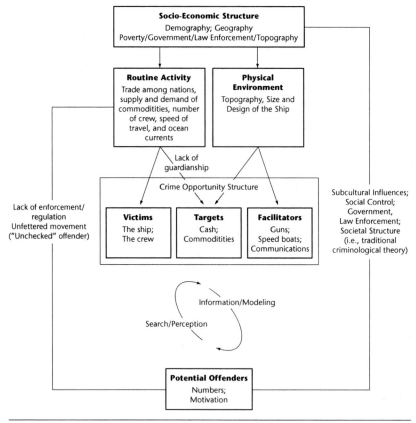

FIGURE 7.6
Situational Crime Prevention. *Adapted from R.V. Clarke (1995).*

ployment, disaffection) sets up a complex interaction that may induce sufficiently motivated offenders into acting while concurrently reducing guardianship, which makes piracy more likely.[29]

Identifying the routine activities associated with shipping and analyzing the situational factors surrounding each act of piracy contribute to the body of knowledge known as environmental criminology. From this analysis, the practical application of situational crime prevention can be undertaken (i.e., vessel security practices). Clarke (1997) identifies several opportunity-reducing techniques, some of which have already been incorporated into the shipping industry's practices; twelve techniques appear here.

The international and dynamic nature of the maritime shipping business and services provided makes the shipping industry more vulnerable to security lapses than most other industries. The number of variables involved in protecting a ship are, by far, greater than protecting a stationary building. With a comprehensive security program a company can limit access to both the ship and the terminal or port facility the vessel is calling on. Shipping companies can review the content of the policies, plans, and procedures in their management systems to verify they adequately address elements, such as training, communications, key procedures, and emergency preparedness, that apply to security issues. Clarkson (2003)[30] identifies some improvements of a comprehensive management system for shipboard security, which includes access control, entry/exit screening, surveillance by employees, and rule setting, all aspects of situational crime prevention:

1. **Gangway Security**—A vessel's gangway is the easiest
   point of access to a vessel when she is moored at berth.
   Too often, the crew member assigned to monitor gangway
   access is not given clear instructions for boarding procedures and when to call for the assistance of an officer.
   Furthermore, decreased staffing levels on ships often
   result in the gangway watchman taking on additional
   responsibilities that require leaving the gangway unattended for periods of time.

   Vessel operators need to emphasize the security aspects
   of the gangway watchman in procedures and training.
   Items to be addressed should include Embarking/
   Disembarking procedures (for crew, guests, and
   contractors), communication procedures (internal and

---

29. Clarke, 1997: 12–13.
30. Clarkson (2003).

TABLE 7.5	Opportunity-Reducing Measures for Vessel Security		
Increasing Perceived Effort	**Action Taken**	**Increasing Perceived Risks**	**Action Taken**
Target Hardening	• Using containers instead of bails or loose cargo • Fortified/reinforced bridge and engine room • Storing money in hidden safe	*Entry/Exit Screening*	• Embarking/disembarking procedures • Proper I.D. • Proper ticketing of passengers • Captain's interview of crew members • Certificate validation
Access Control	• SecureShip© electrified fence • Ship-board security measures to control sensitive areas (the bridge, the engine room, the gangway)	*Surveillance by Employees*	• Vigilant anti-piracy watch by crews while underway • CCTV while berthed or anchored • Perimeter patrols • Hand-held radios
Deflecting Offenders	• Sailing farther from coastline of source countries (Somalia) • Buffer zones for ships (Yemen 3,000 meters) • Escorts to open waters	*Formal Surveillance*	• ShipLoc© • Satellite Monitoring • IMB Piracy Reporting Centre • IMB Rapid Response Investigative Service

ship-to-shore), Stores and Package Receiving procedures, and Security Equipment (lighting, CCTV's, hand-held radios, etc.)

In many ports, the terminal or a third party provides a security officer. In such cases, the vessel should have procedures to familiarize the security officer with his responsibilities to the vessel. In all cases, the master of the vessel must ensure that this security is adequate and that security personnel know and understand shipboard requirements and procedures.

TABLE 7.5	Continued		
Reducing Anticipated Rewards	*Action Taken*	**Removing Excuses**	*Action Taken*
Identifying Property	• Unique owner-applied numbers to the containers or to cargo (DataDots©) • Requiring containers to be registered	*Rule Setting*	• International legislation against piracy and terrorism • Written vessel security plans and procedures • Maritime regulations • Regulating the sale of certain merchandise
Reducing Temptation	• Destroying pirate hide-outs • Creating secure anchoring areas • Carrying little or no cash • Establishing "no slowing" zones/minimum speed limit	*Stimulating Conscience*	• Posting anti-piracy warnings • Publishing results from piracy arrests/prosecutions • Public service announcements against piracy
Denying Benefits	• Ink merchandise tags • "No cash" sales or transfers of merchandise • Merchant agreements not to vend except with established clients	*Facilitating Compliance*	• Clearly marked shipping lanes preventing wrong turns • U.S.C.G./U.S. military to train foreign governments in anti-piracy • Creating incentives • Adopting a foreign policy

2. **Modified Pre-Departure Checklists**—Most shipping companies have a pre-arrival/pre-departure checklist for entering and leaving port. Sometimes these checklists are forms that must be completed and filed for verification purposes.

  Others act as guidelines and the recording mechanism for completion is a log entry stating that the items on the checklist were inspected and/or tested and in good working order. Companies should review these checklists to verify they provide adequate attention to security related issues. Items like stowaway search and securing restricted access spaces are examples.

3. **Modified Vessel Familiarization Tours**—A standard requirement for ISM Code compliant safety management systems is a familiarization tour for crew members new to the vessel. Security requirements such as the conduct of a proper gangway watch, security rounds, recognition of an intruder alarm, and station bill duties for an emergency involving an intruder or hostage situation need to be included in the orientation process.

4. **Certificate Validation**—One of the most difficult processes to carry out aboard a vessel is validation of a crew member's certification. Forged and illegally obtained documents are widespread and must be dealt with through a cooperative effort from several sources. Validation procedures should include input from the vessel, vessel management, manning agencies or unions, and, in some circumstances, flag-state administrations.

5. **Captain's Interview of Crew Members**—Ship's masters should conduct one-on-one interviews with each new member of the crew as they sign on. A thorough interview will give the master insight to the capabilities and attitude of the crew member and provide the opportunity to immediately establish policy and expectations aboard the vessel.

6. **Security Tours and Contingency Plans**—Crew members' rounds, both at sea and in port, should always include elements of security. Tours and inspections throughout the vessel can include checks for intrusion and piracy, lock and key control, and adherence to limited access spaces. Also, vessel management systems should be examined for content of their Emergency Response Plans. Most vessels have plans for emergency items such as pollution events (hazmat, oil spills), medical emergencies, fire, abandon ship, man overboard, and many others. However, few vessels have contingency plans for bomb threats, dealing with intruders, or hostage situations.

One of the first tasks that must be undertaken when designing security responses is to analyze the universe of incidents. Naturally, before any analysis can occur there must be accurate reporting and indexing of the offenses, preferably in some sort of a central repository. Outrage in the shipping industry at the alarming growth in piracy on the world's oceans prompted the creation of the IMB's

Piracy Reporting Centre in October 1992 in Kuala Lumpur, Malaysia. The Piracy Reporting Centre responds immediately to acts of piracy to collect and analyze data as well as evidence for law enforcement agencies and is a form of formal surveillance. Rapid reporting by shipping companies has been credited with many foiled piracy attempts and multiple victim vessels being recovered. The IMB has been moving forward to create a variety of public and private programs designed to combat piracy.

One program about to be launched by the IMB is the "Rapid Response Investigative Service." Teams of trained anti-pirate investigators will mobilize within hours of an incident to complete criminal investigations that often require many days on the part of poorly trained port officials. The program is not only designed to bring more criminals to justice, but also will hopefully address the problem of under-reporting.

Conclusion

Controlling piracy has as much to do with improving social conditions in politically unstable regions of the world as it does with manipulating the immediate environment. A multi-faceted effort will include international government participation in destabilized regions of the world[31] and maritime industry security improvements of the type defined by situational crime prevention. In the international community, the United States will have to convince the governments in regions most affected by piracy that it is in their long-term economic interest to adopt more proactive measures against piracy, dismantle corrupt maritime forces, and secure their ports and waterways from the threat of piracy or risk economic sanctions.[32] This will require some measure of nation building[33] from the industrialized democracies of the world, which will remove the excuses for piracy. Removing military regimes and corrupt governments such as the one that exists in Somalia is a long-term endeavor, but as part of a multi-prong anti-piracy effort it is worth the investment. The more immediate and less distant response to high-seas terrorism rests with the shipping industry. On a daily basis shippers are confronted with the realities of piracy. Only through

---

31. Rand, 2003.
32. Dillon, 2000.
33. Fritz and Menocal, 2007; Organisation for Economic Cooperation and Development, 2008.

consistent, vigilant, proactive security measures, such as those out-lined previously, will the shipping industry reduce the rewards and incentives for pirates to strike.

The international trend is clearly towards defense collaboration driven by political, economic, and military factors. States ignore this trend at their own peril. It remains to be seen whether Asian States will replicate the trend of international defense collaboration; how-ever it is doubtless in their best interest. Yemen, for example, announced new restrictions for vessels traveling to that country.

The restrictions are for vessels approaching commercial ships with-out authorization and [they] will open fire on any ship violating the restriction. Other craft must maintain a distance of 3,000 meters from any tankers and 250 meters from any general cargo ship. Fishing boats are to be licensed for the first time and the govern-ment has banned the unauthorized transport of boats by land. This latter restriction follows Yemeni declarations that the boat that rammed the Limburg was transported over land on a trailer with foreign license plates.

John Mo of *Sea Grant Law and Policy Digest* concurs that the most effective means to controlling piracy is international coopera-tion. Mo argues that

. . . government cooperation involving most of the governments of the Southeast Asian region is the best way to combat maritime piracy, although it is not an easy task due to various political, eco-nomical, and historical reasons. A unilateral and expedient arrangement by one or a few governments to combat maritime piracy may be convenient but may also encounter resis-tance or raise suspicion from other governments.

In order for the maritime community to realize substantial secu-rity gains, anti-piracy must have at its foundation state-sponsored support. Piracy must be thought of as terrorism for two reasons: first, although there is not a consensus among researchers, there is a nexus to established terrorist organizations; second, the proceeds from piracy may be used to finance terrorist operations. In the wake of the attacks of September 11, 2001, the United States is develop-ing a foreign policy on terrorism. The logical corollary is for that policy to extend to piracy.

Terrorists [and pirates] are ruthless but not numerous. They control no territory permanently. If their activities are harassed [and disrupted] by the security forces and administrative organs of all their potential victims—if no country will harbor them—they will become outlaws, increasingly obliged to devote their efforts to their own survival. . . . The key to antiterrorism strategy, therefore, is to eliminate safe havens. . . . The overwhelming majority of safe havens occur where a government closes its eyes because it sympathizes with at least some of the objectives of the terrorists—as in Afghanistan, Yemen, and Somalia. [The United States must create] incentives for the sharing of intelligence. Security cooperation [must be] improved, designed to interrupt the flow of funds, harass terrorists communications, and subject the countries that provide safe havens to pressures, including, in the extreme case, military pressure.[34]

The International Maritime Organization (IMO) is best poised to assume the leadership role necessary for disparate (and suspicious) governments to work cooperatively on this important international issue. The IMO has already made recommendations for a concerted international effort:

1. Inviting governments to cooperate in the interests of safety of life at sea and environmental protection by increasing their efforts to suppress and prevent acts of piracy and armed robbery against ships.
2. Inviting governments to develop, as appropriate, agreements and procedures to facilitate cooperation in applying efficient and effective measures to prevent acts of piracy and armed robbery against ships.
3. Encouraging governments to apply the provisions of international instruments aimed at improving safety of life at sea and the prevention and suppression of acts of piracy and armed robbery against ships.[35]

Piracy will stop when individuals believe there is a greater risk of being captured or killed (pain) than getting rich (pleasure), as the result of committing an act of piracy. The world's democracies should seize the opportunity presented by the IMO and combine

---

34. Kissinger, 2001.
35. Parritt, 2002.

anti-piracy efforts with counterterrorism initiatives. A unified force will be a significant achievement; it will signal the opening engagement of a continuing worldwide campaign of improving life at sea.

References

BBC News. 2009. Country profile: Somalia. April 23, 2009. Retrieved April 29, 2009 from *http://news.bbc.co.uk/2/hi/africa/country_profiles/ 1072592.stm.*

Bateman, S. 2001. Piracy on the rise. Correspondents' Report. Australian Broadcasting Corporation. Retrieved March 15, 2003, from *http://www.abc.net.au/correspondents/s326347.htm*

Brantingham, P. and P. Brantingham. 1984. *Patterns in Crime.* New York: Macmillan.

Brantingham, P., and P. Brantingham. 1975. "The spatial patterning of burglary," *Howard Journal of Criminal Justice,* 14, 11–23.

Brantingham, P., and P. Brantingham, eds. 1991. *Environmental Criminology.* Prospect Heights, OH: Waveland.

Burt, C. 1925. *The Young Delinquent.* London: University of London Press.

Clarke, R. V. 1997. *Situational Crime Prevention.* 2nd ed. New York: Harrow and Heston.

Clarkson, J. S. 2003. Security is synonymous with safety: Integrating security processes into the safety management framework. Modern Maritime Inc. Retrieved February 20, 2003, from *http://www.modernmaritime.com/ SecurityisanAspectofSafety.doc*

Cohen, L. E. and M. Felson. 1979. Social change and crime rate trends: A routine activity approach. *American Sociological Review,* 44: 588–608.

Cornish, D., and R. V. Clarke, eds. 1986. *The Reasoning Criminal.* New York: Springer-Verlag.

Dillon, D. R. 2000. Piracy in Asia: A growing barrier to maritime trade. Heritage Foundation. Retrieved April 29, 2009, from *http://www.heritage.org/research/asiaandthepacific/bg1379.cfm*

Durkheim, E. 1893, reprinted 1933. *The Division of Labour in Society.* Trans. by George Simpson. New York: The Free Press.

Farrington, D. P. and B. J. Knight. 1980. "Stealing from a 'lost' letter," *Criminal Justice and Behavior,* 7: 423–436.

Felson, M. and R. V. Clarke. 1998. *Opportunity Makes the Thief: Practical theory for Crime Prevention.* London: Home Office. Retrieved May 1, 2009, from *http://www.homeoffice.gov.uk/rds/prgpdfs/fprs98.pdf*

Felson, M. and R. V. Clarke. 1998. *Crime and Everyday Life,* 2nd ed. Thousand Oaks, CA: Pine Forge Press.

Fritz, V. and R. Menocal. 2007. Understanding state-building from a political and economic perspective: An analytical and conceptual paper on processes, embedded tensions and lessons for international engagement. Overseas Development Institute. Retrieved on May 3, 2009, from *http://www.odi.org.uk/resources/download/1340.pdf.*

Hartshorne, M., and M. A. May. 1928. *Studies in the Nature of Character,* vol. 1, *Studies in Deceit.* New York: Macmillan.

Hirschi, T. 1969. *Causes of Delinquency.* Berkeley, CA: University of California Press.

Hobbes, T. 1651, reprinted 1994. *Leviathan.* Edited by E. Curley. Indianapolis, IN: Hackett Publishing.

ICC International Maritime Bureau. 2009, April. Piracy and Armed Robbery Against Ships: report for the Period 1 January–31 March 2009.

ICC International Maritime Bureau. 2009, January. Piracy and Armed Robbery Against Ships: Annual Report 1 January–31 December.

ICC-International Maritime Bureau. 1998, The return of the pirates (N. Ryan, ed.). *ForeignWire.com.* Retrieved February 16, 2003, from *http://www.foreignwire.com/pirates.html*

ICC-International Maritime Bureau. 2003a. High seas terrorism alert in piracy report. Retrieved February 9, 2003, from *http://www.iccwbo.org/ home/news_archives/2003/stories/piracy%20_report_2002.asp*

ICC International Maritime Bureau. 2003b. ICC commercial crime services: A division of the international chamber of commerce. Retrieved February 9, 2003, from *http://www.iccwbo.org/ccs/menu_imb_bureau.asp.*

Jeffery, C. R. 1971. *Crime Prevention Through Environmental Design.* Beverly Hills, CA: Sage Publications.

Kissinger, H. 2001. *Does America need a foreign policy? Toward a diplomacy for the 21st Century.* New York: Simon and Schuster.

Maslow, A. H. 1943. A theory of human motivation. *Psychological Review,* 50(4):370–396.

May, L. 2008. History of piracy on the high seas. *The Independent,* November 18, 2008. Retrieved May 1, 2009, from *http://www.independent.co.uk/news/world/africa/history-of-piracy-on-the-high-seas-1023701.html*

McDaniel, Esq., M. S. 2000. Modern high seas piracy. Retrieved April 9, 2009, from *http://cargolaw.com/presentations_pirates.html*

McFadden, R. and S. Shane. 2009. In rescue of captain, Navy kills 3 pirates. *New York Times,* April 13, 2009.

Mo, J. 2002. Options to combat maritime piracy in Southeast Asia. *Ocean Development and International Law.* 33: 343–358. Found at *Sea Grant Law and Policy Digest* 1(1): 22. Retrieved March 16, 2003, from *http://www.olemiss.edu/orgs/SGLC/Digest/Digest.pdf*

Newman, O. 1996. *Creating Defensible Space.* U.S. Department of Housing and Urban Development: Washington D.C.

Newman, O. 1972. *Defensible Space: Crime Prevention through Urban Design.* New York: Macmillan.

Organisation for Economic Cooperation and Development. 2008. Concepts and dilemmas of state building in fragile situations: From fragility to resilience. OECD Discussion Paper, *Journal of Development,* 9(3). Retrieved May 3, 2009, from *http://www.oecd.org/dataoecd/59/51/41100930.pdf.*

Parritt, B. A. H. 2002. The transnational threat from piracy and smuggling. Presentation for the National Defense University Pacific Symposium. February 20, 2002. Retrieved March 16, 2003, from *http://www.ndu.edu/inss/symposia/pacific2002/parrittpaper.htm.*

Rabasa, A. and J Haseman. 2003. The Military and Democracy in Indonesia: Challenges, Politics, and Power. Chapter 12: Strategic scenarios for Indonesia and their implications. Rand. Retrieved March 16, 2003, *http://www.rand.org/publications/MR/MR1599/MR1599.ch12.pdf*

Reppetto, T. A. 1974. *Residential Crime.* Cambridge, MA: Ballinger.

Scar, H. A. 1973. *Patterns of Burglary,* 2nd ed. Washington D.C.: U.S. Department of Justice, National Institute of Justice Law Enforcement and Criminal Justice.

Wilkins, L. T. 1964. *Social Deviance.* London: Tavistock.

Zambito, T., C. Boyle, and T. Connor. 2009. Somali pirate's smile turns to tears; charged with crimes that could send him to jail for life. *Daily News, U.S./World News,* April 21, 2009. Retrieved April 29, 2009, from *http://www.nydailynews.com/news/us_world.*

7.3
Lessons Learned and
Projections for the Future

AGOSTINO VON HASSELL
M. R. HABERFELD

Finally, in 67 B.C., the tribune Aulus Gabinus forced a bill through the popular assembly empowering Pompey to settle the pirate problem. Pompey was still in the East, resettling pirates as peaceful farmers, when in Rome another tribune, Gaius Manilius. . . .[1]

This volume represents a compilation of different perspectives to an old problem that suddenly resurfaced as a phenomenon to be dealt with in an ad-hoc manner, despite its roots in history. What appears to be a very indicative thread of human behavior is our ability for self-deception and insistence that there is not much to be learned from the distant past, as our orientation is primarily rooted in a futuristic and almost hedonistic approach to life. The goal of this last chapter is to bring together some ideas and responses, identified by the various contributors, together with the most recent insights into the problem and, finally, identify a template for a response grounded in the lessons learned from the past, and, at the same time, customized for the future.

The measures passed by the Roman Senate in 67 B.C. have been compared by some as akin to the massive efforts to protect the United States against terrorism after September 11. Keep in mind that the entire grain supply to Rome—all carried by ship—was endangered by pirates. The Roman Republic was truly endangered. A rapid reaction, NOW, against piracy is called for but, as this

---

[1]Encyclopedia Britannica: Pompey the Great.
http://www.britannica.com/EBchecked/topic/469463/Pompey-the-Great

compilation of articles shows, it is neither easy nor simple. Very much like the Roman Senate, the U.S. Senate is reviewing this issue. In May, Democratic Senator Carl Levin[2] expressed his views regarding the recent surge in piracy off the coast of Somalia and in the Gulf of Aden, referring to the growing problem of piracy as moving away from the historical and entertainment arenas and onto the front pages on the world's newspapers. He recognized that although the naval forces of the world do have a critical role to play in deterring and combating pirates, the problem is more complex and requires a holistic approach combining military efforts with deterrence, collaboration with allies, and ongoing diplomatic outreach, very much along the lines of response in other volatile areas of conflict, like Afghanistan, for example.[3]

The ideas and analyses presented throughout the chapters ranged from operational to legal to economic perspectives, and the solutions were roughly sketched on a rather blank canvas. Kraska and Wilson (2009), in a more recently published article (not included in this volume), outlined and summarized some of the ideas presented by different authors. The two identify the operational and legal hurdles that need to be analyzed in order to determine the most viable solution.

Operational Hurdles

1. Combined Maritime Forces (CMF) in Bahrain created Combined Task Force 151, a multinational counter-piracy naval force of more than twenty nations. Previously, coalition efforts against piracy included ships and aircraft from CTF-150, which was established at the outset of Operation Enduring Freedom to conduct Maritime Security Operations (MSO) in the Gulf of Aden, the Gulf of Oman, the Arabian Sea, the Red Sea, and the Indian Ocean. The operational value of these patrols proved to have only some success. Part of the lack of the success was the size of the operational area—2.4 million square miles—and a lack of common rules of engagement as well as proper sharing of intelligence.
2. Merchant ships taking additional steps by avoiding the problematic areas all together and taking a longer and more costly trip instead. Many ship owners decided to

---

2. Levin, 2009.
3. *http://levin.senate.gov/senate/statement.cfm?id=312458*

avoid Aden and would send ships around the Horn of Africa, adding eleven to twelve days of sailing time. However, piracy is emerging off the cost of western Africa (Nigeria, Sierra Leone, Angola), and this may defeat this operational change.

3. Some vessels increase the passive and non-lethal security measures, like ringing lifelines with concertina wires, fire hoses to repel boarder, bright lights, or the Long-Range Acoustic Device, but all are limited in their deterrent value.

4. Piracy is a battle not restricted to the high seas. "Pirates don't live at sea. They live ashore. They move their money ashore. You can't have a discussion about eradicating piracy without having a discussion about the shore dimension."[4]

According to Kaplan (2009), CTF-151 is likely to become a permanent fixture in the Somali region, as piracy is the maritime ripple effect of land-based anarchy, and for as long as Somalia is in the throes of chaos, pirates operating at the behest of warlords will infest the waters far down Africa's eastern coast. However, he advocates that a different and accordingly better approach would be to rely on multiple regional and ideological alliances in different parts of the Indian Ocean. The navies of Thailand, Singapore, and Indonesia exemplify this approach in their banding together to deter piracy in the Strait of Malacca. According to a model proposed by an Australian commodore, a network of artificial sea bases supplied by the U.S. Navy should be created, which would allow for different permutations of alliances: frigates and destroyers from various states could "plug and play" into these sea bases as necessary and spread out from East Africa to the Indonesian archipelago. These "sea bases" are an old concept pioneered by the former Chief of the Joint Chiefs of Staff, Admiral Owens. However, this concept has since been dismissed by the U.S. military as too costly.

Legal Hurdles

1. What to do with the caught criminals or the "persons under control" (PUC)?
2. What should be done with the victims?

---

4. *Washington Post,* 2009, May 4. Fight against pirates also needed ashore. Statement by Chief of Naval Operations Admiral Gary Roughead; Shelal-Esa, 2009.

3. What should be done with the injured?
4. Who will prosecute the pirates?

Possible Solutions

1. During armed conflict, merchant vessels may be boarded under the right of visit and searched to determine the neutral character of the goods on board, but that rule of naval warfare does not apply to maritime piracy.
2. In peacetime, a vessel may be boarded by the naval forces of a state other than the state of registry with the consent of the flag state under articles 92 and 94 of the Law of the Sea Convention.
3. The United States recognizes that the master of the vessel also may provide consent to a boarding of his vessel.
4. Under article 51 of the UN charter and customary international law, all nations may exercise of the right of individual or collective self-defense against a vessel committing a hostile act or demonstrating hostile intent.
5. Naval forces also may board merchant vessels under the right of approach and visit pursuant to article 110 of the Law of the Sea if there are reasonable grounds to suspect the vessel is engaged in piracy.
6. The extension of port state control measures may be used by the port state authorities to board a vessel that has declared a nearby port.
7. The UN Security Council may authorize all states to take action against piracy under chapter VII of the UN charter, providing yet another potential authority for boarding pirate vessels.[5]
8. Study of history is essential. For example, how did Pompey Magnus defeat the pirates? Apart from the military response based on a legal authorization, he arranged for land grants and other economic opportunities. An example from the more recent past is found in the battle against the Barbary Pirates in the early part of the nineteenth century when the war was carried ashore by United States Marines in Tripoli. This was yet another response that produced the desired results.

---

5. Kraska and Wilson, 2009.

According to Meade (2009), the European Union is close to creating a legal framework that will allow naval forces operating in the Gulf of Aden to prosecute the perpetrators of maritime attacks. Some of the potential jurisdictions that have been identified are Kenya, Tanzania, Ethiopia, and Egypt. However, no overarching legal framework has yet been established. This solution would be especially welcomed by the International Chamber of Commerce Shipping told *Lloyd's List,* which is obviously a major stakeholder in these legal developments. In May 2009, Russian President Dmitry Medvedev instructed Prosecutor-General Yuri Chaika to contact his foreign counterparts to devise a mechanism of bringing to justice those responsible for piracy, including creation of an international criminal tribunal.[6]

Owens (2009) posits that one school of thought argues that we should do little or nothing because the cost of stamping out piracy again is too high. The critics of a more concentrated effort to combat maritime terrorism point out that some 21,000 ships transit the Gulf of Aden every year and maintain that 50 successful pirate attacks doesn't really constitute much of a threat, certainly not one worth expending the resources necessary to eliminate it. Finally, piracy in this part of the world does not appear to be a U.S. problem; it might create an annoyance, but it doesn't, for the most part, affect U.S. shipping. Thus focusing on piracy is an example of overreaction to a series of events that should not even be defined as a problem. On the other end of the spectrum, though, some experts point out that piracy is a threat to a peaceful, commercial "liberal world order," especially during the economic crisis of the early twenty-first century.

One might agree with both notions as contributors to this volume have made valid arguments on both ends of the spectrum. The most recent capture of eleven Somali pirates by a French naval ship adds yet another layer of considerations to the debate between those who perceive maritime terrorism as a real threat and the ones who prefer to treat it as a mere nuisance.[7]

When the pirates mistake the French naval ship for a commercial vessel the nuisance has the potential for far-reaching consequences with much deeper political ramifications. There is no guarantee that the military response of a naval ship under attack will always end with the given incident, without using it as a precedent for a much more complex action-response. Dunnigan (2009) points to the fact that the Somali pirates are now operating as far as

---

6. *http://www.itar-tass.com/eng/level2.html?NewsID=13903497&PageNum=0*
7. Reuters, 2009.

1,500 kilometers from the African coast. Their sophistication extends to the use of the media as a force multiplier when they attempt to portray themselves as patriots who are getting a pay-back from the foreigners who are illegally exploiting the Somali waters. If this label catches the minds and the hearts of the local populations in the feral cities and the larger audience around the world, we will truly find ourselves in a bind in terms of acceptable and accepted operational and legal response.

The very cliché notion of freedom fighters versus terrorists has a real potential of impeding the efforts of many nations in their attempt to curb maritime terrorism. It is almost a compulsory obligation to look at the developments of modern piracy and maritime terrorism in the twenty-first century as a paradigm and extension of the problems that plagued the Roman Empire and learn from their response—legal, military, and socioeconomic—to draw some parallels for our times.

While building upon the criminological theories of crime prevention, the response of the Roman Empire appears to tackle the hurdles identified at the onset of this volume and throughout its contributions. As the democratic foundation for the nations involved in the response to maritime terrorism problems, the authors suggest the legal framework should be the one addressed first. The Roman General Pompey should be credited with providing a template for a response in the twenty-first century. His three-pronged approach to the maritime problem can and should be replicated today.

In 67 B.C., the tribune, A. Gabinus, proposed to pass a law (lex Gabina) that would require the Senate to appoint a commander of consular rank with some extraordinary powers, for three years by land and by sea, to suppress the piracy that, at that time, infested every part of the Mediterranean. Pompey managed to take the proper advantage of this law (the first of the three prongs) and in merely three months (using the second prong of the approach—the military might) had the seas completely cleared from the piracy threat.[8]

The third part of his three-prong approach was Pompey's success in managing the infrastructure of the lands that produced the maritime threat and the encouragement of agricultural rebirth and economic thrive and prosperity.[9] By using the three-pronged approach introduced by the Romans, we might learn that the lesson we can take from the ancient history is the following formula that the authors propose as the most adequate solution for the future.

---

8. *www.uah.edu/society/texts/latin/classical/cicero/promanilai.html*
9. *http://www.britannica.com/EBchecked/topic/469463/Pompey-the-Great*

Legal Framework→Military Response→Economic Development

The formula above appears to be the mostly widely advocated by many contributors of this volume and the one that logically extends the democratic principles rooted in legalization of concepts, suppression of violent and illegal resistance, and development of the sustainable infrastructure. The international cooperation and response, be it military or economic, cannot and will not be achieved without a template that will commence with the internationally recognized legal framework that will provide the legitimate authorization for a military response to be followed by a swift (as swift as possible) commitment to economic development. Nothing short of these combined efforts will bring about the desired solutions. As history taught us, chaotic and unstructured responses to violent problems do not generate peaceful solutions. Terrorism, be it on land or at sea, when not confronted in a structured and comprehensive manner, has the potential to grow out of control, and it is the hope of these authors that this volume will contribute, in whatever miniscule manner, to the creation of this uniformed response.

References

Dunnigan, J. 2009. Why the pirates are immune from attack. *Strategypage,* May 5, 2009. Retrieved May 8, 2009, from *http://www.strategypage.com/*

Encyclopedia Britannica: Pompey the Great. Retrieved May 1, 2009, from *http://www.britannica.com/EBchecked/topic/469463/Pompey-the-Great*

Greenough, J. B. and G. L. Kittredge (eds.) (1902) Select Orations and Letters of Cicero. *The Society for Ancient Languages.* Retrieved May, 1, 2009 from *http://www.uah.edu/society/texts/latin/classical/cicero/promanilia.html*

House Armed Services Committee. 2009. Statement of Admiral Gary Roughead, Chief of Naval Operations, before the House Armed Services Committee on FY10 Department of Navy Posture. May 14, 2009. Retrieved May 18, 2009 from *http://www.navy.mil/navydata/people/ cno/Roughead/Testimony/Roughead_Testimony051409.pdf*

Itar-Tass News Agency 2009. Retrieved May 4, 2009 from *http://www.itar-tass.com/eng/level2.html?NewsID=13903497&PageNum=0*

Kaplan, R. D. 2009. Center Stage for the Twenty-first Century: Power Plays in the Indian Ocean. *Foreign Affairs,* March/April, 2009. Retrieved May 16, 2009, from *http://www.foreignaffairs.com/*

Kraska J., and B. Wilson. 2009. Fighting piracy: International coordination is key to countering modern-day freebooters. *Armed Forces Journal.* Retrieved May 16, 2009, from *http://www.armedforcesjournal.com/ 2009/02/3928962*

Levin, C. 2009. *Opening Statement of Senator Carl Levin, Senate Armed Services Committee Hearing on Ongoing Efforts to Combat Piracy on the High Seas.* May 5, 2009. Retrieved May 16, 2009, from *http://levin.senate.gov/ newsroom/release.cfm?id=312458*

Meade, R. 2009. EU close to legal framework on piracy prosecutions. *Lloyd's List,* February 27, 2009. May 3, 2009. Retrieved May 16, 2009, from *http://www.lloydslist.com/ll/news/viewArticle.htm?articleId=20017622826& src=rss*

Owens, M. T. 2009. What to Do about Piracy? *Foreign Policy Research Institute.* April 2009. Retrieved May 16, 2009, from *www.fpri.org*

Reuters. 2009. France captures 11 suspected Somali pirates. May 3, 2009. Retrieved May 16, 2009, from *http://www.reuters.com/article/ worldNews/idUSTRE5421QE20090503*

Shelal-Esa, A. 2009. Fight against pirates also needed ashore. *Reuters.* May 4, 2009. Retrieved May 16, 2009, from *http://www.reuters.com/article/ worldNews/idUSN0440838820090504?sp=true*

APPENDIX

Discussion Questions

DISCUSSION QUESTIONS

2.2
The Challenges of Modern Piracy

1. How do Somali pirates pick up their targets?

   _____

   _____

   _____

   _____

   _____

   _____

   _____

2. Discuss some of the possibilities for misinformation that would divert the pirates from attacking a specific ship. Is there a specific technology that could be used to achieve this goal? Base your answer on the chapter material as well as additional research of this field.

   _____

   _____

   _____

   _____

   _____

   _____

   _____

3. Once on board, the pirates, sometimes numbering as many as 100, can easily overcome the crew. What strategies would you suggest for counter resistance on the part of the crew?

_____

_____

_____

_____

_____

_____

_____

4. Discuss the importance of the ties that the pirates have to other terrorist groups and our ability to intervene in this arena.

_____

_____

_____

_____

_____

_____

_____

_____

Name: _____ Date: _____

DISCUSSION QUESTIONS
2.3
What Makes Piracy Work?

1. Using bullet points, outline the historical timeline of piracy in
    the modern world.

    _____

    _____

    _____

    _____

    _____

    _____

2. Looking at the bullet points of the historical timeline discuss
    the turning points during which the modern world lost the con-
    trol over its maritime transportation system.

    _____

    _____

    _____

    _____

    _____

    _____

    _____

3. Address the issues of recruitment into a pirate-terrorist group. Do you see it as an organized network or a loose-end enterprise that encompasses a few disorganized individuals?

_____

_____

_____

_____

_____

_____

_____

_____

4. Based on your previous answer, what strategies would you suggest to curtail and or discourage the recruitment?

_____

_____

_____

_____

_____

_____

_____

_____

Name: _____ Date: _____

3.1
Armed Robbery and Piracy in Southeast Asia

1. There is a noticeable downtrend in piracy in Southeast Asia—
   list the reasons the authors attribute to this phenomenon.

   _____

   _____

   _____

   _____

   _____

   _____

   _____

2. Discuss the Malacca and Singapore Straits' strategic locations
   that make them an attractive target for maritime terrorists.

   _____

   _____

   _____

   _____

   _____

   _____

   _____

3. Discuss the possible links between the attacks around the Indonesian waters and the terrorist groups active on land in Indonesia. Draw the possible nexus of connections between the two.

_____

_____

_____

_____

_____

_____

_____

_____

_____

_____

_____

_____

_____

_____

_____

_____

_____

DISCUSSION QUESTIONS
3.3
The Overstated Threat

1. What is the difference between pirates and water-borne terror?

_____

_____

_____

_____

_____

_____

2. Discuss the economic and human costs of piracy. Which one—the economic or the human—will, eventually, lead to a more concrete response on the part of the injured parties and the countries they represent?

_____

_____

_____

_____

_____

_____

_____

3. Discuss the role of International Maritime Organization (IMO) and its ability to influence the scope and intensity of modern piracy.

_____

_____

_____

_____

_____

_____

_____

_____

_____

_____

_____

_____

_____

_____

_____

_____

_____

_____

Name: _____ Date: _____

DISCUSSION QUESTIONS

3.4
The Threat to Maritime Domain:
How Real Is the Terrorist Threat?

1. According to the author only a few terrorist groups have developed the capacity to mount attacks on maritime targets. List the groups identified in the article and the reasons they have the capacity to engage in maritime terrorism.

   _____

   _____

   _____

   _____

   _____

   _____

2. Discuss how the capabilities of the groups differ and what kind of specific threats they can pose to American maritime interests. Do you see any ways of countering their activities?

   _____

   _____

   _____

   _____

   _____

   _____

   _____

3. How do you perceive the role of Al Qaeda in the future developments of maritime terrorism? Do you consider it a major opportunity venue for this terrorist organization or a possible peripheral engagement only?

_____

_____

_____

_____

_____

_____

_____

_____

_____

_____

_____

_____

_____

_____

_____

_____

_____

Name: _____ Date: _____

DISCUSSION QUESTIONS

4.1
Legal Interoperability Issues in International Cooperation Measures to Secure the Maritime Commons

1. Define the problems of legal interoperability as presented by the authors of this chapter.

   _____

   _____

   _____

   _____

   _____

   _____

2. Looking at the above problems discuss whether they resemble legal interoperability problems we face in other areas of criminal justice prosecutions? If yes, how? If not, why not?

   _____

   _____

   _____

   _____

   _____

3. Discuss the problems inherent in legal interoperability with regard to intelligence matters. How do you propose to solve them?

_____

_____

_____

_____

_____

_____

_____

_____

_____

_____

_____

_____

_____

_____

_____

_____

_____

_____

_____

DISCUSSION QUESTIONS
4.3
Feral Cities—Pirates Havens

1. In bullet points, outline the support systems in place on land that serve as the lifelines for the pirates.

_____

_____

_____

_____

_____

_____

2. Looking at the bullet points of the most important support systems on land, discuss the possibility of curtailing or eliminating some of the ancillary structures that enable the pirates to operate successfully before, during, and after committing their acts of terror.

_____

_____

_____

_____

_____

_____

3. Address the issues of varying logistics that appear to be conducive to the creation of the land support systems as they differ in various geographic locations mentioned in the chapter. Do governments of these countries do enough to prevent these save heavens from flourishing?

_____

_____

_____

_____

_____

_____

_____

4. What are the main lessons learned, based on the information provided in this chapter, and do you agree with the premises of these recommendations?

_____

_____

_____

_____

_____

_____

_____

Name: _____ Date: _____

DISCUSSION QUESTIONS
5.1
Piracy, Policy, and Law

1. Discuss the definitional challenges inherent in identifying what constitutes maritime terrorism.

   _____

   _____

   _____

   _____

   _____

   _____

2. Looking at your answers to the previous question, discuss the possible remedies to the definitional challenges and their legal ramifications. Differentiate between conceptual and legal challenges.

   _____

   _____

   _____

   _____

   _____

   _____

   _____

3. Outline in bullet points the advantages of the prevention and deterrence techniques outlined in the chapter. Base your answers on the policy and legal challenges that always accompany any prevention and/or deterrence action.

_____

_____

_____

_____

_____

_____

_____

_____

4. What are the main advantages and disadvantages of creating a task force of Regional Cooperation on Combating Terrorism?

_____

_____

_____

_____

_____

_____

_____

_____

Name: _____ Date: _____

DISCUSSION QUESTIONS

5.3
The Law of Piracy in Popular Culture

1. List in bullet points the timeline of writings on piracy between the seventeenth and twentieth centuries.

   _____

   _____

   _____

   _____

   _____

   _____

   _____

2. Looking at the timeline in question 1, discuss the development of popular perceptions about maritime terrorism and piracy. What was the role of these writings in creating a misconception about the concept of piracy and modern maritime piracy?

   _____

   _____

   _____

   _____

   _____

   _____

   _____

3. Discuss the role of the media in the twenty-first century and its influence on the way the phenomenon of modern piracy and maritime security is responded to by various countries and their respective governments. Specifically concentrate on the way the media can and, possibly will, influence the court proceedings of the captured pirates brought for trial in the United States.

_____

_____

_____

_____

_____

_____

_____

_____

_____

_____

_____

_____

_____

_____

_____

_____

Name: _____ Date: _____

DISCUSSION QUESTIONS

7.1
Maritime Terrorism: Risk and Liability

1. In bullet point, outline the risk factors identified by the authors.

   _____

   _____

   _____

   _____

   _____

   _____

   _____

   _____

2. Looking at the bullet points of risk factors identified by the authors, discuss the liability issues that accompany these risk factors.

   _____

   _____

   _____

   _____

   _____

   _____

   _____

   _____

3. Address the issues of risk and liability within the context of the proliferation of piracy attacks in the year 2009 and the larger impact of these attacks on the economic recession and the overall political situation around the world.

_____

_____

_____

_____

_____

_____

_____

_____

4. Based on your previous answer, what strategies would you suggest to curtail and/or discourage the recruitment?

_____

_____

_____

_____

_____

_____

_____

_____

INDEX